THE ENDING OF
ROMAN BRITAIN

THE ENDING OF
ROMAN BRITAIN

A.S. Esmonde Cleary

B.T. Batsford Ltd, London

Typeset by J&L Composition Ltd, Filey, North Yorkshire
and printed in Great Britain by
Mackays of Chatham plc, Kent

for the publisher, B.T. Batsford Ltd
4 Fitzhardinge Street, London W1H 0AH

CONTENTS

Acknowledgements   *vi*

List of illustrations   *vii*

Preface   *ix*

Introduction   *x*

1 The Structures of the State   *1*

2 The Continental Background   *16*

3 Britain in the Fourth Century   *41*

4 The Passing of Roman Britain: 380–430   *131*

5 Britons in the Fifth Century   *162*

6 Postscript: Continuity and Change   *188*

References   *206*

Bibliography   *219*

Index   *236*

ACKNOWLEDGEMENTS

The author would like thank the following individuals and organizations for permission to reproduce copyright material: Phil Barker and S.C Renow (Figs. 38, 39, Pl. 10), Birmingham University Field Archaeology Unit (Fig. 48), Centre Nationale de la Recherche Scientifique (Fig. 7), Council for British Archaeology (Fig. 43), Professor B.W. Cunliffe (Fig. 37, Pl. 11), Dorset Natural History and Archaeology Society (Figs. 33, 40), Professor M. Fulford (Pl. 9), Giraudon (Pl. 2), Hampshire Field Club and Archaeological Society (Fig. 29), S. Johnson (Pl. 4), Kent Archaeological Society (Figs. 36, 45), Leicester University Press (Fig. 47), D.F. Mackreth (Fig. 17), Lincoln Archaeological Trust (Fig. 14), Museum of London (Pl. 1), Oxford University Press (Fig. 34), Royal Archaeological Institute (Fig. 5), Roman Research Trust (Pl. 7), Royal Commission on Historical Monuments for England (Pl. 6), Society of Antiquaries of London (Figs. 13, 16, 18, 19, 20, 27, 30, 31, 35, 44), Society for the Promotion of Roman Studies (Figs. 12, 26, 28, 42), Suffolk County Council and R. Mowett (Fig. 32), Thames and Hudson Ltd (Fig. 41), Trustees of the Barber Institute, University of Birmingham (Pl. 3), Trustees of the British Museum (Pl. 8).

I am also very grateful to Harry Buglass for drawing Figs. 1, 2, 3, 4, 8, 10, 11, 15, 21, 22, 23, 24, 25, 46 and for enhancing the other figures, and to Graham Norrie for his photographic work in reproducing all the figures.

LIST OF ILLUSTRATIONS

Figures in the text   *page*

 1 Map of the late Roman empire   3
 2 Map of administrative divisions of western empire in fourth century   19
 3 Map of military commands in west in fourth century   21
 4 Map showing principal sites mentioned in Ch. 2   23
 5 Late Roman town walls in Gaul   25
 6 Amiens in second and fourth centuries   26
 7 The villa at Montmaurin   31
 8 The churches of fourth-century Trier   37
 9 The cemetery church at Xanten   39
10 The northern frontier of Britain in the fourth century   49
11 The Saxon Shore   52
12 Wallsend in the second and fourth centuries   58
13 The internal buildings of Portchester   60
14 The defensive sequence at Lincoln   62
15 Map of towns in fourth-century Britain   65
16 Verulamium in second and fourth centuries   67
17 Water Newton   69
18 Silchester basilica   70
19 Silchester general plan   76
20 'Strip-buildings', Caerwent   79
21 Find-spots of imported pottery   84
22 Location of major pottery industries in Britain   87
23 Distribution of fine wares in southern Britain   89
24 Fourth-century hoards   97
25 Rural sites mentioned in text   101
26 Plan of Woodchester   107
27 Plan of Keynsham   109
28 Plan of Bradley Hill   112
29 Plan of Chalton   113
30 Plan of Lydney   118
31 Plan of Silchester church   122
32 Plan of Icklingham church   123
33 Plan of Poundbury cemetery   126
34 Plan of Lankhills cemetery   133
35 Verulamium Insula XXVII   149
36 Fifth-century burials from Canterbury   150

37 The Bath temple precinct   156
38 Wroxeter baths basilica   176
39 Wroxeter baths basilica reconstruction   177
40 Plan of Poundbury settlement   180
41 The gate at South Cadbury   181
42 Plan of Lamyatt Beacon   182
43 Plan of Cannington   183
44 Location of Caistor-by-Norwich cemetery   190
45 *Grubenhauser* at Canterbury   192
46 Dorchester-on-Thames   194
47 Plan of Orton Hall Farm   195
48 Plan of Wasperton   202

Photographs (between pages 116 and 117)

 1 Medallion from Beaurains, Arras. The obverse showing a
    forceful Constantius I, the reverse the relief of London in 296

 2 Silver *missorium* showing Theodosius I

 3 Coins of the principal emperors and usurpers relating to late
    Roman Britain

 4 The late Roman walls at Le Mans

 5 The Saxon Shore fort at Portchester

 6 The mosaic from Hinton St Mary, Dorset

 7 The mosaic from Littlecote, Wiltshire

 8 Gold buckle from the Thetford treasure, fourth-century

 9 The forum-basilica at Silchester

10 The baths-basilica at Wroxeter

11 The temple precinct at Bath

PREFACE

Any book such as this one will inevitably betray the results of its author's archaeological and intellectual upbringing, and the hands of those who have had a part in this. As a schoolboy I was very fortunate to be in Winchester in the late 'sixties. There for five summers I worked on the late Roman cemetery at Lankhills and on the Roman and mediaeval town site at Lower Brook Street. Digging in Winchester in those days one could not but help be made aware of the immense potential of archaeology as a source of information. I am ever grateful to Don Mackreth, site director at Lower Brook Street, for tolerating and encouraging my early archaeological enthusiasms. As an undergraduate at London I was taught by Richard Reece, and in common with all others who have sat at his feet I was always interested and stimulated by what he had to say, and sometimes provoked or outraged. From him I learnt always to question, but also to have a care for the evidence. As a postgraduate at Oxford, my supervisor Sheppard Frere and his then Research Assistant Roger Goodburn held me on a loose rein, giving me ample time to explore the magnificent collection of the Ashmolean Library. Thereby I learnt a great deal more archaeology than I ever would have from sticking to my research topic. Since coming to Birmingham several generations of students with their uncomfortable questions and their expectation of being coherently taught have forced me to discriminate between what I thought I knew and what I could actually demonstrate. At Birmingham I have also been extremely fortunate to have as long-suffering colleagues Steve Bassett, Martin Goodman and Chris Wickham. They have all read this book in draft and commented extensively on both form and content. Each of them stands outside Roman Britain looking in, and is thus generally better able to see the wood for the trees than the habitual toiler in this (dis)Enchanted Forest. Their comments have improved this book beyond all measure. To these three, to the others mentioned here, and to a host of others my thanks are due. They may recognise their imprint here; whether that is a bitter or a sweet experience I leave to them to decide.

Books are not just intellectual abstractions: they are also concrete objects which need to be realised. Peter Kemmis Betty at Batsford has my gratitude not only for having the courage and taste to commission this book, but also for his encouragement along the way and his treatment of the deadline as a metaphysical rather than a real-life concept. And finally my thanks go to Philip Farrar who bore the latter stages of the writing of the book with a fortitude and placidity which in themselves did much to help in getting the book finished.

INTRODUCTION

This book seeks to deal with what was happening in Britain between the years AD300 and 500. At the beginning of this period Britain was an unexceptionable part of the Roman empire, but by the end of it Roman rule was a thing of the past. In place of a widespread and centralised Roman culture there was a multiplicity of localised territories, some of them Celtic, some of them Anglo-Saxon. In place of the plethora of settlements, structures and objects which characterised the Roman period in Britain, there was a lack both of quality and quantity in the buildings and the finds, reflecting the technological and social collapse that had taken place.

The collapse of great civilisations provokes nowadays an uneasy fascination. This is the more so when the civilisation in question is the one which shaped much of the culture and religion of the western world down to the present day. Moreover, out of the disappearance of Roman Britain were to grow the states which eventually gave rise to modern England, Scotland and Wales. For these reasons and others the period covered in this book has already been covered by many other books with a variety of perspectives. What are the perspectives of this book to justify yet another assault on the subject?

The first is that the ending of Roman Britain can only be explained within the context of the fall of the western part of the Roman empire and the rise of the barbarian successor states. Too often attempts have been made to try to explain the end of Roman Britain in insular terms. Such attempts have tended not to explain much because the causes of the end of Roman Britain lay outside the island and not within it.

The second point is that it was the peculiar nature of the late Roman economy which sustained late Roman culture in Britain, and that the removal of that economic system knocked away the supports of what was Roman about Roman Britain. This collapse was a consequence of the weakness of the Roman state in the early fifth century.

A third point is scepticism about the value of the written sources, particularly for the fifth century. Because of the poverty of the archaeological record for this century the written sources have achieved a dominant position in the study of the period. But this work will seek to examine the reasons for the composition of these sources (usually much later than the events they purport to describe), and whether they should therefore be taken at face (or any) value as historical sources. The answer will usually be No.

As a fourth point, the conclusions of the third point necessarily promote the archaeological evidence to centre stage. The archaeological evidence for the fourth century is often bewildering in its quantity and complexity, so one purpose of this work is to try to make some of it more accessible to the reader and to explain current work on its potentials and pitfalls. In contrast the archaeological evidence for the fifth century (other than Anglo-Saxon — and that has its problems) is pitiful, but it does exist and needs to be considered independently of the supposed historical framework. As most readers of this book will be non-specialists I have tried to avoid the more abstruse and self-defeatingly jargon-ridden reaches of modern archaeological theory and expression.

The fifth point is that traditionally the end of Roman Britain has been seen as having something to do with the invasions by the Anglo-Saxons. One of the effects of relating the causes and dating of the ending of Roman Britain to that of the western empire is that it opens up a chronological gap between late Roman Britain and the arrival of the Anglo-Saxons. There is a discernible post-Roman but non-Saxon interlude over most of the country of half a century at least; much more in the west. Of interest as a society in its own right, it also has far-reaching consequences for the vexed question of continuity from Roman Britain to Anglo-Saxon England. That there was some such continuity is a current orthodoxy. But if the Roman and the Anglo-Saxon periods are seen no longer to overlap, but indeed to be separated, then the channels of continuity will have to be completely re-assessed. In this respect also the comparison and contrast with processes on the Continent are instructive.

These are some of the ideas which underlie, and themes which inform this book. They will, I hope, justify the appearance of another work in addition to those already dealing with the period.

Simon Esmonde Cleary
Birmingham
The Feast of St Paulinus of Trier

ONE

The Structures of the State

Roman Britain had by AD300 been part of the Roman empire for two and a half centuries. She was tightly bound into the political, military, economic and social meshes that held the empire together. The actions of the imperial government in any of these spheres might well have their repercussions in Britain, and any innovation might well affect Britain. Moreover, changes affecting the fabric of the whole empire or its institutions would have a knock-on effect in Britain. This being so, we must appreciate the imperial background for late Roman Britain, both for how the island functioned, and as a means of discriminating between the general and the insular in the passing of the Roman order of things.

The half-century prior to AD300 had seen great changes and upheavals in the Roman world, as a result of which the empire of the fourth century appears markedly different from that of the second. The 'third-century crisis' is usually seen as having affected three main areas of the empire's life: political, military and financial.

In the half-century from the death of Severus Alexander in 235 to the accession of Diocletian in 284 there were some twenty recognised emperors (many of them just successful usurpers) as well as a host of usurpers and men who ruled over part of the empire.[1] In this time no emperor survived long enough to implement coherent policies, let alone found a dynasty to carry through his work and provide a measure of political stability.

At the same time pressure on the frontiers from hostile peoples became well-nigh insupportable.[2] The 250s and 260s saw a succession of invasions deep into imperial territory in the west, in the Balkans and on the eastern frontier. Whereas the empire's defensive strategy as it had developed in the late first and second centuries had implicitly assumed that the army would only have to mount major operations in one theatre at any one time, the empire was now faced with simultaneous threats from several points around its perimeter.[3] The effects of this pressure were made the worse by the fact that Rome now had new and more potent enemies to face. In Europe the old tribal divisions were increasingly disappearing into large new confederations such as the Franks and the Alamanni, and new peoples such as the Goths were making their presence most unwelcomely felt. In the east the torpid Parthian empire under the Arsacid dynasty was replaced by the resurgent Persian empire under the Sassanids. This was proving too much for the Roman strategic system, which started to come unravelled, reaching its nadir in the 260s with the western part of the empire under the usurping regime of the Gallic Empire, the Danube frontier under desperate pressure, and large parts of the east of the empire under the control of Palmyra following on the defeat and capture of the Emperor Valerian by the Persians in 260. In addition to the external threat the army was ever being divided and drained by the seemingly never-ending intestinal wars of the claimants to the imperial purple.

To political and military weakness is usually added financial turmoil. The evidence cited in support of this is the coinage. During the third century gold coins virtually ceased to be minted. The silver *denarius* and the new double-*denarius* coin, usually called the *antoninianus*, suffered a debasement from *c.* 70 per cent silver to 5 per cent or less by the 270s, becoming in effect bronze coins and driving out the old base-metal coins such as the *sestertius* and the *as*. This has been held to be symptomatic of massive and destabilising inflation, especially by those scholars who had seen the financial and political fate which had followed comparable monetary inflation in Weimar Germany. There is now some doubt as to how cataclysmic such inflation of the coinage really was, since it appears that in terms of the amount of gold required to buy a given amount of staples such as grain, prices at the end of the third century were much the same as at the beginning. Modern experience has also shown that people adapt to such inflation by a variety of strategies. It must also be borne in mind that coin-use was not universal in the Roman empire; there would have been significant geographical areas and social groupings where the economy was not monetised. So though the effect of coin debasement would have been serious in certain fields, such as the payment of troops, it should not necessarily be seen as a general evil.

Overall, though, the picture of the empire in the third century is one of profound stress affecting the principal organs of government and defence, and at times looking as though the very continuance of the empire might be under threat. To deal with this it was not an option to try to revert to the practices of the early empire; these had failed. A new order was needed.

As the fourth century opened, the main agents of the third-century crises had been tamed, and a bruised and battered empire set on its feet again. On the political front, the accession of Diocletian in 284 was to mark a turning-point, though there was no particular reason at the time for thinking that it would. He came to power by the time-honoured route of assassinating his predecessor and patron; but, realising the limitations of one mortal in the face of the empire and its problems, he appointed a colleague, Maximian, who was to have responsibility for the western half of the empire, whilst Diocletian retained that for the eastern. To try to provide for an uncontested succession he and Maximian each co-opted a junior colleague with the right of succession when his senior retired. Diocletian and Maximian were each styled *Augustus* and their juniors, Constantius in the west, Galerius in the east, were styled *Caesar*. In the face of the family and kin loyalties bred in the bone of any Roman the longer-term success of this 'Tetrarchy', or rule of four, was always a dubious prospect, relying as it did on altruism rather than personal loyalties. Diocletian and Maximian retired in 305. In 306 Maximian's successor in the west, Constantius I (Chlorus), died on campaign at York. His son Constantine,

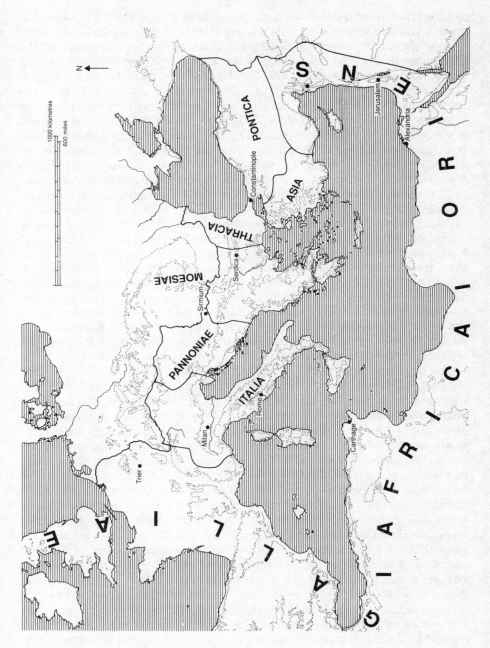

Fig. 1 Map of the late Roman Empire

ignoring the constitutional niceties, had himself proclaimed Augustus. For twenty years of sporadic internal warfare it must have looked as though the bad old days were returning. But by 324 Constantine was sole master of the Roman world. He then consolidated his success by living a further thirteen years, and by his death in 337 his dynasty was assured, with his sons Constantine II (337–40), Constans (337–50) and Constantius II (337–60) succeeding him. Even after the death of the last male of the House of Constantine, the emperor Julian (360–3), a smooth transfer of power was engineered to avert military conflict. The rest of the century, and beyond, was to be dominated by the linked dynasties of the House of Valentinian and the House of Theodosius. Both Valentinian I (364–75) and Theodosius I (378–95) were successful generals and effective rulers, but both had ineffectual male heirs (the womenfolk of the House of Theodosius were quite another matter). Nonetheless the restored dynastic principle provided a great measure of political stability down into the fifth century. Usurpation did not, of course, go out of fashion, but after Constantine I in 306 treason did not prosper.

Once he had secured the throne the overriding duty of any emperor and the continuing concern of his administration and subjects was the safeguarding of the empire, and finding the means to pay for that. Rome was fortunate that Diocletian, Constantine I, Valentinian I and Theodosius I were all experienced and able generals. They all maintained a close interest in the performance of the army, not only as a political but also as a military force. Constantine I in particular reorganised the army, the better to respond to the changed strategic circumstances which the third century had thrust upon it.

The emperors of the third century had been essentially conservative in their view of the organisation, strategy and tactics of the army which they had inherited from Augustus and his successors. In the 270s and 280s strong, if short-lived, emperors such as Aurelian (270–5) or Probus (276–82) had been able to use it to good effect to start to stabilise the military situation. This work was carried to a conclusion by Diocletian and Maximian, so that by 300 the barbarians on the Rhine and Danube were quiescent, and the Persian empire under the Sassanid kings had been pushed back more or less to the frontier line established in the early third century. During the later third century, from the time of Gallienus (260–8) on, two important modifications had been introduced into the army. The first was the appearance of a body of troops in direct attendance upon the person of the emperor himself, his *comitatus*. The second was the increasing importance of cavalry, like the *comitatus* detached from the frontier armies. These prefigure far-reaching changes under Constantine I, but affected only a small part of the army and must not be allowed to obscure the fact of the essential conservatism of third-century military organisation and strategy.

Constantine I himself spent much of his long reign campaigning, either against his enemies within the empire, or against the peoples who threatened its frontiers. In that furnace he forged the new model army of the late Roman empire.[4] Gone was the old two-fold division into legions (Roman Citizen heavy infantry) and auxiliaries (non-Citizen light infantry and cavalry); in its place was a new two-fold division between *limitanei* (lower-grade frontier troops) and *comitatenses* (higher-grade mobile field-armies). The *limitanei* were the lineal descendants of the units which had manned the frontiers from the beginning of the second century or earlier. In areas such as Britain which had been little troubled by the military upsets of the third century, the ancestry is evident in the continued use of the old unit titles. Elsewhere new unit types such as *cunei* and *vexillationes* bear witness to the changes wrought by unremitting frontier warfare. The *comitatenses* developed out of the emperor's *comitatus* of the later third century. Under Constantine I they were expanded greatly in number whilst keeping their close physical link with the person of the emperor. But as the fourth century wore on, detachments of the *comitatenses* were increasingly stationed away from the emperor and became instead regional field armies. Both the *limitanei* of the various frontiers and the *comitatenses* to their rear came under the command of separate hierarchies of local commanders, styled variously *dux* or *comes*, and both ultimately responsible to the emperor's chief commanders, the *magister peditum* (master of the infantry) or *magister equitum* (master of the cavalry), sometimes combined as the *magister militum* (master of the soldiers).

The strategy of the remodelled army was simple.[5] The *limitanei* were charged with policing and holding the frontier both against small-scale acts of aggression and, where possible, against major incursions and invasions. If they failed in the latter duty the *comitatenses* were there to intercept the invaders and throw them back out of imperial territory. Nor should the *comitatenses* be seen simply as a passive defensive force awaiting the inevitable. On occasion they were used to mount expeditions across the boundaries of the empire, most often against Persia, and in the west as late as Valentinian I's expeditition across the Rhine in 369. They were also available for the support or the suppression of claimants to the purple.

Though many units of the late Roman army bore the titles of old-style units such as legion or cohort, this should not fool us into thinking that their size and internal organisation remained the same. Clearly the new-style units such as the *cunei* can be expected to have had new structures. The incipient debate on unit-size in the fourth century is much hampered by a shortage of evidence. Nonetheless, literary, papyrological and archaeological evidence are all combining to suggest that unit sizes had come down considerably since the days of the second century.[6] Partly this was the result of the common third-century practice of vexillating units, that is, splitting off part of the unit for use elsewhere; increasingly such detachments were not returned to their parent unit and acquired a life of their own, sometimes retaining the titulature of the parent unit. The suggestion now gaining favour is that the comitatensian units styled legion may have been of the order of one thousand men rather than the five thousand or more of the early empire. *Limitaneus* legions may only have been some five hundred strong. The size of the other types of unit, including those still styled cohort, is even less certain, but a comparable reduction may be envisaged, and would not be at odds with the archaeological evidence: forts built *de novo* in the later Roman period tend to be smaller than their earlier equivalents, and re-used or maintained earlier forts were often reduced in size. In the interior of these forts archaeology is increasingly showing a much smaller provision of accommodation than in the early period. Thus, though the number of units in the late Roman army may be consider- ably increased over that of the second century, the actual number of troops may not have gone up all that greatly since the individual units were now so much smaller.

The quality of the troops in the late Roman army is often contrasted unfavourably with that of their better-known predecessors in the first and second centuries. Partly this is the result of viewing the late army as essentially defensive, so much less heroic than the expansionist glories of the Principate. Partly it is the result of a misinterpretation of some late laws, which have given rise to the impression that the *limitanei* were some sort of part-time peasant militia.[7] Moreover what little we know of the arms, armour and equipment of the fourth century shows it to have been less sophisticated than that of the second — indeed the late Roman army would probably have looked more like something off the Bayeux Tapestry than off Trajan's Column. But this unflattering view of the late Roman army is in large measure the result of the scant attention paid until recently to the late army as compared to the early. As the balance is redressed it becomes clearer that though different in many ways from the army of the second century, the late army was nevertheless a permanent standing body of men, adequately trained and equipped for its purpose. It kept the empire safe throughout the fourth century and was often able to defeat large enemy forces through its good training, equipment and generals. The Franks and Alamanni found this to their cost at Strasbourg in 357 when confronted with the Caesar Julian's numerically much inferior forces. Against the well-equipped armies of Persia the Roman army also had more successes than failures.

A contributory factor to the view that the late army was an unworthy successor to that of the Principate has been that it employed troops from beyond the boundaries of the empire. This is seen as a 'barbarisation' of the army, with all the pejorative overtones of that word. Undoubtedly as the fourth century progressed the empire experienced increasing difficulty in recruiting enough troops from amongst its own people, perhaps due to manpower shortage, certainly due to unwillingness in certain areas to enlist.[8] It is incontrovertible that 'barbarians' were increasingly used at all levels in the army. Many of the ablest generals of the century have names attesting to their barbarian origins, including the great Stilicho, Vandal-born and *de facto* ruler of the western empire at the turn of the fourth and fifth centuries under the feeble Honorius. Ordinary troops also could be of non-Roman origin. There were two common types of such troops: *laeti* and *foederati*.[9] *Laeti* were barbarians who had surrendered to the empire. They were settled in ethnic groups in areas of the western empire, and in return for permission to settle and for their land they had to supply a regular stream of recruits to the Roman army. Legislation was enacted to keep this valuable source of soldiers from intermarrying with the provincial population and losing its identity,[10] but once in the army soldiers from this source would be indistinguishable from Roman-born troops. *Foederati* on the other hand were bands of barbarians who entered the empire under a treaty arrangement (*foedus*), and retained their ethnic identities, methods of fighting and leaders. The use of non-Roman troops in this way has precedents which go back far into the army of the Republic. In the fourth century it was regularly used, but until late in the century the bulk of the army was still Roman-born. It was probably only after the obliteration of the eastern field-army by the Goths at the disastrous battle of Adrianople in 378 that widespread use of barbarian troops became the norm, at first in the east, and increasingly in the west towards the end of the century — a growing reliance on barbarian troops was a charge levelled against the western emperor Gratian (375–83). It should be noted, however, that there is no evidence for federate troops proving unreliable or deserting to the barbarian side in peace or war. Over a period of some thirty years in the mid-fourth century Ammianus only enumerates four occasions on which non-Roman troops were held to be responsible for Roman military reverses, and one of these was through negligence rather than malice. Tribal antagonisms may well have been stronger than ethnic identity: moreover what most barbarians wanted was a share in the Roman system, and this is what the federate troops had gained.

The defensive posture of the empire is visible in the fortifications constructed at this period, and in the overall strategy to which they contributed. As the invasions of the latter part of the third century had made disastrously clear, the defensive system put in place during the course of the second century had a major flaw. It was too much like a lobster: once through the armoured outer carapace there was nothing but undefended fleshy parts. Thus the late-imperial strategy sought not simply to reinforce the effectiveness of the outer shell, but also to minimise the destructive potential of invasion and the time required to expel the invaders.[11] Deep into imperial territory cities and towns were now fortified and new strongpoints (*burgi*) constructed along the roads. Defensively these were to hamper enemy advance within imperial territory, particularly by impeding use of the road-system which had so speeded the progress of the third-century invaders; into these fortifications could be gathered stores and supplies, both to safeguard them and to deny them to the enemy. Offensively they could be used as assembly-points for troops and as places for which advancing troops could make; the stores would enable the comitatensian forces to make full use of their mobility, unencumbered by a slow-moving baggage train.

The military architecture of the late Empire is as distinctively defensive as the strategy.[12] In place of the familiar 'playing card' shape forts (rectangular with rounded corners and internal towers) of the first and second centuries, which were little more than defensible accommodation, we find installations taking advantage of naturally advantageous sites and making use of an expressly defensive architecture. The common features of late-Roman defences include thick, high walls, small, heavily-defended gates and projecting towers from which archers or artillery could keep attackers at a distance or enfilade the front of the walls. Though these defences do not exhibit the sophistication of the fully-developed medieval castle, they were perfectly adequate for the job they had to do. The form defences take is a reflection of the perceived ability of a potential enemy to attack them. In the Europe of the late Roman empire the barbarian rulers might command thousands of ferocious warriors, but they had neither the technological nor the logistical ability to mount a siege. The words of the Gothic chieftain Fritigern well encapsulate this: 'I am at peace with walls.'[13]

The equipping, paying and provisioning of the army was the single largest head of expenditure for the empire. In addition there was a considerable bureaucracy to support and there was the imperial court, though this latter could draw upon the yield of the vast imperial estates. The City of Rome herself, and to an extent the New Rome, Constantinople, also had to have their food supplies (*annona*) assured at state expense. There were in addition non-recurrent items such as public works. Under the Republic and early empire the Roman economy had been expanding, partly by the simple means of more-or-less continuous conquest, which caused the inflow of booty and resources; partly because of the quantum increase in economic potential provided by the political unification of the Mediterranean basin.[14] This had meant that relatively low levels of personal taxation had been sufficient for the needs of the state in the first two centuries AD. But in the later empire the Roman world was no longer expanding, nor it seems was its economy: Rome had to learn to live within her existing means. Granted, certain areas of the late Roman world such as Africa and Syria had become much wealthier than in the early empire, but on the other hand Italy had undergone a secular decline in her agriculture and trade, and some areas such as the Danubian provinces had certainly suffered badly as a consequence of the military failures of the third century. So though there had been changes in importance and wealth or shifts in the axes of trade, the overall prosperity of the empire was at best unchanged. It was at precisely this point in Rome's economic development that we find resources increasingly called on to ensure the empire's own survival. It is generally agreed that the combined effect of the various late Roman taxes in coin, in kind and in labour represented a far greater proportion of product than did those of the early empire. In the fourth century productive capacity, fiscal requirements and the ability to levy tax seem to have been broadly in equilibrium. But any disturbance to one would jeopardise the other two, and this is what happened in the fifth century. Invasion and lapses in political control diminished the tax yield, this in consequence diminished the state's ability to discharge its functions (particularly security), this in turn led to further loss of revenue. Thus military and political weakness fed upon themselves and locked the empire in the west into a self-perpetuating cycle of decline.

In the late Roman empire revenue was from taxation,[15] aided by occasional windfalls such as Constantine I's confiscation of pagan temple treasures. The most important taxes were the *iugum* and the *capitatio*, essentially a property and a poll tax respectively. The burden of this fell squarely on the rural population. This may seem inequable, but is a reflection of two overriding facts: first, the vast bulk of the empire's population (of the order of 90 per cent) lived on the land; second, land was the only real source of wealth in this pre-industrial society. Other taxes show a similar incidence: local aristocrats had long been in the habit of presenting gifts of gold (often in the form of a crown) to an emperor upon his accession and at other auspicious times; this was regularised as the *aurum coronarium* (crown gold), a tax. The aristocrats of the empire, the senators, also were liable for special taxes (the *aurum oblaticium* and the *collatio glebalis*) levied on their income and on the vast estates scattered across the empire which yielded that income. In contrast there was but one tax levied on the urban population of the empire. Its Latin name, *collatio lustralis*, shows its purpose; a *lustrum* is a period of five years, so it was linked to the quinquennial donatives. Its Greek name, *chrysargyron pragmateutikon*, the tax in gold and silver on artisans, shows its target. The rural peasantry was exempt as were urban 'professionals' such as doctors and lawyers. The government, though, had no qualms about living off immoral earnings; prostitutes were specifically liable.[16] The tax was unpopular and does not seem to have yielded much revenue compared with the problems of collecting it.

The payments and provisions for state employees, and the consequent need to raise equivalent income both in coin and in kind from the populace, were far and away the most significant economic activity in the empire, and its most important economic motor. The scale of late Roman taxation is remarkable even to those used to the levels of exaction common in modern industrialised societies. Precise figures are hard to come by, and moreover they tend to relate to areas of the empire outside our immediate concern.[17] But given the general uniformity of taxation structures throughout the empire they may furnish a rough guide. They suggest that between a quarter and a third of gross yields might have been exacted in tax. For peasants one must add to that the exaction of rent, with the result that a half or more of their produce might have been forfeit. Obviously such rates of taxation were burdensome in the extreme and would have had a profound effect on the rural economy since so much effort had to be devoted to meeting the tax requirements. It would also have led to the desire to avoid the payment of tax whenever and wherever possible. But on the other hand the state depended on these revenues and would do its utmost to ensure them, and if non-payment increased then it would try to make up the shortfall by further calls on those whom it could still force to pay. This was already apparent in the fourth century in the form of superindictions, extra payments demanded over and above normal taxation. Much of this huge volume of revenue had to be turned into coin to be acceptable to the state. The need to obtain coin would thus be an enormous economic dynamo. This was even appreciated by writers at the time, who commented that the state's needs and expenditures dominated the economy. The obvious way to convert produce into coin was by commercial transactions in the towns. Moreover it was through the towns that the taxation system was mediated, so towns had a central rôle in the late Roman taxation cycle, and the late Roman taxation cycle had a central rôle in the economy of the towns. Again, fourth-century sources specifically mention towns, forts and the stations of the *cursus publicus* (the state postal service) as places particularly involved in the taxation system.[18]

No one likes paying tax, and tax evasion was a persistent feature of the period. The initial collecting of taxes was the responsibility of local

(margin note, handwritten) Urban Function of Urban Continuity → Rural Conservatism + Continuity of Urban Function

landowners in their capacity as *curiales*, the members of the local councils. What it seems happened was that they coerced their peasantry into paying over the odds, and then tended to decline to contribute themselves. Both operations were facilitated by bands of armed retainers. Since remonstrations against this occur in imperial legislation, it undoubtedly went on. But imperial legislation was concerned with the system when it was not working. What we do not have is any indication of how widespread abuse was. Nevertheless the cancellation of outstanding tax arrears in one of the provinces of Gaul (Belgica II) by the Caesar Julian, and the introduction of a fairer method of assessment, suggest that the problem was considerable. Not for nothing is inequable and coercive taxation often cited as a major contribution to the depressed state of the peasantry (*coloni*) in some areas during the fourth century.

The raising of revenues and their disbursement was the province of two of the most senior of officials: the *comes sacrarum largitionum* (count of the sacred largesses — finance minister) and the praetorian prefects (*praefecti praetorio*). Each had a hierarchy of officials, which ran roughly in parallel. The *comes* had officials responsible for the finances of each diocese and province of the empire. Within the regional hierarchies there were also officers who ran the various state factories which fell to the *comes*, such as those making armaments, fine armour or clothing.

As a rule of thumb it can be said that payments in specie were the responsibility of the *comes sacrarum largitionum* and those in kind of the praetorian prefects. The former was also responsible for the minting of coin in gold and silver, and the latter for the minting of bronze. The principal outgoings of the *comes sacrarum largitionum* were the salaries, the *stipendia et donativa*, for state servants. The *stipendium* (annual salary) was a hangover from early imperial days, when it had been the principal means of payment for the army and others. But the monetary inflation of the third century had rendered it of little value. To make up for this the *donativa* (donatives) issued on the accession of the emperor and every fifth anniversary thereafter, and on occasions such as when the emperor held the consulship, became a major source of income. The more senior the officer or official, the larger was the donative. The basic donative paid by Julian on his accession in 360, of five *solidi* (gold coins) and a pound of silver, was to become standard; the amount of the quinquennial and other donatives is not certain. If there were more than one Augustus or Caesar earnings could improve. In addition to these money payments, state servants also received payment in kind, an annual ration of food (*annona*) and of fodder (*capitus*) — officers and higher officials earning multiples of the basic unit. As the fourth century wore on there was a tendency for payments in kind increasingly to be adaerated, that is paid in coin at a set rate of correspondence with produce in kind.

A particular feature of the late Roman revenue and expenditure cycle was the central rôle accorded in it to gold and silver. Donatives were payable only in these metals, and much tax could only be rendered in them. Both disbursements and renders were payable either in coin or in bullion. Thus we find in addition to precious-metal coins, decorated *largitio*-dishes and stamped silver ingots, all of a certain weight in pounds and used for payments.[19] Equally bullion (such as plate) given in payment had to be assayed, giving rise to the system of control-stamps (*OB*[ryzatum] for gold and *P*[u]*S*[ullatum] for silver) on both plate and coin from the reign of Valentinian I on. In these and other ways the Roman state went to great lengths to maintain its supply of bullion and to add to it. Indeed, much bullion appears to have circulated in what was virtually a closed cycle, being paid out by the state with one hand and taken back in tax with the other.

It is against this background that we must see the minting of coin. The Roman empire, like other pre-modern states, did not strike coin as a act of fiscal philanthropy, but as an instrument of state policy, principally the payment of its servants. The monetary chaos of the third century had seen the virtual cessation of the minting of gold and silver, the bulk of what was emitted from the mints being bronze with a small percentage (< 5 per cent) of silver. Diocletian reformed the currency and introduced new gold and silver issues. These were not maintained, but in 310 Constantine I introduced a new gold coin, the *solidus*, which became the standard gold issue of the late Roman and then the Byzantine empire. From *c*. 325 he issued quantities of silver (in denominations called the *siliqua* and the *milliarense*), and this also was maintained through the fourth century.[20] As has been stated, the minting of gold and silver coin was the responsibility of the *comes sacrarum largitionum* and was carried out at so-called 'comitatensian' mints. Increasingly these were the mints nearest to where the emperor was to be found, underlining the fact that this coinage was closely tied to the requirements of the central authority. By contrast the bronze coinage (the names of various denominations are known, but how they relate to actual types of coins is uncertain) was the responsibility of the praetorian prefects, and their mints operated according to a different rationale, but one still connected with the taxation/payment cycle. Some base-metal coin was struck to pay the nearly worthless *stipendia*, but the bulk of the bronze coin was struck to enable the state to recover gold and silver. The principal agents for this were the *nummularii* or *collectarii*. They bought gold and silver coin from taxpayers, and then had it bought off them by the state; and they also seem to have sold gold and silver to those wishing to have the appropriate means to pay their taxes. These transactions were carried out in bronze at set rates, and in the discount between one and another the *nummularii* made their profit. Once the bronze coin had performed this primary function the imperial government seems to have lost virtually all further interest in it; if people then wished to use it for day-to-day commercial transactions that was their business.[21]

Clearly these considerations must have a considerable effect on the archaeological presence and absence of the various metals. Not only were gold and silver intrinsically valuable, but they were also sought after by both the state and private individuals because of the finance system. We may therefore expect them to be rare as site-finds, which is indeed the case. But what this masks from us is the extent to which they were in common use, which could have been considerable. That there was a large volume of both coin and plate in private hands is amply demonstrated by the hoards of coin and/or plate regularly found. Bronze coin, though, was of minimal intrinsic value and could be lost or discarded more freely. This is the observed archaeological situation, but it may not be easy to interpret its meaning (*cf.* p. 91).

In addition to the coin/plate nexus, there was also the system of payment in kind. Much of the property and poll taxes was payable in kind throughout the fourth century.[22] This went to feed and equip the army and the civil service, which will inevitably have meant that large quantities of material had to be transported over long distances under the supervision of the provincial *primus pilus* (originally the senior centurion of a legion, but by now a provincial official responsible to the praetorian prefect) and the receiving body. The transport itself could be imposed on provincials as a form of tax (a *munus*). Such state-directed transport is the only way a pre-industrial society has of regularly moving quantities of goods over a long distance. In this case it must principally have consisted of grain and other foodstuffs. Given the existence of such movement, it would not be at all surprising to find evidence allied to it of 'trade', that is, goods moved for resale at a profit. An instance both of the bulk movement of goods at the state's behest and of the trade parasitic on it can be seen in the west in the first two centuries AD. The distribution of certain types of amphorae (large pottery containers for the bulk transport of goods) of south Gaulish, Italian and south Spanish (Baetican) provenance is markedly skewed.[23] As well as being found local to their areas of production, there is a long-distance pattern of find-spots which concentrates along a corridor formed by the rivers Rhône, Saône, Moselle and Rhine, apparently with few outliers in the rest of Gaul. What we have here is the movement in bulk of Mediterranean commodities to the army on the north-western frontiers. These goods were being transported as part of the taxation/supply system, and the amphorae must stand proxy for other staples, particularly grain, which were also being moved along the same axis and for the same reason. Associated with this distribution pattern was one in luxury goods such as metalwork, glass and pottery, where the *negotiatores*, the middlemen, were latching onto the transport system which was thus made available. Interestingly, in the late empire a rather different situation is observable, with the system associated with the north-western armies atrophying, and a system linking the areas lying around the Mediterranean rising to prominence. Again it is archaeologically visible through pottery, in this case African Red Slip Ware (ARSW). In the late empire north Africa was the granary for Rome and the Roman state, and also produced vast quantities of olives and olive oil. This was shipped at the state's behest to feed to the populace of the City of Rome and for the army, and the existence of this free or low-cost transport network gave other African products such as ARSW a head-start over those of other areas. In consequence we find the widespread distribution of this pottery in the Mediterranean basin, but reflecting the power of the state-directed economy rather than simple 'trade'.

In parallel with the financial administration was the civil.[24] The empire was divided into some half-dozen huge territorial circumscriptions, each of which was responsible to a praetorian prefect (*praefectus praetorio*). A praetorian prefecture was divided into a number of dioceses ruled by a *vicarius* and covering the territory roughly of a second-century province. The diocese was further sub-divided into a number of provinces, governed usually by a *praeses* (sometimes a *consularis* for the more important). All these officials with their staffs were responsible for the good order and administration of their areas, including judicial functions. As outlined above they also had important rôles to play in the taxation and supply system, having responsibility for the parts of these in kind, through the medium of the provincial *primi pili*.

At the local level administration was carried out by the *civitas*, the area of land dependent on a principal town. Here the local landowners formed the *ordo* or council, and their functions were again administrative and fiscal. In the first two centuries AD service on the *ordo* had been a matter of honour, and in some parts of the empire there developed a tradition of public service and civic euergetism (public works and benefaction) which led to the provision of public buildings and facilities, shows and spectacles by the civic aristocracy. For the late empire the picture appears rather different.[25] A whole series of imperial enactments suggest that curial duties were increasingly unattractive to the landed classes and were increasingly evaded. At the end of the third century Diocletian legislated to make membership of the curial class and performance of curial duties an hereditary obligation; but as he did so for almost all professions and trades in the empire, this really tells us nothing in particular about whether there was dereliction of curial duty. Constantine I legislated to make service as a *curialis* a 'punishment' for evading military service. But it is to the latter part of the fourth century that the bulk of imperial legislation concerning non-fulfilment of curial duties dates, and most of it is directed to officials in the eastern part of the empire. In the west the evidence of inscriptions and buildings in Italy is that the fourth century saw a sharp decline in the provision of new buildings (except churches) and aristocratic expenditure increasingly being turned to private luxury.[26] In Gaul the writings of men such as Ausonius and Paulinus of Nola in the fourth century, and Sidonius Apollinaris in the fifth century, display no marked aversion to the obligations imposed by their local standing; nonetheless they concentrate on their doings at their country estates, and affairs in the town take them away from this preferable retreat. Archaeologically the late empire is notable for the decline of the traditional means of expressing civic pride and personal glory, that is public buildings and amenities, and in Gaul and Britain there is evidence for new uses for, or decline of, the existing public buildings (*cf.* pp. 71). But there is an important exception: in the European provinces the fourth century sees the private financing of church-building, some of it patronage as lavish as that for a second-century secular basilica.[27] Certainly in the fourth century the *curiales* did not like their rôle as tax-gatherers, especially as they were liable for any shortfall. But that does not mean that they had lost all sense of the obligations of their rank. Rather it seems to have been differently expressed, in expenditure on private rather than public magnificence. A response to the disinclination of local landowners to undertake the more irksome duties of local administration was the appointment by the imperial government of an official (a *corrector*) to oversee the proper administration of a *civitas*.

Such were the structures by which the late Roman state was administered and by which it sought to ensure its own survival. In general the provision of the officers and officials of the various departments seems to have been relatively uniform across the empire, though of course the need for military commitments will have varied from the frontier through to the interior of the empire. But all this was imposed on a set of local conditions formed in and inherited from the earlier history of the empire, and it is at some of the outlines of this that we must now look. Late Roman society was intensely hierarchical and was operated through a web of kinship and patronage relationships. One hierarchy was that of the established nobility, whose status and power derived from the ownership of land and their authority over the people who lived on their land or otherwise worked for them. At the highest level were the senatorial families, usually commanding considerable landed wealth, often great riches.[28] Many families had almost innumerable ramifications, including branches in the provinces, and many senatorial families were themselves of provincial stock. Within the provinces the local aristocracy, even if not elevated to senatorial status, still exercised considerable powers of local patronage, though now it less often took the form of public works and benefactions. Both the senatorial and provincial aristocracies regularly sought places in the imperial service, thus maintaining their usefulness to the emperor and their influence in his councils. It was also one of the ways to try to improve one's standing.

As well as the established hierarchies of landed wealth there were three other principal routes by which the ambitious might seek preferment. These were the imperial service, the army and the church. Acquisition of the imperial favour could unlock the way to rank and fortune, as is well shown in the west by the career of Ausonius, who from being a provincial professor at Bordeaux was made tutor to the young Gratian, son of Valentinian I. Under Valentinian, Ausonius became *quaestor sacri palatii* (comptroller of the household). Gratian succeeded his father in 375 and in 378 Ausonius was appointed praetorian prefect of the Gauls, and in the following year consul. In 376 his son Hesperius was appointed proconsul of Africa, in which post he was succeeded by his brother-in-law Thalassius. In about 375 Ausonius' father, then aged nearly ninety, was given the honorary codicils of appointment as praetorian prefect of Illyricum. Those who rose in the imperial service would then hope to marry and/or buy into the senatorial order to become part of the traditional aristocracy. The beneficial effects of imperial patronage may be seen not only in the careers of individuals but also in the fortunes of communities. The city where Ausonius served Valentinian, Trier, is a remarkable example of this. In the early empire it had been a *colonia* and the seat of the *procurator Belgicae et duarum Germaniarum* (the financial administrator for northern Gaul and the Rhineland), and it had grown rich on the traffic passing down the Moselle to the frontier armies. Nonetheless, it was only a provincial city, albeit a wealthy and well-appointed one. But with the arrival of the imperial presence and court the face of the city was changed.[29] Along the eastern side of the city centre there now stretched that huge complex of buildings proper to the housing of the emperor and his court, to say nothing of the praetorian prefect of the Gauls and his staff, the *praeses* of Belgica I and the officials of the financial administration. In addition there were a variety of state factories with their installations and storehouses. Thus adorned, and benefiting from the inflow of state expenditure to the city, Trier was without parallel amongst the cities of central and northern Gaul.

Equally, meritorious service in the army could lead to senior appointments which would give the prospect of social advancement. Even middle-ranking officers could expect to become at least local notables. All of them, of course, wielded powers of military patronage which could be used to their own advantage and that of their families and retainers. To judge by papyrological evidence from Egypt, the local military commander was a person of consequence in the locality, well beyond the walls of his fort.[30] Likewise advancement in the Church led to positions of power and patronage in the local community, especially for the bishop. Some bishops, such as the contemporaries Ambrose of Milan and Martin of Tours could be actors on the imperial stage.

Clearly there was a tension between those who owed their position to inherited wealth and those who had made their way through ability. But the common aim of both was ownership of land, and the security of income and the power that went with such ownership. A landowner had a very direct effect on those who lived on his estates and a significant part to play also in his local community both through his position and through the money at his disposal. Our sources, though these are mainly from the eastern parts of the empire, tend to suggest that in the late Roman period the gap between haves and have-nots was becoming more marked and that society was becoming polarised. Though all free people in the empire were now citizens, there was nevertheless a legal distinction between the land-owning classes and the broad mass of the populace. The former were classified as *honestiores*, the latter as *humiliores*, and their legal rights in such matters as imprisonment, corporal punishment, torture and execution differed considerably. For many peasants life was brutal, and the landowners acquired increasing power over their lives and property, reducing them to the status of *coloni*, labourers tied to the land.

Many aspects of the late Roman empire offend modern sensibilities, but it was a pre-industrial society with a relatively undeveloped economy and a traditional social basis. It was also under immense external threat. The measures taken by Diocletian and his successors were aimed at one thing above all others — the prime responsibility of the rulers and the prime concern of the ruled — the continued existence of the Roman state.

What we have seen here is essentially the eagle's-eye view of the empire, from the top down. It outlines how the late empire might be expected to operate in general terms. But the Roman empire was not a homogeneous unity. It was made up of a mass of differences imposed by geography, by climate, by resources, by wealth, by history, by culture, by belief. All of these had to be compromised with in the actual local administration and make-up of the empire. In the next chapter we shall outline how the special circumstances of Gaul and Germany were reflected in their development in the fourth century as the essential backdrop against which events and trends in Britain may be properly assessed.

TWO

The Continental Background

The previous chapter examined the structure of the late Roman state to an extent as an idealised construct: this was how the state should run. In this chapter we move to examining a particular area of the empire in the west, principally Gaul and Germany. We shall see how the imperial structures and institutions were put in place here and discuss how the area reacted to them. This is necessary in order to provide an immediate context for late Roman Britain, since events in these areas were the most likely to have directly-related repercussions on the island. Geographically, they are of course the areas of the empire closest to Britain. Historically, they had been linked by common ethnic and cultural ties since well before Britain became a part of the empire. The advent of Rome had imposed an administrative, cultural and economic unity which could transcend local and regional boundaries. In the late empire all these areas depended on a common hierarchy of administration, lived under the same laws, endured the same taxation, were protected by the same armies and shared common cultural values and religious beliefs. Yet the general view has been that the lands to either side of the Channel differed profoundly in the later Roman period. Comparisons of late Roman Gaul with Britain have been essays in contrasts: both have towns but they are unlike; both have villas but they differ; both are subject to the same fiscal and economic imperatives and pressures but these are responded to in different forms. Overall, the fourth century is seen as a time of prosperity for Britain, partly profiting from the misfortunes which had blighted her continental neighbours from the middle of the third century.

Militarily, the western provinces had had their fair share of the problems of the third century. In the early part of that century the familiar tribes along the Rhine frontier, such as the Chauci and Cherusci, long under Roman tutelage, had coalesced into the new and decidedly less amenable confederations of the Franks and the Alamanni on the lower and middle Rhine respectively. In 235 the threat of the latter brought the emperor Severus Alexander to Mainz. His assassination there set in train the political instability of the ensuing half century. In the 250s there were again problems on the Rhine. The emperor Gallienus conducted a series of successful campaigns in 255–7, but was unable to avoid having to abandon the *Agri Decumates*, the re-entrant of land between the upper Rhine and the upper Danube. He was in Germany in 260 when news came of the capture of his father the emperor Valerian by the Persian Great King Shapur I. On his departure he left his son the Caesar Saloninus in his stead at Cologne. This was to prove the boy's death-warrant;

he was murdered and replaced by the general Postumus. For the next fourteen years Postumus (260–8) and his successors Victorinus (268–70) and the Tetrici father and son (270–4) ruled from Hadrian's Wall to the Straits of Gibraltar and the Alps. Though not recognised by Gallienus and his successors, this 'Gallic Empire' was not a separatist movement designed to split the west from the rest of the empire. Rather it was the result of the increasing inability of any one emperor to look after the interests of all his subjects equally. Instead the provincials and provincial garrisons set up emperors whose prime loyalty would be to their area, and whose prime concern would be the security of the people who had placed him on the throne. In this endeavour the Gallic Empire had mixed fortunes. On the one hand new fortifications were built along the Rhine and the Channel coasts of Britain,[1] but on the other the 260s saw a series of barbarian invasions across the Rhine and into Gaul. In 274 the elder Tetricus surrendered his charge to the legitimate emperor Aurelian on amicable terms, suffering nothing worse than exile and subsequent promotion to a provincial governorship. The years immediately following on the surrender of the Gallic Empire saw what were later regarded as the most devastating of the third-century invasions of Gaul; in its aftermath the emperor Probus was said to have had to restore some seventy cities. Through the 280s the Alamanni remained restive until they were utterly crushed by the western Augustus Maximian in 293. The same year saw military success against another episode of usurpation in the west. In 286 Carausius, commander of the Channel fleet, had revolted from his allegiance, apparently in advance of intended disciplinary action by Maximian. From 286 to 293 he controlled Britain and the north-western parts of Gaul.[2] In 293 he lost his Gallic possessions, including the great fleet base at Boulogne, to Maximian's Caesar Constantius I (Chlorus), and soon after his life. His supplanter, Allectus, was suppressed by Constantius Chlorus in 296 and Britain restored to the light of legitimate authority (Pl. 1).

Politically, the episodes of usurped imperial authority seem to have done the western provinces no lasting harm. More problematic are the effect of the third-century barbarian invasions and how we measure that effect, for on our view of this depends much about our perception of the fourth century on the continent. The most commonly held view is that the damage went deep, and that Gaul and Germany never really recovered. There is evidence for destruction at many sites in the mid to later third century, though not perhaps as much as is generally thought. There has been a tendency to ascribe any third-century burnt deposit to this period and to put it down to barbarian attack. Buildings, especially timber-framed ones, do burn down for other causes. Likewise the spate of coin hoards in the west dated to the 260s and 270s is taken to be a reaction to the threat or actuality of invasion from beyond the Rhine rather than political or financial instability within the empire.[3] But whereas in the short term the effect of an invasion can be devastating, and takes some recovering from in the medium term, what about the long term? Is it plausible that the events of the later third century should depress the economy and society of Gaul right through the fourth century?

We shall turn first to the level and nature of state involvement in late

Roman Gaul and Germany. The fourth century saw a level of direct imperial interest and imperial presence north of the Alps unlike anything that had gone before. The retirement of Maximian in 305 was followed by the accession of Constantius Chlorus, whose death at York in the following year brought his son Constantine I to the throne. For much of the next decade Gaul was Constantine's base, and it was probably he who commissioned the grandiose palace buildings in his capital, Trier. After Constantine became sole master of the Roman world Trier was still the residence of members of the imperial family, and it was there that his wife Fausta died in suspicious circumstances in 326. After Constantine I's death in 337 his sons and successors in the west, Constantine II and Constans, continued to favour Gaul and particularly Trier. The city went into relative eclipse in the 350s, but in the 360s, 370s and 380s it was again the principal imperial residence successively of Valentinian I (364–75), his son Gratian (375–83) and the usurper Magnus Maximus (383–88).

In the first part of the fourth century the presence of the emperor would have involved the presence of a force of *comitatenses*, presumably based in and around Trier. As the century progressed Gaul was afforded a significant regional detachment of the comitatensian army as well as *limitaneus* commands (*cf.* p. 20). The known history of the fourth century shows that it was basically a time of military stability along the Rhine. From Maximian's defeat of the Alamanni in 293 until 350 we have no record of a serious breach of the Rhine frontier. In 350 this was upset; in that year in the course of his bid for power the British usurper Magnentius had the western Augustus Constans killed at Elne. The surviving son of Constantine I, the eastern Augustus Constantius II, determined to avenge his brother. According to some accounts it was he who instigated a major barbarian invasion across the Rhine to weaken and distract his opponent. If so, it proved too successful, and even after the overthrow of Magnentius in 353 Constantius was unable to expel the Alamanni and their allies. In desperation he appointed his young and untried kinsman Julian as Caesar in Gaul in 355. Julian proved to be a surprisingly able commander, and in 357 brought the Alamanni to battle and soundly defeated them at Strasbourg. In the following year he brought the Franks on the lower Rhine to heel. For the next half century there is again no record of any serious breach of the Rhine frontier. Only in the extreme north-west did the Salian Franks gradually establish themselves in Toxandria, within the line of the *limes*. Given the great measure of security from external threat during the course of the fourth century it would seem that a necessary, if not of itself sufficient, precondition for a recovery in the fortunes of Gaul and Germany was in place.

Within these secure frontiers the administrative reforms of Diocletian were put in place as in any other part of the empire (fig. 2). Britain, Gaul, Germany, Spain and a small chunk of western north Africa now comprised the praetorian prefecture of the Gauls. The praetorian prefect had his seat at Trier, where he could be in attendance on the emperor when the latter was in residence. The city was also well-placed for communications with the Rhine, Britain and the interior of Gaul. The praetorian prefecture consisted of four

Fig. 2 Map of administrative divisions of western empire in fourth century

dioceses, each with its *vicarius*: *Britanniae* (Britain), *Galliae* (northern Gaul and Germany), *Viennensis* (later *Septem Provinciae* — southern Gaul) and *Hispaniae* (Spain and Mauretania Tingitana in north Africa). Each diocese originally contained about four of the new, small provinces ruled by a *praeses* or a *consularis*. The prefecture also contained mints for the striking of bronze coin at Trier, Lyon and Arles as well as London (to 326) and Amiens (350–3). Through the *primus pilus* in each province the prefect was responsible for the collection and transport of some of the taxes in kind. This proliferation of administrative subdivisions and officials has been seen by some as representing the fragmentation of the late empire; in fact it was a mechanism to exercise close supervision of the entire empire to bend it to the imperial priorities.

In parallel with the hierarchy of the civil administration under the praetorian prefect was that of the financial administration responsible to the *comes sacrarum largitionum*. In each diocese there was a *rationalis* responsible for the taxation in specie and the disbursements in his area. There were *thesauri* (treasuries) at London, Trier, Lyon and Arles. Comitatensian mints struck gold and silver at Trier (most often) and occasionally at London, Lyon and Arles. Throughout Gaul (though not Spain) there were the various state factories for the production of clothing and weaponry as well as official metalwork, along with fine armour and uniforms for senior officers and officials. The largest concentration of these installations was at Trier, further underpinning the city's economy. Not far behind was Arles in southern Gaul, and it was to this city that the seat of the praetorian prefecture was transferred at the turn of the fourth and fifth centuries.

The *Notitia Dignitatum* reveals that by the end of the fourth century there were three major and two minor *limitaneus* commands in Gaul and Germany. Along the Channel coast there were the *dux tractus Armoricani et Nervicani* (Brittany and Normandy) and the *dux Belgicae* (the Pas-de-Calais). On the Rhine was the command of the *dux Moguntiacensis* (the central Rhine) as well as the curious little command of the *dux Sequanici* (on the upper Rhine). There were also the two *limitaneus* commands in Britain discussed below (p. 50). With the development of regional field armies in the latter part of the century we find the *Notitia* listing a substantial force in Gaul under the *magister equitum per Gallias*, with lesser forces in Britain, Spain and Tingitana (fig 3).[4]

The successive military construction campaigns under the Gallic Empire, Maximian, Constantine I and Valentinian I resulted in the Rhine frontier being strengthened overall and individual forts being brought up to date in their defensive architecture. By the end of the fourth century there was a more-or-less unbroken chain of forts, fortlets and watchtowers, and a frontier road, from the North Sea to the Alps.[5] As with the rest of the empire we are still woefully inadequately informed about the nature and size of the units which manned these installations. In the interior, the newly-defended towns and cities of Gaul and Germany not only offered protection to local interests and personnel, but also discharged functions in wider imperial strategy by defending internal lines of communication and acting as fortified bases. This

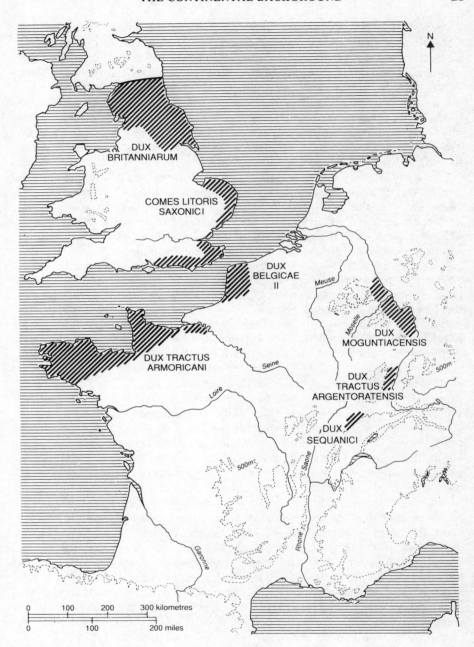

Fig. 3 Map of military commands in west in fourth century

latter function may be seen in the use made of the towns by Julian and Valentinian I when on campaign. In addition, the interior of Germany and the eastern parts of Gaul saw the widespread use or re-use of hilltop defended sites, many of them Iron-Age hillforts.[6] Some of these, to judge by the quality of the defensive works and the associated structures and artefacts, were purely civilian initiatives. But the masonry of the defences of others is of much better quality, and these are often associated with cemeteries containing weapon graves (*Waffengräber*), at sites such as Furfooz[7] or Vireux-Molhain[8] (*cf.* p. 33). These suggest that bodies of troops (possibly federate barbarians) were being stationed in the interior.

The civil, financial and military structures characteristic of the late Roman empire can thus be seen to have been in place in the late Roman west as elsewhere. But the structures of the state were not all that there was to the late Roman empire; as we have said they operated alongside and over a mass of local conditions. It is the condition of late Roman Gaul and Germany apart from their official institutions that we must now examine.

We may start with that most characteristic of Roman institutions, the town, especially the towns of late Roman Gaul. Until recently there was little debate on the nature of these towns, a view established in the earlier part of this century having long held sway.[9] This may be summarised, and I hope not unduly caricatured, as follows. The invasions of the 260s and 270s were knock-out blows from which the expansive, classicising towns of the early empire never recovered. In their place arose tiny, heavily-fortified *cités administratives* set amid fields of ruins, in which lived the *corrector* of the *civitas*, the bishop and perhaps some other notables. Whereas the *civitas*-capitals of the early empire had been sprawling, undefended settlements of 100 ha. (250 acres) or more, the defended enceintes of the late Empire covered only a fraction of this area, of the order of 4–10 ha. (10–25 acres), rarely more. The new walls were in the standard late-imperial defensive idiom, thick and high with regularly-spaced, externally-projecting towers and small, heavily-defended gateways. The lowest courses of these walls often consisted of ashlars and architectural stonework re-used from the civic buildings and monuments and the tombs of the earlier town; this was taken as clear evidence that the towns had been sacked and that such structures were good for nothing but spoliation. The desecration of tombs showed total disruption of the earlier pieties and of family reverence for forebears. Moreover, at some towns the former civic buildings were actually incorporated into the defences — at Bavai the forum, at Périgueux and Tours the amphitheatre, at Amiens both. The coins along with the milestones and other inscriptions incorporated into these walls all pointed to a date late in the third century. The walls were thus seen as a hasty response to the barbarian invasions. The defended area was assumed to be all that was left of the town, and it could not have housed anything like the population of the earlier town. The small size of the defended area coupled with the re-use of stone from earlier buildings led to the conclusion that the area outside the defences was derelict. The written sources refer to the continuing administrative functions of the towns, and in the late Roman period the bishops are placed at towns.

Fig. 4 Map showing principal sites mentioned in Ch. 2

Since most of the cathedrals of mediaeval France stand within the late Roman enceinte, it was assumed that this was a situation which had developed in the fourth century when bishops were instituted in the *civitates* of Gaul.

This picture of physical, social and economic collapse in the towns of late Roman Gaul contrasts strongly not only with that for the earlier Gallo-Roman town, but also with that for the towns of late Roman Britain. We have already noted that conditions in late Roman Gaul, particularly away from the Rhine frontier, were generally peaceful. Furthermore, administrators and bishops with their entourages represented sources of patronage and money, as did remaining local aristocrats. Some towns also had state factories whose labour force would be in receipt of regular pay. The taxation system for Gaul, which was no different for that of the rest of the empire, was administered through the towns and required quantities of surplus production to be turned into gold and silver coin. In addition the rural population would still be in need of specialist goods and services which they could not provide for themselves but which town-based artisans, merchants and professionals could. All in all it would seem that the general preconditions necessary to the functioning of a late Roman town, and which elsewhere in the empire supported such towns, were in place in late Roman Gaul. If this is so, is the view of these towns as poor, withered things still tenable?

To take the defences first (fig. 5). Examination of some of the late Roman circuits suggests that they were not in fact built in haste.[10] Above the lower courses of reused monumental stonework, the upper parts of the walls were built in the time-honoured style for Gallo-Roman public buildings: a core of coursed rubble (undressed stone) faced on either side with a skin of *petit appareil* (small rectangular blocks of masonry) with regularly-spaced bonding-courses of flat, Roman bricks. At a few towns, such as Le Mans, the external face of the wall was decorated in patterns made of different-coloured stones (Pl. 4). At other towns the facing stones were carefully dressed and laid. At Tours the stone for the *petit appareil* was all freshly quarried.[11] The lowest courses of re-used ashlars and architectural stonework were in fact fitted together with considerable care. These defences were not works of hasty improvisation, but were planned and constructed with care and expertise. Their date too is being reconsidered. The most spectacular case is at Tours,[12] where excavations within the north-eastern corner of the late Roman *castrum* yielded a stratified sequence of coins pre-dating the construction of the wall, including one of 364–75 from the actual foundation trench of the defensive wall. It may be no coincidence that in 374 Tours was created the capital of the newly-constituted province of Lugdunensis III. At other sites also a late third-century date will no longer hold. At Beauvais there are coins of the House of Constantine associated with the construction of the defences, suggesting a date of 320 or so.[13] Beauvais is one member of a group of stylistically-linked late defensive circuits in Belgica,[14] so presumably the other members such as Senlis and Soissons must also be re-assigned to the fourth century. At Auxerre there is a record of a coin of Magnentius (350–3) from the walls.[15] So not only were these defences a more carefully-executed phenomenon than has previously been thought; they were also not all grouped together in the

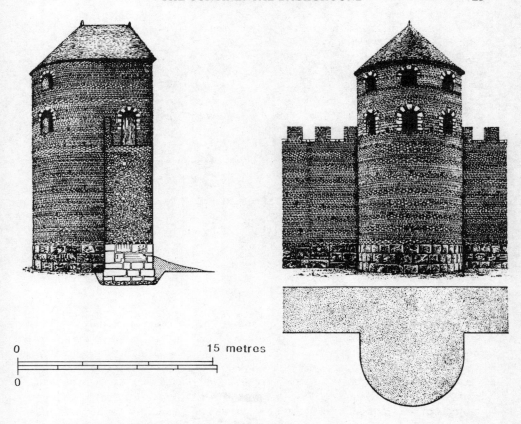

Fig. 5 Late Roman town walls in Gaul

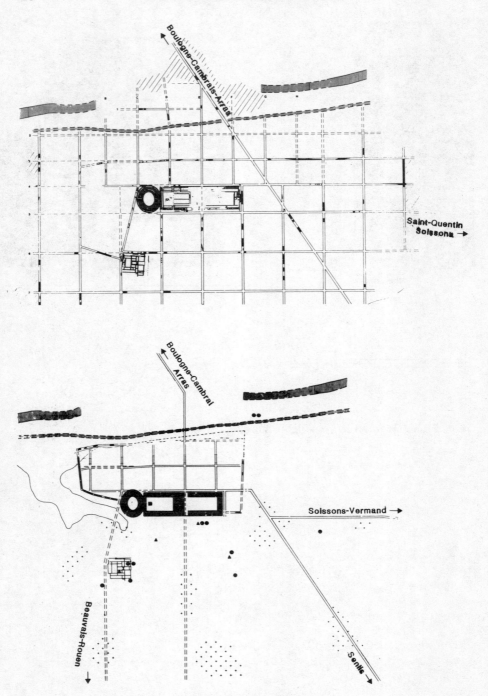

Fig. 6 Amiens in second and fourth centuries

late third century, some at least were constructed well into the fourth. That it was the sites of towns that were chosen to receive defences so long after the third-century invasions must mean that there was something more there than fields of ruins.

What of the view that the defended area was all that there was of these late towns? This has been decisively shown to be not the case at one *civitas*-capital in Lugdunensis: Paris.[16] There the early imperial city lay on the south (left) bank of the Seine. In the fourth century the Ile de la Cité was surrounded by a set of new defences (if this is not a quay), but significant areas of the settlement on the left bank continued in use, as did much of the earlier cemetery area. At Amiens (fig. 6) the defences enclosed a larger-than-usual 20 ha. (50 acres), in itself more than would be needed simply to house officials and ecclesiastics. In addition, an area of up to 10 ha. (25 acres) outside the southern walls was occupied in the fourth century. The town was probably the manufacturing centre for so-called 'Frontinus' bottles.[17] The rest of the area of the earlier town seems to have been abandoned, with cemeteries encroaching on the formerly occupied areas. At Reims,[18] where the excavator remarks that the size of and the care taken over the defences suggest that they were constructed in a period of prosperity, there is now also evidence for extra- as well as intra-mural occupation in the fourth century, with the cemeteries at a remove from the walls. At present these are but straws in the wind, but they do suggest that the received view may be too restrictive, and that the walled area was not necessarily all that there was of the town. Outside the walls also lay the cemeteries, and for these still to be in use there must have been an urban population dying off through the fourth century. There are also a few literary straws that may be clutched at. In his account of the life of St Martin of Tours, Sulpicius Severus speaks on more than one occasion of the people of Tours. Ausonius also refers to the people of his native Bordeaux, and the panegyricist from Autun performing before Constantine I nonetheless lets slip that the population still thrives.[19]

So far we have been discussing the higher-order towns such as the *civitas*-capitals; the fate of the smaller market towns, or *vici*, is even more obscure. In the first and second centuries these had proliferated as centres of manufacture and redistribution serving the local rural population, like their cousins across the Channel.[20] The assumption often made is that they suffered as badly as, if not worse than, the large towns in the invasions of the third century. In support of this, much evidence for burning or abandonment has tended to be dated to the period of the invasions, whether justifiably or not. But a survey of the fates of the small towns of Belgica[21] has shown that this assumption needs modifying. Of the eighty-seven sites attested in the early third century, thirty-one did not see out the century but fifty-six did. Of the fifty-six all had been affected by the events of the later third century; all had been reduced from their earlier extent and some had become little if anything more than fortified strongpoints, *burgi*. Some though have yielded structural and artefactual evidence to suggest that they did to some extent perpetuate their former rôle in the socio-economic hierarchy.

One of the established ways of assessing the place of a town in the economic hierarchy is the study of artefact distributions, particularly for pottery because of its survival rate. In theory, if the town is acting as a market or distribution centre the pottery from it should differ in quantity and/or quality from that from the rural sites it served. Unfortunately there is as yet not a sufficient data-base from which to draw reliable conclusions for late Roman Gaul. One may point to the apparent urban bias of the distribution of Argonne wares,[22] both in overall volume and in range of types, but this remains subjective until quantifiable. One area where pottery distributions do differ from those of the earlier empire is that of long-distance trade, particularly from the Mediterranean. In Chapter 1 (p. 12) we noted the epigraphic and artefactual evidence for a clear axis of movement up the Rhône and Saône to the Moselle and thence down the Rhine and to Britain.[23] The axis was clearly inspired by the need to transport grain and Mediterranean goods to the frontier armies, and on the back of this bulk transport rode other trade goods.[24] In terms of the overall volume of goods moved north of the Alps in the early imperial period this was probably trivial; the vast majority of trade would have been constrained by competition, transport costs and other factors to remain resolutely local. Its significance lies in the fact that it represents tangibly the linking of the Mediterranean world with the north-west. In the late empire this link was feeble. Apart from a small amount of ARSW found on the upper Rhine[25] and some amphorae from Spain, there is little material of identifiably Mediterranean origin north of the Alps. On the other hand the Mediterranean basin seems to have been closely bound together by maritime commerce, to judge by the distributions of ARSW and north African amphorae.[26] Another major absentee from the late as compared with the early empire is samian, the red-gloss fine pottery of Gaul. Manufactured and exported in huge quantities, it saturated the western provinces in the first and second centuries. In its own right it generated a volume of trade; but if like other pottery such as amphorae it is in fact indicative of trade in other perishable goods it is all the more significant. The causes of its decline and disappearance are still imperfectly understood,[27] but it occurred in the early part of the third century. Thereafter this trade which had linked the western provinces was no longer present. In general it appears that a shear-line was developing between the economy and trade of the Mediterranean and those of the north-west, and that in the north-west long-distance trade was becoming even more uncommon. While the political and cultural unity of the empire was maintained over and above regional tendencies this would not have mattered too much. But once that unity started to disintegrate, separation of economic spheres would hasten and perpetuate the disintegration, and lack of long-distance contacts would hardly impede further fragmentation within those spheres.

As with the towns, so with the country. The consensus that has built up over the years sees decline, impoverishment, depopulation.[28] This rests essentially on literary evidence, backed up by the prevailing view of the seriousness of the third-century invasions and supported by the deficiencies of the archaeological record. The main literary props are *coloni* (serfs), *agri deserti* (abandoned lands), *bacaudae* (or *bagaudae* — bandits/brigands) and *laeti* (barbarian settlers). The overall picture is that the harsh oppression of the *coloni* drove them to flee from their masters wherever possible, giving rise to *agri deserti*. Some of the ex-*coloni* formed or attached themselves to bands of *bacaudae*. These are first attested in eastern Gaul in the decades following the great third-century invasions, and reappear sporadically down to the mid-fifth century in Armorica (Brittany and adjoining areas of Gaul). It is difficult to establish a reliable picture of the causes and nature of bacaudic outbreaks because of the unremittingly hostile bias of our sources. Modern writers tend to see them as bands of dispossessed peasants living by exacting what they wanted from settled agriculturalists, or else living with their connivance;[29] sometimes with uncomfortable overtones of Robin Hood or Che Guevara. In their turn they contributed to the problem of *agri deserti*. One partial solution to this was to settle *laeti* on the land, both to bring it back into production and to furnish military manpower.

Recent re-examination of the literary texts on which this gloomy picture is based has shown that, as usual, they should not be taken at face value. Though the laws and rescripts speak of *coloni* and their problems in particular locations and at particular times, there is never any mention of the colonate as such. It is therefore unwise to assume that there was a uniform, empire-wide institution of the colonate and that therefore the problems of one area illuminate those of others. A simple, universal picture of a depressed peasantry is too simple. Localised references must be considered in their local context.[30]

The question of *agri deserti* has been shown to be linked to the particular outlook of the authors who mention it, Christian and pagan. The Christian writers were operating within an established millenarian tradition, which saw this world in irretrievable decline towards Armageddon and the Parousia (the Second Coming). Any feature of society which showed this world to be a vale of tears would be pressed into the service of this view. Equally, pagan writers tended to view this age of the world as in decline from previous happier ages (sometimes due to the malign influence of Christianity), therefore they also were interested in painting a particular picture of the world rather than the true state of affairs. Actual evidence for *agri deserti* being a widespread and significant phenomenon is hard to find, especially in Gaul. For instance one of the few occurrences of the term from fourth-century Gaul is in a panegyric asking the emperor for remission of taxes to the city of Autun: presenting such a case brings out the special pleader in us all.[31]

Bacaudae likewise have been undergoing re-examination.[32] Even given the weaknesses and biases of the sources, all from the 'official' side, certain things may be said. First of all, it is manifestly unsatisfactory to assume that because a phenomenon of the late third century in eastern Gaul and one of the early to mid-fifth century in western Gaul are called the same thing, they necessarily are the same thing. Moreover, because they are encountered in the third and the fifth century it is assumed that they are endemic through the fourth century. Yet there are no references to them from that century; indeed they seem to show an interesting negative correlation with the presence of an emperor in Gaul. Such evidence for what the phenomenon actually was as we may glean from the hostile commentaries which survive suggest that the *bacaudae* were not just dispossessed peasants terrorising the countryside, but that they could include, certainly in the fifth-century version, a significant proportion of members of the minor land-owning classes. These may have fallen on hard times or been pushed off their land by the wealthy. They would have had no redress through the traditional land-dominated structures of society, but may have had through the alternative channel of power represented by the imperial presence during the fourth century. The literary sources do not allow us to argue that the *bacaudae* were a regular feature of late Roman Gaul or that they had a general depressive effect on the rural economy.

Agri deserti, bacaudae, coloni, laeti all existed in certain places and at certain times. But we may doubt whether they all co-existed in fourth-century Gaul in the significant relationship postulated for them. If we no longer take the texts at face value, we see that they do not give us a framework for the understanding of late Roman rural economy and society in Gaul. If this is so we need to start again, and to lay more emphasis on the archaeological evidence and problems arising from it.

It has long been known that there is a strand of literary evidence actually from late Roman Gaul which runs counter to the supposed evidence for decline discussed above. This derives from the writings of a group of Aquitanian nobles of the second half of the fourth century,[33] chief amongst them Ausonius and Sulpicius Severus, but including others such as Paulinus of Nola. In the early and mid-fifth century respectively, Rutilius Namatianus from Narbonensis and Sidonius Apollinaris from the Auvergne echo this world. In it we find a countryside of commodious villas at the centre of large, well-stocked estates giving their owners the time and means to pursue literary and theological pastimes or the traditional thrills of the chase. Clearly there is the problem that we are seeing this world through the eyes of the fortunate, and we must also beware of the rose-tinted Roman literary tradition of rural *otium cum dignitate* (useful and cultured leisure), but nevertheless the fourth-century texts are markedly devoid of reference to barbarian threat, internal dissent or rural privation. Since the last war archaeology has come to support this picture with the excavation of Aquitanian palace-villas such as Chiragan and Montmaurin (fig 7).[34]

For central and northern Gaul the picture to be gained from archaeology is still profoundly incomplete. To an extent preconceptions are still dominated by the idea of *honestiores* and *humiliores* and the growing divide between the rich and the poor. This had led to an expectation that the rural settlement hierarchy should be bi-polar, some rich sites and a lot of poor ones. Moreover the rich sites (the villas) would have been much affected by the third-century barbarian invasions. Work on the late Roman countryside in the north has therefore concentrated on one class of site: the villas. Attempts have been made to try to assess how many villas suffered or were extinguished in the later third century, and how many there were in operation in the fourth. These figures are then compared with those for the later second century to assess the extent of the decline. So far, though, we have few regional surveys

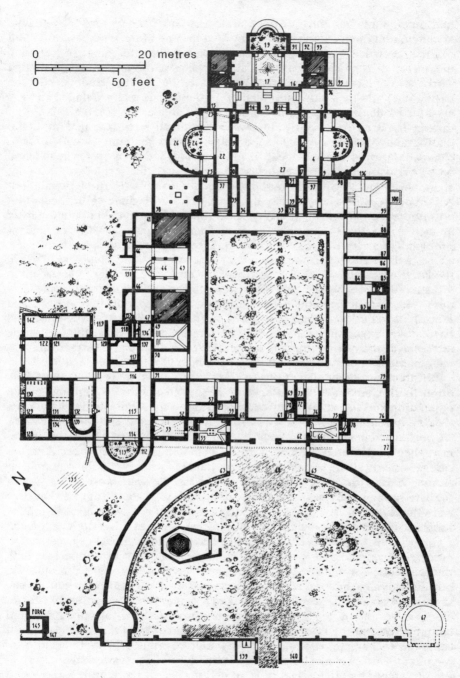

Fig. 7 The villa at Montmaurin

that provide much usable information. In Brittany[35] the picture is one of the abandonment of most of the villas known at the end of the second century and of the regrowth of woodland at the expense of cultivated land. In Belgica[36] the overall picture is of destruction at many sites in the third century (though workers may have been too willing to ascribe this to the handiwork of the barbarians) and their non-reoccupation in the fourth. More detailed surveys exist for particular areas within Belgica. In the area of the Somme valley,[37] of the six hundred or so early imperial villas of all sizes revealed by aerial photography, very few have yielded fourth-century material, though it is not clear what proportion have been examined and whether by surface collection or by excavation. It is nevertheless assumed that this fertile area was not abandoned and that there must have been a continuing rural population. Alternatives as to where it may have been located include continuing villas now under mediaeval and modern Picard villages, or that the population lived in crude structures (*cabanes*) of *pisé* (rammed earth), with consequent problems of archaeological recognition. Elsewhere in Belgica work on villas suggests that between 10 and 20 per cent of second-century sites were in use in the late Roman period. One exception is the area around Trier,[38] where up to 40 per cent of second-century sites were still in use, along with some new ones. These range from the probable and possible imperial villas at Konz and Pfalzel, through well-appointed ones such as Wittlich, to simpler farms. Evidently the quantity and quality of the Treveran villas is a testimony to the influence of the nearby imperial and prefectorial seat (and a further interesting comment on the potency of such patronage).

But there are other classes of site known from the late Roman countryside of northern Gaul, and the existence of these both confirms a continuing rural population and suggests that by concentrating on the villas we may have been looking in the wrong place. We have already noted the hilltop fortifications (re-)furbished in eastern Gaul and the Rhineland, some of whose cemeteries have been excavated, some of these containing *Waffengräber*. Another category of rural site which was in part functioning was the rural temple or shrine. In Belgica[39] several dating from the early empire were still in use in the late, and as they were off the beaten track this would suggest that they were the centre of devotion for the local rural populace. A similar picture for Lugdunensis can be gained from Sulpicius Severus' descriptions of the combats of St Martin of Tours against rural paganism. Rural cemeteries too occurred in numbers in fourth-century northern Gaul.[40] In comparison with the cemeteries of the first and second centuries they were fewer in number, but individually they tended to be larger. They were also often not on the same site as the earlier cemeteries. Taken together these categories of site are eloquent testimony to the continuing presence of the rural population and labour force, but their different nature and location from the settlements and cemeteries characteristic of the early empire argue for a relocation of population and a change both in the nature of settlements and in the nature of the settlement hierarchy. It can be argued that in northern and eastern Gaul this third-century shift in the nature and location of rural settlement was more profound and significant than that of the fifth and sixth centuries. By concentrating on villas and villa continuity we may have been looking in the wrong places for the wrong type of settlement.

In support of a continuing, functioning rural population we may cite not only the physical evidence but also the fiscal. There is no mention in the surviving written sources of there being a systemic inability of Gaul to pay its taxes; it was probably still the wealthiest area of the west, even though grain was regularly imported from Britain to help supply the army of the Rhine, a well-known instance of this being after the recovery of the Rhineland by the Caesar Julian.[41] It was also Julian who experimented with the taxation of Belgica II,[42] showing that by not allowing the customary abuses and by instituting equable practice the required returns could be brought in without trouble: there was no inherent inability to pay.

As with the towns, so with the country: the traditional picture of death and disaster has been over-drawn and needs toning down. Clearly much had changed between 200 and 350, and much would never be the same again, but change does not necessarily entail discontinuity or disaster. We need to recognise that the aspect of the late Roman countryside in northern and central Gaul had changed radically, and we need to devise programmes to identify the settlement pattern, the economic régime on which it was based and the social structures it supported. Then we shall be able to reassess the place of the countryside in late Roman Gaul.

One topic which has already been mentioned deserves a slightly fuller discussion because of its potential significance for Britain; that is the issue of weapon graves, *Waffengräber*. We have noted that at certain of the hilltop fortifications of eastern Gaul and Germany the cemeteries contained male burials with weapons — shields, spears, swords, throwing-axes (*franciscas*), knives — in varying combinations. These are usually accompanied by more or less elaborate bronzework, usually associated with belt-buckles, belt-stiffeners, decorated buckles and buckle-plates and strap-ends. In addition some of them, and some of the associated female graves, have brooches of non-Roman manufacture best paralleled in the settlements and cemeteries beyond the lower Rhine.[43] These cemeteries were by no means confined to the hilltop sites and occur across Gaul north of the Loire. No representative of this class has yet been found in Britain (*cf.* p. 55).[44] The practice of burying weapons was not characteristic of the provincial Roman population in the west, nor of excavated cemeteries outside some late Roman forts, such as Oudenburg.[45] The combination of the burial rite and the non-Roman metalwork has led to the conclusion that these are the burials of Germanic people in the service of the Roman state. In this case they are most likely to be *laeti* or *foederati*. Of the two it is felt that the *laeti* are less likely, partly because they seem to have been of low social status, whereas some of these burials contain prestigious objects; partly because the recruits they provided were absorbed into the regular Roman army and did not remain distinct. Also the *Notitia* lists *laeti* in Belgica I and II, Lugdunensis I, II and II, Aquitania I and II and Germania II, that is most of Gaul, whereas the cemeteries are mainly in the north. Furthermore, *laeti* are known to have been settled in the first half of the fourth century, yet these graves date from the 370s on, which is precisely the time at which the emperor Gratian was accused of increasingly relying on barbarians. Given the wealth and warlike nature displayed in these graves it is more likely that these are of *foederati* recruited in the homelands of the Anglo-Saxons, the Franks and the Alamanni. Because of the association of the distinctive belt-suites with Germanic burials inside the empire, and their appearance in burials in the Germanic homelands and the influence the decoration on this metalwork had on the development of Germanic art-styles, it came to be thought that this type of metalwork was made in the empire specifically for issue to Germanic troops.[46] This view is now discounted. In the first place, in the late Roman empire the belt was a symbol of office, indeed the phrases *cingulum sumere* and *cingulum ponere* (to put on and take off the belt) came to be synonymous with joining and leaving the civil service:[47] so they are not even specifically military. Their distribution in Europe concentrates along the Rhine and the Danube, where the bulk of the Roman forces in Europe lay.[48] They are depicted on representations of late Roman civil and military personnel.[49] In sum, this metalwork is late Roman official-issue and has no special link with particular ethnic groups. Some of the people who wore it and took it to the grave with them will have been Germanic, but they had had these belts because, like thousands of non-Germanic personnel, they had been in the service of the Roman state, not because of their ethnic origins.

Finally in this necessarily very partial review of late Roman Gaul and Germany, there is one important topic that remains to be discussed: religion, in particular Christianity. Though Christianity in fourth-century Gaul and Germany was probably only practised by a minority of the population it has received enormous attention and detailed study. This is in part a reflection of its importance in mediating the change from antiquity to the Middle Ages in areas as diverse as administration, culture and settlement, to say nothing of religion. It is also in part a reflection of the fact that western Europe is still, if only nominally, Christian, so the study of how this came about exercises a particular fascination. The danger remains of over-emphasising what was only one religion among many, albeit one under imperial patronage and with influential adherents.

After the Peace of the Church in 312/3, which rendered it a licit religion, and with the conversion of Constantine I and the approval and backing of all subsequent emperors (with the unimportant exception of Julian), Christianity faced up to the need to match its responsibilities in its organisation. Long before Constantine it was widespread in the eastern parts of the empire, where its chief strength lay in the cities. In the west it was less ubiquitous, but again a city-based cult. In the fourth century, therefore, its organisation in the west was an urban one and consciously and closely paralleled the secular administrative hierarchy.[50] In Gaul and Germany (and probably Britain, *cf.* p. 12) each *civitas* was to have a bishop, as were the major extra-territorial administrative units such as the larger tracts of imperial estate or major military installations. Within each province the bishop at the provincial capital would be styled the 'metropolitan', and have a certain jurisdiction over the church in that province. Each bishop would have his see at the principal town of his area, where there would be a church (*titulus*) with a staff (*canon*, *cardo*) of clergy (*canonici*, *cardinales*) who, like the estates and revenue of this church, would be under the bishop's control. As well as episcopal churches there would be other churches (*parochiae*) endowed by private benefactors, whose clergy were not members of the episcopal household. Though the word *parochia* gives us our word parish we must not imagine that there was anything like the fully-developed mediaeval parish system in operation at this date.

For Gaul we have a certain amount of documentation which sheds light on the organisation of the Church at this date. Names of bishops from various towns are subscribed to the *acta* of church councils held in the west. Many dioceses also preserve lists of bishops stretching back into late antiquity (though mediaeval fabrication, interpolation and 'improvement' make these a source to be approached with caution). There is also the document known as the *Notitia Galliarum*, apparently compiled about the turn of the fourth and fifth centuries. This is a list primarily of the *civitas*-capitals of Gaul along with some other places such as forts. There is argument over whether this is a document reflecting secular or ecclesiastical administration;[51] whichever it is, that such a debate can take place shows the close parallelism to be expected between the secular and ecclesiastical administrations. The references to bishops in the histories of the period touching upon the area always link them with towns. Besides the documentary evidence there is the evidence referred to above (p. 24) of the location of cathedrals within the enceintes of the late Roman period. Merovingian sources show that an intra-mural location was the norm in that period, and it has been assumed that this was a practice established in the fourth century. There is thus an idealised model for the ecclesiastical hierarchy north of the Alps and Pyrenees of a bishop for every town and in every town a *titulus*. Alongside these documents we have those relating to the Church in fourth-century Gaul which emanate from the Aquitanian writers of the late fourth century. Chief amongst them for our purposes here is Sulpicius Severus, a disciple of St Martin of Tours, who wrote the *Chronicon*, a history of the people of God from the earliest times to his own day, and a *Vita* (an edifying Life) of Martin himself. Both contain much on the state of the Church in fourth-century Gaul. Other members of this group such as Ausonius and Paulinus of Nola offer us titbits in the course of their other concerns.

If we collate the evidence from these varying sources and try to establish how far the idealised structure for the Church was actually in place, we find it to have been far less uniform than might be supposed. Of particular interest for students of Roman Britain is a recent penetrating analysis of the situation in Belgica,[52] the region of Gaul nearest Britain. For Belgica, only the bishops of Reims and Trier were present at the council of the western Church at Arles in 314. This may be because they were the metropolitans of their provinces and thus representing their colleagues. The names of these bishops reappear in the bishop-lists for these cities, helping partially to verify and to date them. In neither case is it the earliest name on the list. Otherwise the bishop-lists for Amiens, Cambrai, Châlons-sur-Marne, Metz and Verdun start in the mid-fourth century, which is also the date of the only known fourth-century bishop of the Nervii. Several *civitas*-capitals in Belgica II have no known bishop in the fourth century. Given that Victricius, bishop of Rouen at the turn of the fourth and fifth centuries and a disciple of Martin of Tours, felt compelled to undertake campaigns of evangelisation in Belgica, such evidence as there is suggests that in the fourth century these northern provinces did not see as uniform an ecclesiastical presence and hierarchy as did those further south.

The evidence for the location of episcopal *tituli* is by no means as reliable and consistent as has been supposed. The sole archaeologically-attested, fourth-century, intra-mural cathedral is the imperial double church at Trier, which dates from about 330.[53] Bishops of Trier are reliably attested for before then and must have had their seat elsewhere in or around the city. Otherwise there is no reliable documentary or archaeological evidence for intra-mural *tituli* in Belgica before the Merovingian period. For Lugdunensis there is the story preserved in the *vita* of Amator, bishop of Auxerre, who died in 418. He wished to extend his church, but because it was outside the defences beside the river Yonne, the river constrained the site. It was only when he was offered a vacant plot inside the defences that he could build as he wished. This throws interesting light not only on the location of early churches, but also on the relationship between intra- and extra-mural areas. For many towns in the centre and south of Gaul there is good evidence for the intra-mural location of the fourth-century cathedral, and it will presumably turn out that this is the case at some northern towns also. But to assume it on present evidence would be unwise, and we must also bear in mind the possibility of early churches being in other types of location.

Another type of church which has attracted a good deal of attention because of its rôle in late-antique and early-mediaeval topography is the cemetery church. It became the custom to commemorate the site of the passion or burial of a martyr with a shrine, a *martyrium* or a *cella memoriae* (or simply a *memoria*). This latter term also came to be applied to a shrine over the burial-place of other significant members of the Christian community who died more peaceful deaths, such as bishops. Since burial was by Roman law extra-mural these churches lay outside the defences of their respective towns. At some — the best-known are probably Bonn and Xanten in the Rhineland — the post-Roman occupation focused on the cemetery church, and that is where the mediaeval town grew up rather than within the Roman defences.[54] The late Roman shrine therefore initiated a process of settlement shift. An alternative is seen at Tours, where there is a particularly well-documented case of a cemetery church (that of St Martin) becoming a separate focus alongside the defended area.[55] At other towns, such as Cologne or Trier, the settlement focus remained intra-mural, despite the presence of cemetery churches. The significance of the cemetery church may be seen to mirror in physical form the importance of the Church as mediator of continuity from late Roman to early mediaeval.

The impression that cemetery churches were a regular and significant element of the topography of the towns of Gaul and Germany is one that has

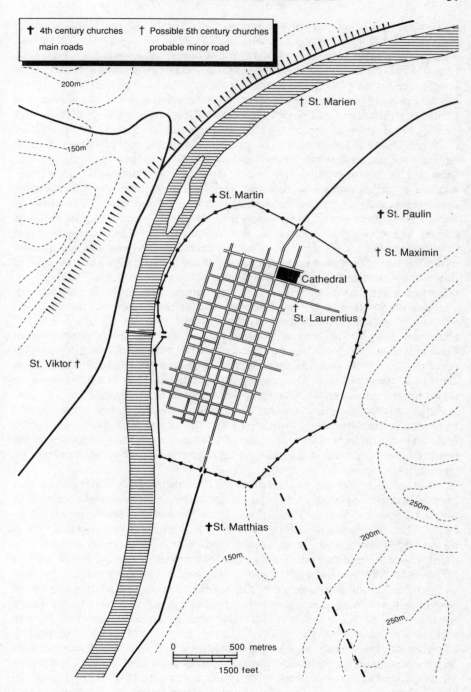

† 4th century churches   † Possible 5th century churches
main roads   probable minor road

† St. Marien

† St. Martin

† St. Paulin

† St. Maximin

Cathedral

†
St. Laurentius

St. Viktor †

†St. Matthias

200m

150m

150m

250m

200m

250m

0   500 metres

1500 feet

Fig. 8 The churches of fourth-century Trier

gained considerable currency amongst workers in Britain. But again a consideration of the evidence available to us must prompt us to be less dogmatic. Of the halo of nine extra-mural churches attested around Trier (fig. 8) by AD1000, only three, St Matthias, St Martin and St Paulin, can with confidence be assigned to the fourth century.[56] The archaeological remains at the first two are of small chapels, little more than mausolea,[57] and would have been little different from pagan cemetery shrines fulfilling similar functions. Trier was an imperial capital with a Christianised court and all the material resources that implies. If such a city had only a small number of unpretentious cemetery churches, what should we expect at less-favoured towns? For instance, at the two Rhineland towns cited above, Bonn and Xanten, the fourth-century structures were of the simplest, at Xanten (fig. 9) a wooden mausoleum with no stone structure before the middle of the fifth century. At Bonn the basilica is first recorded in 691. At the important city of Cologne there is the substantial late Roman phase of St Gereon, and the simple shrine over the grave of the martyrs Asclinus and Pamphylius, which was only extended at the end of the fourth century when it became the burial-place of the bishop whose name the church now bears, St Severin.[58] Given the situation at such major centres as Cologne and Trier it is perhaps not surprising that there is no convincing evidence for cemetery churches anywhere in Belgica in the fourth century, except Trier and perhaps Metz.[59] Cemetery churches are a manifestation of the cult of relics. For the north of Gaul this seems to have been introduced at the turn of the fourth and fifth centuries under the inspiration of Victricius of Rouen (author of the sermon *De Laude Sanctorum* — On The Praise Of The Saints). Since, as we have seen, Victricius seems to have been responsible for initiating the effective evangelisation of Belgica, it seems *a priori* likely that cemetery churches and their rise to prominence in northern Gaul should be a phenomenon of the fifth century and later. Certainly most of the known cemetery churches of the north cannot be traced in the documents or the archaeology back before the Merovingian period.

Like so many before we have been concentrating on Christianity. But fourth-century Gaul was still largely pagan. This is clear in the narrative of Sulpicius Severus' *Vita* of St Martin of Tours. During his episcopacy (*c.* 371–390) Martin is consistently shown as having to combat the worship and priests of the old gods and to try to obliterate or Christianise their symbols and shrines, which were still prevalent in the countryside.[60] Indeed the very word *paganus* literally means countryman; it acquired its meaning 'pagan' because that is what the countryfolk were. One of the purposes of Martin's religious community at Marmoutier, just outside his episcopal city, was to train men for the work of evangelisation. We have already encountered one of these Christian shock-troops, Victricius of Rouen. Because of the attention paid to Christianity, the archaeology of late-antique paganism in Gaul has received short shrift. But the archaeological evidence cited above (p. 32) for the persistence of rural sanctuaries in Belgica accords with that gleaned from the pages of Sulpicius Severus for Lugdunensis III and parts of Aquitania. Even at the imperial seat of Trier the great pagan sanctuary-complex of the

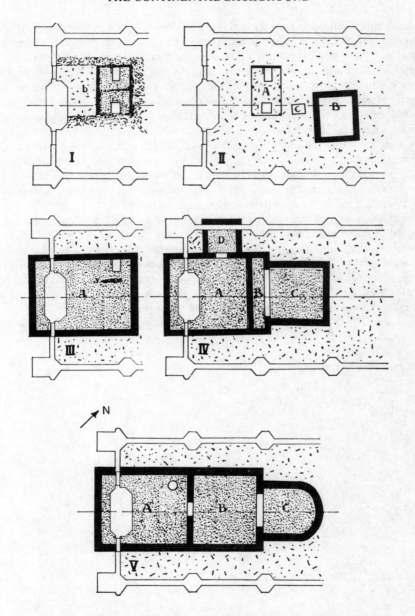

Fig. 9 The cemetery church at Xanten

Altbachtal remained in untroubled use until the reign of the fervent Christian Gratian. His successor, Theodosius I, did not outlaw the public performance of pagan observance until 391. Through the fourth century, and particularly away from direct imperial influence, paganism seems still to have flourished. As is clear from the distribution both of people and things Christian and pagan, Christianity remained essentially town-based and did not make much headway in the countryside. Only in Aquitania do we have evidence for a largely Christian aristocracy, and through their estate churches and chapels they may have been an important channel for the spread of the new religion to their clients, workers and dependents. What the incoming and pagan Franks would have found in northern Gaul was a land where the bulk of the population lived on the land and was pagan, but with an influential, Christianised minority and their leaders in the towns.

Clearly it is impossible here to examine more than a few topics relating to the late Roman west. But they demonstrate that while the required imperial structures of administration, finance and defence were firmly in place, local response varied. Moreover, the themes we have looked at will recur in our study of late Roman Britain, and will form an essential background both to developments in the island in the fourth century, and to the nature of the changes of the early fifth century on both sides of the Channel.

THREE
Britain in the Fourth Century

Fourth-century Britain affords us a huge body of evidence of many disparate types, and from which many different views of the island can be written. Britain's appearances in the histories and the official documents of the fourth century are sporadic and not particularly informative; in the literary sources the diocese appears something of a backwater. But to the archaeologist the fourth century can be seen as the golden age of Roman Britain because of the sheer number of sites of all types occupied and the quantity of finds from those sites. It will be our concern here to examine the various sources of evidence both for their potential and for their shortcomings. From these we may try to construct a picture of late Roman Britain and its place in the wider Roman world.

In the late Roman period Britain was still strongly defended by two *limitaneus* commands, in the north based on Hadrian's Wall and its forts, and along the south-east coasts on the chain of forts guarding the approaches from across the North Sea — the 'Forts of the Saxon Shore'. In due course it also acquired a detachment of *comitatenses*. Behind these defences was an enormous range of settlements. There was a hierarchy of towns from the large and administratively-important such as the diocesan capital London, through the provincial capitals and the *civitas*-capitals, to the lesser market towns. This period is seen as the heyday of the villa in Roman Britain, with the best part of a thousand populating the landscape south-east of a line from Exeter to York. Here too there was an enormous range from the great palace-villas such as Woodchester, comparable with a Chiragan or a Montmaurin on the continent, down to simple farmhouses built in a plain but Roman style. For the first time in Britain these late villas saw the widespread laying of mosaics, and coins and other objects were commonplace. But villas were only one strand in the tapestry of rural settlement; far more common were the 'farmsteads' — the steadings which showed little or no sign of romanised plan or buildings. Even in the south-east they were far more numerous than villas, and in the north-west they were the only form of rural settlement. In the fourth century their occupants too acquired the pottery and other artefacts characteristic of the period, and their retrieval through excavation or field-survey has revealed to the archaeologist the ubiquity of these settlements. Indeed one of the hallmarks of the fourth century when compared even with the rest of the Roman period, let alone the Iron Age or the Saxon period, is the sheer quantity of artefactual material available and being lost or discarded. The disadvantage is that the number and range of types both of settlements and of material bring with them the risk of not seeing the wood for the trees.

In this chapter, therefore, we shall be principally concerned with archaeological evidence. Given the sheer volume of this, some form of selection will have to be exercised if discussion is not to degenerate into cataloguing and argument is not to be overborne by detail. Three principal criteria of selection have been employed. The first is of particular importance since it bears on the whole question of the ending of Roman Britain and is therefore worth some discussion; it is to study that which makes Roman Britain distinctively Roman and whose disappearance sees the disappearance of Roman Britain. The question of what makes Roman Britain Roman is one that is usually ignored. To some this is because it seems a silly question eminently worthy of being ignored: Roman Britain was Roman when and because it was part of the Roman empire. This is essentially a historical and legalistic definition which works well enough for the beginnings of Roman Britain in the years 43 to 86 since one can see most of the island passing by stages under Roman domination. But for the end of Roman Britain it is unhelpful; on the legal side it is highly doubtful whether the Roman state ever *de facto* or *de jure* ceded control over the island. Historically, as we shall see (p. 138), it is impossible to put one's finger on a moment at which Roman Britain can be said definitively to pass out of Roman control, though 411 was clearly a turning-point. But to an inhabitant of Roman Britain what made the island Roman was only theoretically to do with historical events and legal definitions; in practice it was to do with the presence of Roman institutions, values and norms and the fact that these may well have influenced the lives of the bulk of the population. This is not to deny the importance of continuing (if modified) physical, religious, social and cultural patterns inherited from pre-Roman Britain which form the substrate of the Romano-British synthesis; indeed much of this and subsequent chapters will be devoted to this question and the evidence for it. But that is what made Roman Britain British. In the period we are examining Britain remains British but ceases to be Roman; this is the justification for regarding the Roman traits as particularly important. To our theoretical inhabitant of late Roman Britain the Roman-ness of the diocese was manifested in many forms; in the buildings, goods, coins, clothes, languages, laws, religions, cultural values used and shared by the people. Many of these accord with the perception of the modern archaeologist. To him Roman Britain is instantly recognisable by a settlement pattern, a range of settlements, a range of building types and a range of artefact types distinctively and characteristically different from those of any other period of British prehistory or history. To the archaeologist, as these disappear so does the Roman-ness of Roman Britain; it is this disappearance that has to be charted and explained. If we have considered this first criterion at some length it is because it is central to the argument of this book, and the working-out of that argument will in great part be in terms of the how and the why of the ending of what is archaeologically distinctive about Roman Britain. The other two criteria for inclusion in discussion in this chapter can be more succinctly expressed. The first is to try to give as comprehensive an overview of late Roman Britain as is consonant with the argument remaining clear of overmuch detail. The second is that those categories of evidence which are discussed shall contribute something to the 'how' of late Roman Britain as well as to the 'what'.

The structure of the chapter will therefore be as follows. The historical and other documentary evidence will be reviewed for what it tells us of the history of Britain in the fourth century and the extent to which the institutions of the late Roman state were in place. In particular the military dispositions in the diocese and their physical manifestations will be considered, making use of the archaeological evidence. The bulk of the rest of the chapter will rest on the archaeological evidence and be more concerned with the evolution of the society and culture of late Roman Britain. We shall examine that most characteristic of Roman settlements, the town, and its functions. Arising out of this will be discussions of particular classes of artefact, such as pottery and coins, which have a functional relationship with towns. We shall then examine the evidence for the nature of the rural settlement patterns and hierarchies and how they may have related. Finally we shall look at the evidence for religion in late Roman Britain, with Christianity again being accorded a prominent position. As appropriate, the evidence for Britain will be compared with that for the continent outlined in Chapter 2.

Literary evidence

As has been said we have few historical notices of Britain in the late period. The island seems to have been a complaisant part of the Gallic Empire from 260 to 274, and was the power base for the successive illicit régimes of Carausius and Allectus from 286 to 296. Neither episode is recorded as having occasioned large-scale reprisals against the provincial population after the recovery of power by the central authorities. Because of her geographical position Britain had not been affected by the invasions of the 260s and 270s which had so damaged Gaul and Germany. She was, though, under increasing threat of raiding and piracy from the peoples along the North Sea littoral outside the Roman frontier on the lower Rhine, the forebears of the Anglo-Saxons. This resulted in the building of the forts of the Saxon Shore from the early third century on,[1] and at the time of his rebellion in 286 Carausius was commander of the fleet charged with keeping the British seaways clear. By contrast the northern frontier of Britain seems to have passed the third century in a state of torpor.[2] This did not last; in 296, after he had restored Britain to imperial rule by the suppression of Allectus, the Caesar Constantius Chlorus campaigned in the north and instituted the rebuilding of some of the forts on Hadrian's Wall. He returned to Britain in 306, now as Augustus, and died on campaign at York. His son Constantine was proclaimed in his stead in violation of the rules of succession of the Tetrarchy (in this an Alamannic chieftain called Crocus took a prominent part.)[3] Constantine quickly left for the continent to consolidate his power. The issuing of gold by the mint of London in 312 and 314 suggests that

Constantine was revisiting Britain, with London acting as the comitatensian mint,[4] and in 315 Constantine took the title *Britannicus* (conqueror of the Britons). Thereafter the only member of the House of Constantine to come to Britain was Constans, Augustus in the west from 340 to 350. In the winter of 342/3 he came to Britain for a reason which is unclear.[5] Hazarding the sacred person of the emperor in a mid-winter crossing of the Channel was not an enterprise lightly to be undertaken, so something of importance must have been happening on the island.

In 350 Britain was involved in another episode of usurpation, when a cabal of military and civil notables in Gaul overthrew Constans and had him put to death at Elne. The emperor they proclaimed in his place was an army commander in Britain, one Magnentius who proclaimed as Caesar his son Decentius. Defeated at Mursa in Pannonia in 351, Magnentius was not finally suppressed until 353 by Constantius II, last surviving son of Constantine I, who thus became sole Augustus until his death in 361. In the aftermath of the suppression of Magnentius reprisals were visited upon the usurper's supporters in Britain by one of Constantius II's trusted agents, the *notarius* Paul. He initiated a reign of terror, executing some, and falsely imprisoning others on trumped-up charges. Even the *vicarius* of the Britains himself, Martinus, was appalled, and after remonstration had failed tried to assassinate Paul.[6] For one senior administrator to try to do away with another must be a measure of the havoc being wreaked on the political classes of Britain.

In 360 the Caesar Julian, then based at Paris, sent his *magister militum* Lupicinus to Britain with four comitatensian units, of Heruli, Batavi and two of Moesiaci. The occasion for this given in the sources has been questioned. Ammianus states that it was because of trouble on the northern frontier caused by the Picts and the Scots. But it has been suggested that it was because in Paris events were moving towards Julian's proclamation as Augustus and Julian wanted Lupicinus out of the way. True, Lupicinus had been wished on Julian by Constantius II and was promptly arrested on his return to Gaul,[7] but there were other ways of neutralising him than giving him four of Julian's scarce comitatensian units. There must have been some real military problem in Britain. Thereafter, through the 360s there were rumours of trouble on the north British frontier, in particular in 364. But in this passage Britain features as only one of a series of points around the imperial perimeter under pressure, which suggests that Ammianus was making a point about the general strategic situation of the empire rather than one specifically concerning Britain. In 367 the dams burst and the diocese faced military collapse. In that year the separate predators on Britain, the Franks and Anglo-Saxons from across the North Sea, the Picts and Attacotti from Scotland and the Scotti, then in Ireland, did what they had never done before; they combined in a co-ordinated attack on Britain (and the coastal regions of northern Gaul): the *barbarica conspiratio*, the barbarian conspiracy.[8] In the north their task was eased by the fact that the *arcani* or *areani* (the reading is not certain, either way it seems to mean some sort of spies) were suborned. As a result the *dux* Fullofaudes — presumably *dux Britanniarum*, the commander of the northern frontier – was ambushed or besieged. Nectaridus, described as *comes maritimi tractus* (the commander of the coastal area) — presumably the *comes litoris Saxonici*, the commander of the Saxon Shore forts — was killed. Military discipline dissolved, and to bands of raiding barbarians were added those of Roman troops who had deserted the colours. News of the disaster was brought to the western Augustus Valentinian I who was *en route* from Amiens to Trier. After a couple of false starts he appointed one of his most able commanders, the *comes* Theodosius, to restore the situation. Landing at Richborough with four comitatensian regiments, the Heruli and the Batavi (again) and the Iovii and Victores, he made for London. From there he mounted a campaign of force to expel the barbarians and of conciliation to recall Roman deserters to their colours. This was to take two years to accomplish, not helped by an abortive rising led by Valentinus, but was brought to a successful conclusion. It is perhaps worth making the point that the defences of Britain were only overwhelmed by a combined attack; against these peoples individually they had been adequate.

Ammianus' account makes it clear that the barbarian ravages went deep into Britain. He describes London itself as having been surrounded by bands of plunderers laden with booty and driving captured herds and men. Not unnaturally many archaeologists have sought evidence of the barbarian conspiracy in burnt and ruined sites either on the Wall or in the civilian south. There developed a tendency to attribute any site where there was evidence of burning[9] or where the coin-list stopped in the mid-fourth century to a destruction at the hands of the barbarians. But more recently a reaction has set in against this. Excavation on Hadrian's Wall and on the Saxon Shore forts has failed to yield any convincing evidence of wholesale destruction, even at a single fort, at this time — the unfortunate Nectaridus must have been caught in the open or at sea. No town can be shown to have destruction deposits of the right date. Even for villas, standing unfortified in open country, re-examination of sites which had been proposed as suffering in 367 has shown that the evidence is generally far too ambiguous.[10] The trouble is that the sort of archaeological evidence normally used in this argument is seldom unequivocal. Burnt deposits do come about through causes other than enemy action. Many buildings in Roman Britain contained hearths and ovens, and in a small-scale excavation the ashes and burnt material from their rake-outs could even be confused with a destruction-deposit. In the timber-framed buildings prevalent in Roman Britain such hearths and ovens could cause accidental conflagrations. To be a plausible candidate for enemy destruction a site needs more positive and grisly evidence such as bodies. Coin-lists too are now understood to be more problematical. In general the number of coins from rural sites tends to be low in comparison with the towns (*cf.* p. 94), so an end to the coin-list need not mean an end to the site. Moreover, coins can only give a *terminus post quem* (a date *after* which something must have happened), so a coin-list ending with coins minted in 350 or 360 can never say that 367 is the most likely year for that cessation actually to have occurred. We appear to have a paradox, an event for which there is good literary evidence but no certain archaeological evidence. Much of the paradox may be explained by the natures of the two types of evidence. On the literary side,

Ammianus was writing in the reign of the emperor Theodosius I, son of the *comes* Theodosius of 367. Flattery of the emperor's father by vividly writing up an incident in his career would be tantamount to flattery of the emperor himself. Archaeologically, the problem is the limitations of archaeological evidence in reflecting particular events rather than trends, developments, processes. Even if we had convincing evidence for hostile destruction, we have seen that it would be well-nigh impossible to say that the date of an event on a site is more likely to have been 367 than any other year. Much of the paradox is therefore a conflict of types of evidence. There is no reason to doubt that the barbarian conspiracy of 367 happened; one may, however, question how traumatic it was, and the problems of recognising it on the ground should warn us against expecting particular historical events always to be reflected in the archaeological sequence.

In 383 another army commander in Britain, Magnus Maximus, headed a revolt, and this time the western Augustus who was killed was Gratian, son of Valentinian I and pupil of Ausonius. Maximus ruled the west, principally from Trier, until his death in 388 when Theodosius I avenged his western colleague. Towards the end of the fourth century the court poet Claudian twice mentions Britain in one of his works,[11] a panegyric of the great Vandal-born general Stilicho (d. 408), who was effective ruler of the western empire under Theodosius I's younger son, the feeble Honorius. Britain is depicted as being safeguarded by Stilicho against Picts, Scotti and Saxons. This has led some to suggest that it was Stilicho who was responsible for stationing in Britain the detachment of the *comitatenses* whom we find listed in the *Notitia* under the *comes Britanniarum*; some even link it with a war against the Picts referred to by Gildas (*cf.* p. 166).[12] This is to overstretch a literary device. In Roman literature Britain functioned as a symbol of the far north-west. In both passages of the panegyric where the island is named she could be regarded as doing duty as such a geographical archetype. Indeed in one of the passages the personification of Britannia appears to address the *magister*; it is possible to regard this as a precise geographical formulation, but it could equally be regarded as a literary device. Claudian may just have been showing the all-embracing nature of Stilicho's solicitude rather than an acute awareness of events in Britain, and we should not base too much on these casual references. By chance the early years of the fifth century are better documented, but these are more properly discussed in the next chapter.

The historical sources for fourth-century Britain are therefore sparse and leave us with as many questions as answers. They show that occasionally Britain impinged on central imperial concerns, as did any diocese, but it did so only occasionally and for the rest of the time the island was apparently a decent, law-abiding part of the praetorian prefecture of the Gauls. From other documentary evidence, principally the *Notitia Dignitatum*, we may reconstruct an outline of the civil, financial and military structures put in place after 296 and which ran and defended the diocese down to the early fifth century.[13]

Administration

It is usually assumed that the administrative reforms of the Tetrarchy were put in place immediately upon Constantius Chlorus' recovery of the island in 296. Certainly there was a *vicarius* of the diocese by 319 when Constantine I addressed a rescript (an imperial edict in response to a query from an official) to the holder of that office, Pacatianus.[14] The diocese of the Britains was divided into four provinces: Britannia I, Britannia II, Maxima Caesariensis and Flavia Caesariensis. The derivation of the latter two names is problematical. Flavius was the family name of the Caesar Constantius Chlorus, so Flavia Caesariensis can be plausibly explained in those terms. Maxima might be named after the Augustus Maximian, but why then Caesariensis rather than Augustensis? An alternative is that it referred to the eastern Caesar Galerius Maximianus (usually known as Galerius), but why? In Ammianus' account of the work of the *comes* Theodosius in Britain the creation of a province called Valentia is described; the province also figures in the *Notitia*. The governor of Maxima Caesariensis was a *consularis*, whilst those of the other provinces were mostly styled *praeses*. Maxima Caesariensis was therefore the senior province and must have had its capital at London (now or later officially renamed Augusta instead of Londinium; the name did not catch on), where the *vicarius* also had his seat. The other provincial capitals may be identified with a fair degree of certainty by combining various sources including the list of bishops from Britain subscribing to the *acta* of the Church council at Arles in 314 (*cf*. p. 35). Given the close parallelism we have already seen between civil and ecclesiastical hierarchies in Gaul, it can be suggested that these four were the metropolitans representing the church in their provinces, as Trier and Reims did for Belgica I and II. Unfortunately the surviving version of this list is corrupt and so cannot be taken on its own. It reads:

> *Eborius episcopus de civitate Eboracensi provincia Britannia*
> *Restitutus episcopus de civitate Londiniensi provincia suprascripta*
> *Adelphius episcopus de civitate Colonia Londiniensium*
> *Exinde Sacerdos presbyter Arminius diaconus*

The first bishop is evidently from York, the second from London, the third may be reconstructed as Colchester (*Colonia Camulodunum*) or Lincoln (*Colonia Lindum*). The fourth delegation is of a priest and a deacon; perhaps that see was vacant. York had been the capital of the old province of Britannia Inferior, and was presumably now the capital of Britannia II. From Cirencester comes an inscription (RIB 103) mentioning the *rector* (a generic term for governor) of Britannia I. This places that province in western Britain, and as Cirencester is the town with the largest defended area of the region and evidence for considerable prosperity, it is not unreasonable to postulate that it was actually the seat of the governor. If so it would have been the source of the delegation of a priest and a deacon. This leaves the question of the whereabouts of the fourth capital, that of Flavia Caesariensis. The reconstruction of the third entry in the Arles list which is generally preferred gives Lincoln, previously in the province governed from York. In this way each of the old provinces of Britannia Superior and Britannia Inferior would have been divided into two of the new provinces, which seems sensible. Valiant efforts have been made to locate the apparent fifth province, Valentia, working from no evidence whatsoever.[15] The creation of the province by the *comes* Theodosius is described by Ammianus, and it is clearly named after Valentinian I; it also appears in the *Notitia*, where it is governed by a *consularis*. It has recently been observed[16] that Ammianus' account of the creation of Valentia reads much more like the re-naming of an existing province rather than the creation of a new one. But if this were so it would mean that the entries for Valentia in the *Notitia* would have to be duplications of those for one of the other provinces, perhaps Maxima Caesariensis, which would therefore also be appearing under its old name. Mistakes and dittographies do occur in the *Notitia*, so perhaps the re-naming hypothesis is to be preferred; it certainly minimises the difficulties involved in actually trying to locate the province.

The financial officials responsible to the *comes sacrarum largitionum* listed for Britain in the *Notitia*[17] are headed by the *rationalis* (comptroller) of finances for the diocese of the Britains. He was assisted by the *praepositus* (head) of the *thesaurus* (treasury) at London. These would have been the officials ultimately responsible for the collection and processing of most of the taxes and the disbursement of state payments throughout the diocese. As well as the staff responsible for these activities, there was the *procurator* (director) of the *gynaecium* (state weaving mill) at *Venta*. There are three known places with the name *Venta* in Britain: *Venta Belgarum* (Winchester), *Venta Icenorum* (Caistor-by-Norwich) and *Venta Silurum* (Caerwent). Of the three it is usually Winchester that is thought to be the best candidate, though on no very positive grounds.[18] In Britain there was also a *rationalis* of the Privy Purse,[19] whose responsibility was the supervision of the properties and estates in direct imperial ownership.

There are a couple of sites which should perhaps be considered in the context of the taxation system: Gatcombe and Alcester.[21] At the former site, interpreted by its excavator as a villa, there was a trapezoidal defended enclosure of aproximately 8 ha. (20 acres) within which some twenty buildings have been wholly or partially excavated (there must be more awaiting discovery). The site was laid out *c*. 300 and was in use into the late fourth century. The buildings were either simple rectangular structures or aisled buildings. From them comes evidence for grain-processing and metal-working, along with a limited amount of evidence for occupation. There was no principal residential building, though it is argued that this could have disappeared in the digging of the railway cutting which has removed the southern part of the enclosure. Both in the layout, types and number of buildings, and above all in the provision of defences, Gatcombe differs from most villas, and there must be the possibility that it was a state-controlled depôt for the reception and processing of produce and metal. The excavator argues that if this was the case then there should be artefactual evidence of military involvement, but if it were under the control of either the *rationalis* or the *primus pilus* this need

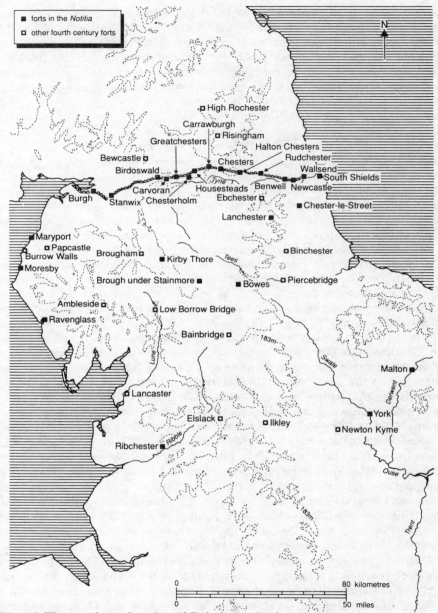

Fig. 10 The northern frontier of Britain in the fourth century

not be so. Such an explanation avoids the considerable difficulties encountered in trying to interpret the site as a villa. A possible parallel could be the site at Orton Hall Farm, Cambridgeshire (*cf.* p. 196). At Alcester there was a large, late third-century granary near the centre of the town, demolished when the town walls were built in the mid-fourth century. Its distinctive plan and its size have led the excavator to suggest that it was a store for taxation in kind.

The army and frontiers

The *Notitia* lists two *limitaneus* and one *comitatensis* commands.[20] In the north the *dux Britanniarum* commanded the troops along Hadrian's Wall (which is accorded its own sub-list in the list of the *dux*) and to its north and south. Round the southern and eastern coasts lay the forts which formed the command of the *comes litoris Saxonici per Britannias*, the Saxon Shore. The *comes Britanniarum* commanded a small detachment of the field army which was stationed in Britain at an uncertain date (*cf.* p. 54).

The two *limitaneus* commands had had rather different histories. The northern frontier (fig. 10) based on Hadrian's Wall had of course been devised and built in the course of the second century, when it had seen a considerable amount of action. After the conclusion of a peace treaty with the tribes of Scotland by Caracalla in 211 the frontier became quiescent. Inscriptions from a number of forts along the Wall and in the Pennines dating to the three decades or so after 211 show that they were being given additional facilities to make them more pleasant places to garrison. In the latter part of the third century there is evidence for considerable dilapidation and disrepair. There is an inscription (RIB 1912) of the Tetrarchy from Birdoswald recording the replacement of buildings which had fallen down through old age and become covered with soil. This accords with archaeological evidence for buildings inside forts such as Halton Chesters[22] and Rudchester.[23] At South Shields[24] and Vindolanda[25] there is evidence for changed and reduced accommodation in the third century and for a decreased standard of maintenance and care of the buildings. Near Birdoswald the Wall itself was allowed to collapse and was not rebuilt until the late third century. The Birdoswald inscription is one of a number of pieces of evidence we have for a major re-commissioning of the installations of the Wall under the Tetrarchy, suggesting that things had indeed been allowed to fall into decay.

One of the occasions for the re-commissioning of the Wall and its associated forts in the late third century may have been a change in the nature of the enemy that had to be dealt with. The tribal names of southern Scotland familiar from the second and third centuries such as the Maeatae and the Selgovae do not persist into the fourth. Instead we find the Picts (*Picti* — the Painted Men), a descriptive name more akin to those of the Franks and the Alamanni of the same period on the continent. Like these peoples, it seems that the tribes of southern and central Scotland had been undergoing internal political development and fusion with other groupings to produce a larger and more hostile nation on Rome's northern frontier.[26] From the Western Isles came the Attacotti, a people renowned to the Romans for their ferocity. The Scotti, then in Ireland, are also mentioned by the Roman sources as attacking Britain. Some Irish sources also suggest attacks on the diocese, but the evidence for this is not conclusive, resting as it does on the largely mythical exploits of early kings such as Niall of the Nine Hostages.[27] The threat to the northern frontier from across the North Sea was, however, negligible; the wide and turbulent waters of this part of the North Sea made such a long crossing far too risky, especially since the crossing of the southern North Sea was so much shorter.

Though the physical installations of the northern frontier of Britain were inherited from the second century, their use in the fourth can be well understood within the framework of late Roman defence strategy (*cf.* p. 7). It consisted essentially of four elements designed either to nip trouble in the bud, or to prevent an invasion into the diocese, or to help the expulsion of a successful invasion. To the north of the Wall there were the *arcani* or *areani*, whom we have already met when they were bribed not to warn of the conspiracy of 367. These would seem to have been agents operating amongst the peoples of the Lowlands in order to try to head off trouble and to warn of any that did develop. In addition there were a number of places (*loca*) where the tribes met at regular intervals under Roman supervision — the Clochmabenstane on the northern side of the Solway may well be the *locus Maponi*. The first element, therefore, was supervision of the tribes to try to prevent trouble in the first place. It was linked with the second element, the outpost forts of Bewcastle and Netherby north of the western end of the Wall, and Risingham and High Rochester north of the eastern. Third was the Wall itself, where most of the forts dating from its construction in the second century were still garrisoned (if somewhat differently, as we shall see) in the fourth. The linear barrier of the Wall itself was back to full order in the fourth century and in itself represented a formidable obstacle to movement, especially of quadrupeds. To the rear of the Wall was the fourth element, the forts still occupied in the Pennines. In the second century these had been designed to supervise the hill peoples. By the fourth these folk seem no longer to have been a threat, and the forts should be seen in the context of late-imperial defensive strategy, hindering the enemy and helping Roman troops on the occasions when the Wall was overrun. There is a discrepancy between the forts listed in the *Notitia* as being garrisoned by the troops of the *dux*, and the evidence of the archaeology, for the latter shows that there were more forts in occupation than are listed in the former.[28] This may be due to the *Notitia* recording a particular series of dispositions at a particular point in time, whereas the archaeology gives a more general picture of occupation during the fourth century. Of course the occupation of the forts of the north was not static through the century; it is possible for instance that the outpost forts may have been abandoned before its end. Late in the century a chain of small fortifications was built along the cliffs of the north-eastern coast within the line of the Wall.[29] These so-called signal stations probably acted as look-out towers for sea raiders, and could have alerted units in the interior by signal or messenger. The enemy must have been from the lands to the north

Fig. 11 The Saxon Shore

of the Wall rather than from across the North Sea. Overall, therefore, the northern frontier dispositions conform well with the general late Roman strategies for the prevention of or for dealing with trouble. The date and circumstances of the abandonment of the northern frontier are dealt with in the next chapter (p. 142).

The Saxon Shore system (fig. 11) was not the product of a single design in the way that Hadrian's Wall had been. Instead it grew up piecemeal in response to the growing threat of raiding across the Straits of Dover and the southern North Sea.[30] Typologically the earliest forts are those at Brancaster and Reculver, which have the 'playing-card' shape, the internal towers and the internal layout and buildings characteristic of early rather than late Roman fortifications. The forts at Burgh Castle and Bradwell, and perhaps also the one at Walton now lost to the sea, are transitional. They have rounded corners, but also have external towers — at Burgh Castle added whilst the walls were still under construction. These five earlier forts all guarded major inlets or estuaries: Brancaster the Wash; Burgh Castle the combined estuaries of the Bure, the Tas, the Wensum and the Yare, where Great Yarmouth now stands; Walton was at the mouth of the Deben and not far from the Orwell and the Stour; Bradwell overlooked the approaches to the Blackwater and the Colne; Reculver protected the southern shore of the Thames estuary and the northern end of the Wantsum Channel between the Isle of Thanet and the coast of Kent. At the other end of the Wantsum Channel was Richborough, which sometime in the third century had an earthen fort placed around the huge concrete base of the late first-century triumphal monument commemorating the conquest of Britain.[31] Under the Gallic Empire this fort was replaced by one in stone and in the defensive style of the late empire with its right-angled corners and projecting external towers.[32] Similar forts were added in the later third century at Dover[33] and Lympne[34] and by Carausius at Portchester (Pl. 5).[35] The date of the fort at Pevensey is still problematical and cannot yet be tied down more precisely than to the late third or early fourth century.[36] These later forts concentrated more on defending the Straits of Dover and the south coast of Britain. The idea that there was a related fort, parts of which may still be seen under the mediaeval castle at Carisbrooke on the Isle of Wight, has been questioned and a case made (though not proved) that it be reassigned to the late Saxon period.[37] The defended promontory of Bitterne at the outfall of the Itchen into Southampton Water has sometimes been considered to be a part of the Saxon Shore system, but there is no evidence that it was other than a fortified civil harbour town. To the east of London a signal tower was built at Shadwell.[38] The date of the formal inception of the Saxon Shore command is unknown. Carausius was responsible for the safeguarding of the Channel seaways, and in 367 the ill-fated Nectaridus is described as having been *comes maritimi tractus* (the commander of the coastal area), which sounds like an approximation to *comes litoris Saxonici*, but the title first appears as such in the *Notitia*.

On the western coast of Britain there are other late Roman defences; these do not appear in the *Notitia*. They are the fort at Cardiff[39] (now the outer walls of the castle), and the fort known as the Werry Wall at Lancaster.[40]

In addition there is the small late landing-place at Caer Gybi (Holyhead), not unlike some of those on the Danube.[41] Recent excavations have shown that there was a fourth-century tower atop Holyhead Mountain, and perhaps also on the Anglesey side of Holyhead Bay.[42] These new fortifications were in addition to those constructed in the second century and still in occupation. Lancaster lay to the south of the chain of forts down the Cumberland coast.[43] Caer Gybi lay near the Roman fort at Caernarfon, which underwent extensive internal modifications in the fourth century.[44] The presence of these fortifications lends credence to the suggestion that the Irish were making the western seaways unsafe. There is also the mosaic from the fourth-century temple at Lydney on the northern side of the Severn estuary east of Cardiff, which mentions a *praefectus reliquationis*, a naval officer.[45]

The whereabouts of the comitatensian troops under the command of the *comes Britanniarum* are much more of a problem, since we lack criteria by which to establish their presence or absence. As we have seen there is no certainty as to when they were first stationed in Britain, and therefore of the point from which we should expect to begin to identify them in the archaeological record. Evidence from the written sources suggests that the *comitatenses* were normaly brigaded in the cities and towns of the interior, sometimes by being billeted on the local citizenry.[46] The abuses of this system and the behaviour of the brutal and licentious soldiery must in large part explain the unpopularity of the army with the literary classes in the late empire. The criteria which one might employ for the recognition of bodies of troops in a late Romano-British town could include a reserved compound, distinctive structures, weaponry and other military accoutrements and perhaps their burials. As yet no such compounds have been recognised, nor have any distinctive structures. This latter is a reflection of the fact that in the late empire the army seems no longer to have used a standard building type utterly different from civilian structures in the way that the first/second-century barrack-block was. Even at Trier, a city which must have held substantial numbers of *comitatenses* for substantial periods, no building has been claimed as comitatensian barracks or accommodation. As we shall see, even within Britain the buildings of the *limitaneus* forts differ widely and are not necessarily that different from some to be found in the towns. Military weapons are rare as site-finds from towns; apart from the *martiobarbuli* (lead-weighted throwing-darts) from Wroxeter[47] there is a distinct lack of military hardware — and the same goes for helmets and armour. But even at the *limitaneus* forts this is also the case; the finds assemblage from, for instance, Portchester is virtually indistinguishable from that from a civil site. The one artefact-group that may be of use here is that associated with the official-issue belts of the fourth century. This material is widely distributed in Britain, but mainly in the civilian interior of the diocese, with comparatively little from Hadrian's Wall and associated forts or from the forts of the Saxon Shore.[48] Of the four types into which the buckles found in Britain are divided, one, Type 2, is an insular British product. Examples of this class are characteristically smaller and lighter than those of the others, and it has been suggested that they were worn by females. However this may be, it is a British phenomenon, and may represent unofficial imitation of a prestige item. Types 1, 3 and 4 are products of the regular imperial equipment factories, as are the associated belt-stiffeners and strap-ends.[49] To whom was this equipment being issued? As has been said its distribution is overwhelmingly on civil sites, principally towns and villas. These are of course the sites on which it was eventually lost or discarded, which need not be the same as those to which it was initially supplied. One possibility is that it reflects the presence of officials of the administrative and financial bureaucracies charged with the smooth running of the diocese, such officials being amongst those entitled to wear such belts. The other is that this equipment was worn by the troops of the *comes Britanniarum*; its distribution would therefore coincide with that to be expected from the written sources. At present there is no way to resolve this question. The shortage of such items from the *limitaneus* forts is curious, as they are common enough on military sites on the Rhine and Danube frontiers. It is worth noting that the belt-suite components from Britain are consistently at the lower end of the range of fineness, being copper-alloy rather than precious metal and of the simpler rather than the more elaborate forms and decoration.[50]

As yet we have no certain comitatensian burials. On the whole it is not that easy to identify the burials of soldiers in Roman Britain,[51] because, as on the continent, they seldom contain weaponry or armour — these seem to have reverted to the army upon death. There are two known burial sites which may be of relevance here; these are Lankhills, Winchester and Dyke Hills, Dorchester-on-Thames. At Lankhills part of the extensive northern cemetery of fourth-century Winchester was excavated.[52] Burial started soon after 300, and the usual burial rite was a coffined inhumation, sometimes with grave-goods such as a pot or a coin or footwear placed inside or outside the coffin. Around 350 a new burial rite appeared. In the male graves there were usually the fittings for an official-issue belt (sometimes with a knife) at the waist, a crossbow brooch at the shoulder and an offering by the right foot. In the female graves there was also the offering, and as well they had bracelets encircling the arm and other items of adornment. Clearly this rite differed from the normal Romano-British rite in the provision of more objects and in the fact that their disposition in the grave suggests that the body had been clothed at burial. Despite the not particularly fearsome knives these cannot be classified as *Waffengräber* of the type we have seen on the continent (p. 33). An extensive search for parallels to the burial rite came up with similar burials inside the imperial frontier in what is now Bavaria and outside it in what is now Hungary.[53] Clearly there is a strong case that people were moved from one of these areas to Winchester, but that does not of itself make them *comitatenses*. Another possibility is that they were *foederati* (*cf.* p. 6), but again the evidence is unsatisfyingly inconclusive. One thing they cannot be, coming from those areas, is Anglo-Saxon. The burials found in the last century at Dyke Hills,[54] outside the defences of the Roman 'small' town at Dorchester-on-Thames have been thought to be such. Discovered along with other burials in the course of earth-moving, the male burial was accompanied by the fittings for the wide, official-issue belt-suite. Nearby was the burial of a

female with the back-plate of an early Germanic brooch. These two burials
are usually treated in association, and the combination of late Roman and
Germanic metalwork is seen as mirroring the *Waffengräber* of northern Gaul,
some (if not most) of which as we have seen (p. 33) were Germanic. Thus
the Dyke Hills burials have acquired enormous importance in the problem of
whether early Anglo-Saxon settlers can be recognised in fourth-century
Roman Britain (*cf.* p. 191), since it is usually assumed that the most likely
source for Germanic *foederati* for late Roman Britain was the Anglo-Saxon
homelands. This need not be the case — for instance we have encountered
Crocus of the Alamanni assisting at the elevation of Constantine I in 306
(p. 43); Germanic yes; Anglo-Saxon no. But the association of the male and
the female burials is not certain; they were just found in the same burial
ground at the same time by non-archaeological methods, as also apparently
were a number of other objects, some of iron. Given the inadequacies of the
records of discovery, three possible interpretations may be offered. One is the
traditional one of an Anglo-Saxon *foederatus* and his family stationed in late
Roman Britain. The second overlaps with it; if some of the metalwork was
weaponry the male burial may be the sole *Waffengrab* so far known from
fourth-century Britain. The third is simply that here we have a burial with an
official-issue belt-suite, a similar situation to that at Lankhills. These burials
have been included in a section on the *comitatenses* under the command of the
comes Britanniarum; this should not be taken to mean that that is what they
must be, it is merely one of the things they *could* be. That this is the best we
can come up with is some measure of the problems involved in identifying and
locating the comitatensian troops in Britain.

Having reviewed the evidence for the strategic dispositions of the commands, we must now consider the units actually in garrison at the forts of the
limitaneus commands and the types of accommodation. In Chapter 1 (p. 5)
we saw that there was mounting evidence that the units of the late Roman
army were much smaller than those of the second century, even where they
bore the same unit-title; is this the case also for Britain? The island was
relatively peaceful in the third century at a time when pressure on other
frontiers was intense. Not surprisingly, therefore, there is evidence for the
large, under-employed garrison of Britain being used as a reservoir from
which troops were vexillated (part of a unit detached) to where they could be
put to good use and probably not returned to their parent unit. Even as early
as the late second century we find *legio* VI *Victrix* from York on campaign
with *alae* and *cohortes* against rebels in Brittany (CIL III 1919).[55] In the third
century we find vexillations of the British legions on the Danube under
Gallienus (260–8) (CIL III 3228 = ILS 546). It is unlikely that the latter were
returned to their parent units after the secession of the Gallic Empire,
especially as that event involved the murder of Gallienus' son. Both the
inscriptions mentioned above refer to the legions being accompanied by
auxiliary troops, *alae* and *cohortes* in the former, *cum auxiliis* in the latter
case. This is entirely logical as the auxiliaries discharged tactical functions for
which the legions were not suited, and auxiliary units were in some sense
'allocated' to legions. So the epigraphic evidence, such as it is, confirms that

the army in Britain was being vexillated in the course of the third century, and we may expect to find evidence for the withdrawal of troops at the fortresses and forts.

The internal layout and buildings of the fortresses and forts of late Roman Britain were indeed markedly different from those familiar from the early empire. To take the legionary fortresses first, in alphabetical order. Caerleon, the fortress of II *Augusta*, underwent major changes in the third century.[56] Near the end of that century the principal administrative buildings were dismantled and robbed; the fate of the barracks is less certain, but there seems to be little going on in them in the fourth century. Occupation associated with fourth-century coins is sparse, consisting only of the odd room here and there in the barrack-blocks. Clearly there had been a great reduction in the level of activity in the fortress, and there is no convincing evidence that it was military rather than civilian re-use of parts of the abandoned fortress. In the *Notitia*, II *Augusta* was listed on the Saxon Shore at Richborough, whose walls enclose only eight acres as opposed to the fifty of Caerleon. Whatever there was left of II *Augusta*, it was a much smaller unit than it had been, though it is of course possible that Richborough held only one detachment of the legion. At Chester the defences and the internal buildings were refurbished at the beginning of the third century,[57] but in the last third of the century there were major changes. In contradistinction to Caerleon it was large areas of the barracks and other buildings that were demolished and not replaced. Only some of the large administrative buildings and the baths were left standing by 300.[58] In one place an early fourth-century building was constructed over the rubble of the earlier fortress buildings. Clearly the accommodation of the fortress had been enormously reduced; indeed, there is hardly any evidence for accommodation, civil or military, within the defences in the fourth century. The Chester legion, *legio* XX *Valeria Victrix*, does not appear in the *Notitia*; it is last attested in a coin issue of Carausius (RIC 82,83,275). Did it survive into the fourth century, and even if it did was it large enough to occupy all the area within the fortress at Chester? York is the fortress of which we know the least. At the beginning of the fourth century the south-western defences, facing out across the Ouse towards the *colonia* and provincial capital on the other bank, were extensively remodelled, with projecting semi-hexagonal interval towers and multangular corner towers.[59] This was more a propagandist statement in the latest defensive language than an attempt to bring up to date the defences of the entire fortress. Excavation of the fortress at York has concentrated very much on the defences, with the result that our knowledge of the interior is very shaky. The only barracks so far excavated were modified in the early fourth century, though it is not clear how.[60] The sewer system and the bath-house were still in commission and the basilica of the *principia* (headquarters-building) was undergoing maintenance.[61] But recent environmental evidence points to dereliction,[62] at least in places. The prefect of the York legion, VI *Victrix*, is listed in the command of the *dux* in the *Notitia*, and the latter was probably based at York, either in the fortress or the *colonia*; the former is perhaps more likely. At two at least of the three of the legionary fortresses of Britain

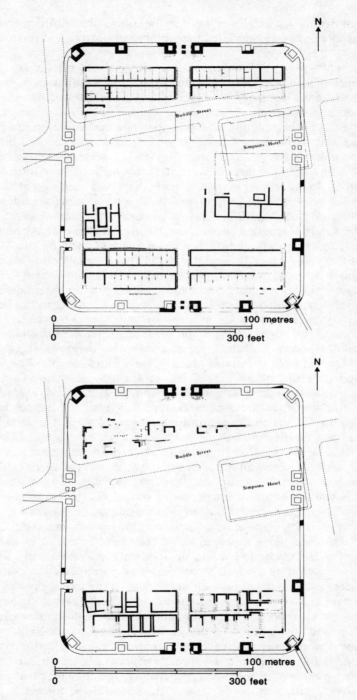

Fig. 12 Wallsend in the second and fourth centuries

such military units as were still in them in the fourth century had been enormously reduced in size.

When we turn to the forts along Hadrian's Wall together with its outpost forts and the forts to its rear in the Pennines, a similar picture emerges. Instead of the barrack-blocks typical of the second century, we find the very different structures usually referred to as 'chalets'. These are linked in date with inscriptions attesting reconstruction under Constantius Chlorus at the end of the third century. Instead of the typical second-century barrack-block holding eighty infantrymen and their centurion, or some sixty cavalry troopers and two decurions, in their place (literally) were small, individual, rectangular buildings separated by narrow eaves'-drip passages. These were the 'chalets'.[63] Three different arrangements have been identified. In the first there was a row of similar-sized 'chalets'; in the second there was a larger 'chalet' at one end of the row; in the third there were larger 'chalets' at both ends of the row. It should not be assumed that all the second-century barrack-blocks were necessarily replaced by a 'chalet' row. At Wallsend (fig. 12) excavation has shown that the barrack-blocks in the *praetentura* (the part of the fort forward of the administrative range) of the second-century fort had been cleared away in the fourth, much of their sites remaining vacant ground, with only a few scrappy structures. In addition, at several forts there were buildings along the inside face of the defensive walls — 'rampart-back' buildings. Again the potential accommodation of the forts had been reduced; the question is to what? One view would have it that each 'chalet' contained the eight men who would have been housed in a *contubernium* (two-room unit) of the second-century barrack (a comparable floor-area). A more radical view is that each 'chalet' housed only one man, perhaps with his family. In support of the presence of families trinkets such as bracelets of a supposedly 'female' nature (to a twentieth-century observer) are cited, and, more importantly, the skeletons of neonate infants from the fort at Malton. There is no evidence that the eight-man *contubernium* survived as a sub-division in the late army, so something along the lines of the latter hypothesis may be the one to be preferred. If so, this would argue for a drastic reduction in the unit sizes, to something of the order of 10 per cent of the second-century complement, or less. So far 'chalets' are only attested from the northern forts, the command of the *dux Britanniarum*, though there are somewhat similar buildings from the fort at Caernarfon in north Wales. Their origins are poorly understood. They are, as has been said, linked with the restoration of the Wall under Constantius Chlorus. But during the third century, rebuilding at South Shields[64] and Vindolanda[65] produced buildings which could be seen as transitional between the conventional barrack-block and the 'chalet'; so not only the reduced garrisons but also the new-style accommodation of the fourth century may have had their origins in the third. It is interesting to note that at none of the forts in the command of the *dux* is there evidence for the addition of projecting towers to the defences (apart from the special case at York). From the early third century we have epigraphic evidence (RIB 1280, 1281) for the construction of *ballistaria* (platforms for field artillery) at the outpost fort of High Rochester. Stone

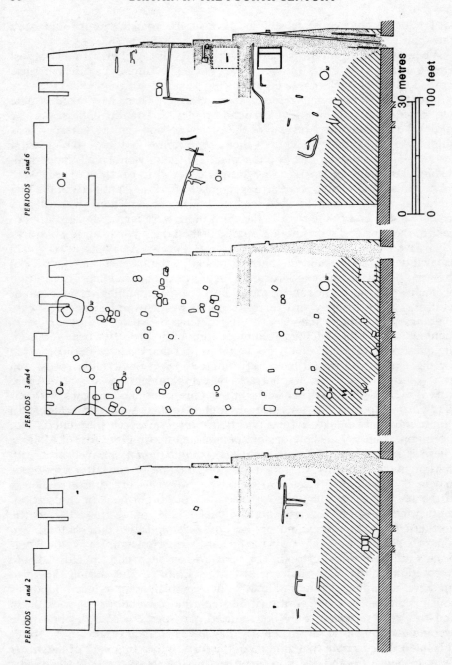

Fig. 13 The internal buildings of Portchester

platforms added to the inside face of the defences at Housesteads may have performed the same function. These are better than nothing, but do not enable the defenders to enfilade the front of the walls. Is this lack of defensive sophistication a comment on the perceived attack and siege abilities of the Picts and other peoples?

Turning to the forts of the Saxon Shore we find an even less certain picture. The evidence from the early forts of Brancaster and Reculver points to standard second-century-type layouts, and in the nineteenth century Roach Smith recorded a structure from Lympne closely resembling the rear range of a traditional *principia*.[66] The evidence from the later forts of the series is very patchy, but indicates something very different from Brancaster or Reculver. At Portchester (fig. 13) the most extensive modern excavations at a Shore fort examined an area along the western side of the metalled road leading in from the postern gate in the centre of the south wall.[67] Three main periods of late third- and fourth-century occupation were recognised: in the first (*c.* 285–90) there were traces of two rectangular timber buildings; in the second (*c.* 325–45) there were only pits in the interior, though some clear spaces could have held timber buildings; in the third (*c.* 345 on) there was a period of ordered occupation with one, possibly two, squarish timber buildings, succeeded by disorderly occupation. None of the structures encountered looks remotely like a traditional barrack-block, nor do they look particularly like the 'chalets' of Hadrian's Wall. The scrappy evidence from Burgh Castle,[68] Pevensey,[69] and Richborough[70] is congruent with this picture of insubstantial timber buildings to no distinctively military plan. As has already been noted the artefact assemblage from Portchester is not distinctively military either, and at Burgh Castle only a helmet gives the game away. For Portchester the excavator suggested that the fort may only have been garrisoned intermittently, so as with the Wall the list in the *Notitia* would be a snapshot in time rather than reflecting the state of affairs throughout the fourth century. It is further suggested that at Portchester some of the phases of occupation may be non-military; again the evidence cited is of 'female' objects and of women's shoes. So far excavation and other research on these installations has concentrated exclusively on the defences and the areas inside them. But all these Saxon Shore forts are presumed to have had a second major function as fleet bases. None of the port facilities associated with any of them has yet been examined, nor do we have any archaeological evidence of the sorts of ships used. A chance remark in an ancient source[71] tells us that the scout-ships which operated in British waters had their sails and rigging dyed sea-green, as were the uniforms of their crews.

The (admittedly incomplete and incompletely understood) evidence from the fortresses and forts of the fourth century in Britain all suggests that the late Roman garrisons and troops were markedly different from those typical of the second century and significantly smaller. A recent estimate[72] is that there were only some 12,000 troops *in toto* under the command of the *dux* and the two *comites*, as opposed to the 50,000 or more postulated for the mid-second-century heyday of the Roman army in Britain. Not only were they numerically fewer, but in appearance and in accommodation they would

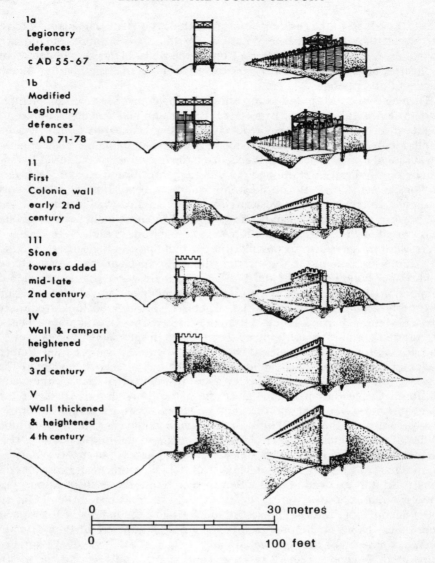

Fig. 14 The defensive sequence at Lincoln

have been almost unrecognisable to a centurion of the second century. In this, though, they merely reflect the late Roman army in general, and we will best regard them in this framework rather than lamenting a decline from the good old days of the second century. It should be noted to their credit that, with the exception of 367, they defended the diocese perfectly adequately.

Before we leave our discussion of the military aspects of late Roman Britain we should consider the defences of the towns, for as we have seen they had their part to play in the overall defensive strategy of the late Roman empire, as well as safeguarding more local concerns (fig. 14). Most of the *civitas*-capitals and some of the lesser towns had received earthwork defences in the later second century.[73] During the third century stone walls were added to the front of the earthen ramparts at most sites, and other sites received defences for the first time. Since by the third century the majority of the *civitas*-capitals had defensive circuits ranging from some 18 ha. (45 acres) at Caerwent up to the 132 ha. (330 acres) of London, the decision to use their lines to determine those of the walls resulted in these late Romano-British *civitas*-capitals having far larger defended areas than their Gallic counterparts. Nor was the opportunity taken to reduce the extent of the defended area as it was at some continental towns which had had early defences, such as Tongeren and Xanten. Even towns such as Canterbury or Leicester, apparently defended for the first time in the third century, conformed to the British practice of enclosing a generous area. Some 'small' towns (for a definition of this term *cf.* p. 64) such as Horncastle (Lincolnshire) and Mildenhall (Wiltshire) were, however, only defended for the first time in the fourth century, the latter *c.* 370 or later; the areas enclosed here were much more in line with those enclosed by defences in late Roman Gaul. At many towns projecting external towers, usually associated with a new, wide ditch, were added in the fourth century. This was not universal; some important sites such as the *civitas*-capitals of Leicester, Silchester and possibly Winchester seem to have managed perfectly well without them. The 1954–5 excavations on the defences of the small town at Great Casterton (Leicestershire)[74] yielded coins apparently associated with the construction of the towers and dating to the end of the 350s. The excavator linked the addition of the external towers to the defences at Great Casterton with the statement of Ammianus describing the work of the *comes* Theodosius after 367: '*in integrum restituit civitates et castra*' ('he fully restored the towns and the forts').[75] The addition of towers was regarded as part of the restoration of the towns, and as subsequent excavations on similar sites did not disturb the dating, a Theodosian date for the addition of bastions became an article of faith. Recently, however, a re-examination of the evidence for the stratification and dating of coins associated with the construction of the towers on the southern walls at Caerwent[76] has shown that they cannot be later than 350, and that the crucial coins at Great Casterton are not as firmly associated with the construction of the towers as had been thought. The universal ascription of these towers to the *comes* Theodosius can no longer hold. Indeed, the linking of Ammianus' markedly unspecific remark about the *civitates* with the specific act of tower-construction was always over-stretching the text.

Nonetheless, even if the towers should no longer be seen as the outcome of a single act, they were built, bringing most of the towns of Britain into line with standard late-imperial defensive practice. These defences would have protected the local populace in time of urgency, and would have also acted as bases for the comitatensian troops of the *comes Britanniarum* and as store-bases.

The towns

We must now turn from the paramilitary defensive aspects of towns in late Roman Britain to their functions within the administration, economy and society of the diocese. Towns had developed in Britain for a variety of reasons and under a variety of influences. Some of these were connected with the ideology and administrative practice of the Roman empire; others represented a response by the indigenous population to the changed circumstances consequent upon inclusion within that empire. In the early empire the Romans regarded the towns literally as the symbol of civilisation, and also as the location through which the local administration of the empire could be carried on. They therefore founded or caused to be founded in Britain a number of towns recognisably constructed to a Mediterranean-derived pattern, with features and structures such as a street-grid, water supply, forum-basilica complex, public baths, amphitheatre, arches. Taken together these were the distinguishing features of the administrative centres in Britain — the *coloniae*, a *municipium*, the *civitas*-capitals, usually referred to together for convenience as the 'large' towns. As well as fulfilling these administrative functions they developed as population centres from the later first and early second centuries, also as centres of production and distribution, either of finished goods imported from the Continent or of goods manufactured in the town itself or in its hinterland. This is characterised by the appearance of the 'strip-building', a long rectangular structure, short end on to street, with evidence for manufacture or trading. From the mid-second century the growing numbers of residences which had little or no commercial function and displayed a desire for spacious and comfortable living, 'town houses', betoken an increasing involvement in the towns by the indigenous land-owning classes alongside the artisan population.

As well as these planned 'large' towns there also appeared the so-called 'small' towns (though there is a measure of overlap in the actual size-ranges). These developed along the main roads and at road junctions or other communication-nodes. Because of this, and because they lacked any formal planning, they usually had a rather straggling form.[77] They lacked not only the street-grids of their larger cousins, but also the public buildings expressive of status and administrative function. These 'small' towns would at best have had very limited administrative duties within the territory controlled from a 'large' town. They also contained very few town houses, both absolutely and also relative to the 'large' towns. The landed aristocracy congregated round the duties and pleasures of the 'large' towns. What the 'small' towns

Fig. 15 Map of towns in fourth-century Britain

overwhelmingly consisted of was strip buildings and other, often very simple, structures. From the building-plans, from artefactual and other evidence from those buildings, and from the evidence of artefact distribution patterns it is clear that the main *raison d'être* of these places was commercial: they were small market towns. So by the end of the second century there was a range of sizes and types of town with differing administrative, artisan and residential functions.

Turning to Britain in the fourth century, there has for some time now been a debate over the nature and function of towns at that period and in comparison with the towns of the second century. As with most debates the protagonists tend to take up positions towards the extremes of their ranges and to find little good in the other point of view. One view[78] is that the towns of fourth-century Britain were unchanged in essentials from those of the second century: the worst troubles of the third century had passed the island by so that uninterrupted development had been possible. The other view[79] looks at the reduced circumstances of late towns on the continent, for instance Gaul, and suggests that as Britain was subject to the same general imperatives then developments in Britain should parallel those on the continent. In this scheme of things the towns of fourth-century Britain were shrunken administrative centres cowering in the shell provided by the earlier defensive circuits. There have been two other problems which have further obscured the issues. The first is enormous uncertainty over what was happening in Britain in the third century. This is to an extent a consequence of poor archaeological data, largely as a result of difficulties in dating deposits (and therefore processes) from *c*. 210–260. The second is the lack of quantified or quantifiable evidence which may be deployed in support of one hypothesis or the other. Accordingly, here we shall first look at some of the evidence for the late third century before passing on to a longer evaluation of the evidence for the fourth century, with objective data when possible (which is all too seldom).

An important site for understanding the 'large' towns is Verulamium, (fig. 16) where excavations in the late 1950s and early 1960s furnish us with one of the few detailed publications of large-scale, modern investigation. The excavations concentrated on a strip running back from the Watling Stret frontage past the north-western side of the forum. *C*. 155 the central area of Verulamium had been burnt down in a catastrophic fire. Until then in almost all the areas investigated there had been timber-framed buildings: closely-packed strip-buildings along Watling Street, larger structures (but not as elaborate as later town houses) with a bit more elbow-room further back from the main street. After the fire, rebuilding was piecemeal, but by the middle of the third century town houses with flint and mortar sill-walls covered up to two-thirds of the area of the former buildings away from Watling Street. Because the individual buildings were larger than their predecessors there were fewer of them. It is interesting to note that the prime commercial site on the Watling Street frontage of Insula XIV remained vacant until *c*. 275, when six strip-buildings were built to replace the twelve burnt down in 155. The majority of these buildings remained in use till at least the middle of the

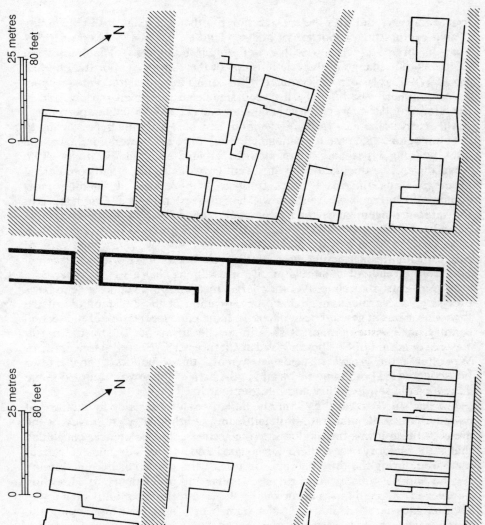

Fig. 16 Verulamium in second (top) and fourth (bottom) centuries

fourth century, and with the construction of other buildings at the beginning of that century the proportion of built-up land to that of 155 was now three-quarters or more, though with fewer, larger buildings.[80] The impression gained is of a change in the relationships of the components of the building stock. Whereas before 155 commercial buildings were the predominant type, at least numerically, after the fire their significance declined sharply, and in the later period they were fewer in number and occupied a smaller percentage of the excavated areas. Instead town houses, which had only been starting to develop before 155, rose to dominance. They were the most numerous of the later building types and occupied a far greater area relative to pre-155. Nevertheless, by the end of the third century we once more find commercial premises along the main street frontage with residential buildings now common to the rear, where there was less pressure on space. One feature of the later arrangement is that areas could remain vacant for considerable periods of time, presumably because the lack of pressure on space made a choice of building-plot possible. This means that we must be wary of simplistically reconstructing the overall development of a town by extrapolation from an individual site within it, or assuming that a vacant plot was a symptom of urban decline. At other 'large' towns it is not yet possible to be as precise as at Verulamium, but the phenomenon of the development of the town house has in general been dated from the later second half of the second century on.[81] At a number of sites in specific towns such as in the north-western quadrant of Chichester[82] and at Cirencester,[83] Exeter,[84] Lincoln,[85] or Wroxeter,[86] the excavated evidence supports the contention that the town house increased both in numbers and in the area of the towns occupied in the course of the third century and into the fourth.

For the 'small' towns the picture is similarly easy to describe in outline, but equally hard to demonstrate in detail from published sites. A survey of the areas of these towns that lay outside the second-century defences concluded that at the majority of sites there was no good evidence for a decline in the occupied area during the third century, or at least that the areas occupied in the second and the fourth centuries were similar and no evidence for desertion intervened.[87] Again this is borne out by the case-histories of individual towns such as Alcester,[88] Braintree,[89] Neatham,[90] or Water Newton.[91] As at the 'large' towns there is a trend from the later second century on to replace purely timber-framed buildings by ones with stone sill-walls at least. It may be, therefore, that further large-scale excavation allowing quantification will show a decrease in building density in parallel with that at the 'large' towns. What is seldom found at the 'small' towns either by aerial photography or excavation, however, is any significant number or area of town houses, so in this respect the 'small' towns cannot have paralleled the effect on the urban layout of the rise of the town house at the 'large' towns. So at present it would appear that at the 'small' towns there was not only little overall change, but less even than at the 'large' towns. One or two 'small' towns, such as Margidunum[92] or Tripontium,[93] can be shown to have declined in the third century, but this does not affect the observation that in the main the third century saw the 'small' towns maintaining both their populations and their rôle.

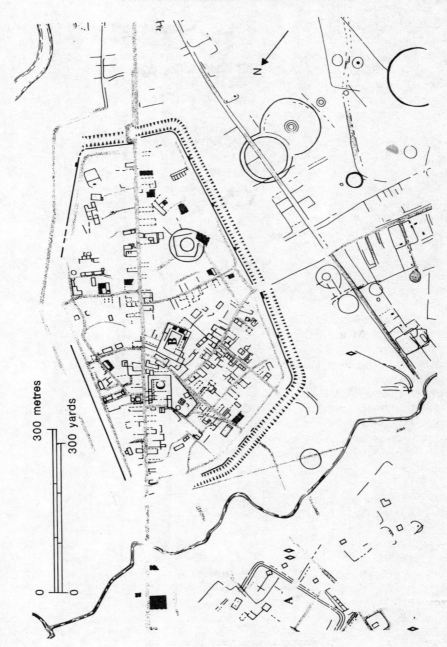

Fig. 17 Water Newton

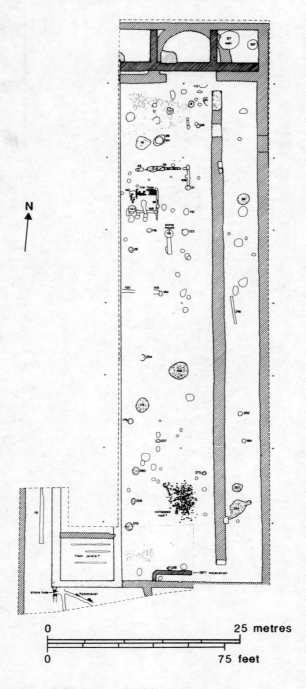

Fig. 18 Silchester basilica

We enter the fourth century with the towns still an active but also dynamic range of settlements. To examine the nature and functions of the towns during the fourth century we may use the broad functional divisions encountered above to structure the discussion and impose a measure of order on a welter of data. The divisions we shall use are administration, production and distribution, and accommodation.

In dealing with administration we shall need to consider two topics; one is the need for a continuing local civil and legal administrative framework, the other is the needs imposed by the late Roman revenue cycle. Discussion of local administration in late Roman Britain has tended to be heavily coloured by considerations imported from the written sources from elsewhere in the Empire, principally the impression that the *curiales* were increasingly unwilling to shoulder the burdens of civic office (*cf.* p. 13). The archaeological record has been read with this in mind, particularly the results of two of the earliest and most extensive excavations on forum/basilica complexes, the epitome of civic status and identity. At Silchester (fig. 18, Pl. 9) the late nineteenth-century excavators[94] showed that in the fourth century the basilica was used for industrial rather than civic purposes. This has been confirmed and amplified by recent re-excavation of the basilica,[95] which has shown that in the late third century the basilica was used for bronze- and pewter-working, and that from *c.* 320–330 on it was used for iron-working on a considerable scale. There is little evidence for subdivision of the interior of the basilica in this phase, so rather than a range of small-scale operations we may envisage centralised, official use of this former civic building. At Wroxeter[96] the inter-war excavations revealed that the forum/basilica complex had burnt down in the late third century and was not rebuilt. In both these cases the archaeological evidence was for the cessation of civic life as expressed in these most characteristic of administrative complexes, and this accorded well with the picture gained from the legislation. But between the excavation of the Silchester and the Wroxeter forum/basilicas, that at Caerwent had been excavated:[97] neither in this campaign of work nor in the re-excavation now under way[98] has there been any evidence for abandonment or change of use of the basilica before the end of the Roman period. The excavator of the Wroxeter forum/basilica also turned his attention to that at Caistor-by-Norwich.[99] Like Wroxeter it had been destroyed by fire in the third century, but unlike Wroxeter it was subsequently rebuilt. At towns such as Cirencester[100] and Gloucester[101] the evidence from partial excavation is that the forum/basilica complex remained in use through the fourth century. At Exeter[102] the excavated, southern end of the basilica was extensively re-modelled in the latter part of the fourth century. The Leicester[103] forum/basilica seems to have been in use to the end of the Roman period. Recent excavation on the London basilica[104] suggests changes in the fourth century. Elsewhere the evidence is too fragmentary to allow conclusions on individual sites, or is simply not present. If one is to equate the maintenance of the principal civic buildings with the maintenance of civic values and practices, the picture from Britain, though mixed, is not unfavourable. But of course, to administer a *civitas* one does not actually need a forum/basilica; a suite of offices will do. At Silchester the basilica had been given over to other uses and at Wroxeter it had been abandoned, yet there is evidence that these towns were still in being in the fourth century.

Forum/basilica complexes were not the only structures reflecting the status of a town which had been provided in the first or second centuries and therefore needed choices made about them by the fourth-century population. The street-grid and the water supply and disposal systems which often ran along the streets were generally maintained in the fourth century, showing that such basic amenities were still felt to be necessary. The most commonly provided public utility apart from the forum/basilica was the baths. At Caistor-by-Norwich,[105] Canterbury,[106] Chichester,[107] Dorchester (Dorset),[108] Exeter,[109] Leicester[110] and Lincoln[111] the evidence is that the baths were maintained and in use as baths well into the fourth century. At Caerwent[112] and Silchester[113] the early excavators did not note anything to suggest an early abandonment of the baths. But at Wroxeter[114] the pottery in the dumps of ash from the hypocaust apparently does not go beyond *c.* 300, though the large, basilican exercise-hall (*palaestra*) attached to the baths is currently thought to have been in use until the latter part of the fourth century[115] before being dismantled and replaced by other structures (*cf.* p. 152). The *macellum* (provisions market) in the corner of the baths insula was refurbished at the turn of the third and fourth centuries.[116] The *macellum* at Verulamium too was in use in the fourth century. Of other public buildings and structures, the amphitheatres at Carmarthen,[118] Cirencester[119] and Silchester[120] show no sign of abandonment before the end of the fourth century.[117] That at Dorchester (Dorset)[121] may have been abandoned as early as the early second century, and at Chichester[122] the arena wall was removed at an unknown (Roman?) date. As yet we know too little about the theatres at Canterbury[123] and Colchester[124] to say anything about their fate in the fourth century. The theatre at Verulamium[125] was only turned into a rubbish dump at the end of the century.

Overall there is no evidence for the widespread dereliction or destruction of civic buildings and monuments in the fourth century — and certainly not on the scale visible in Gaul (indeed masonry reused from such structures in late defences in Britain is a rarity.[126]) This is not necessarily to say that all such buildings retained their original functions; some clearly did not. On the other hand there is no evidence for any new public works (defences excepted as a special case), nor for anything more than partial rebuildings and refurbishments. The civic and legal administration of the *civitates* could still have been carried on and their citizens entertained. These structures do not argue for general dereliction of civic duties; equally they do not argue for any marked enthusiasm. As we shall see (p. 108) there is evidence that, in common with other areas of the empire, aristocratic expenditure was being directed into private magnificence rather than public munificence.

The other administrative function that figured large in the life of the late Roman town was the revenue and expenditure cycle generated by the central government. How this functioned and what its place was in the life of late Roman towns in Britain deserves examination, since it will be argued that its existence was central to the existence of the towns, and they in turn were central to the existence of a romanised economy and culture: to the Romanness of Roman Britain. We have already seen (p. 8) that the main burden of taxation fell on the rural populace, landowners and peasants alike. Also, the proportion of tax payable in specie had to be turned into gold or silver coin or bullion to be acceptable to the authorities. Therefore, there had to be in existence some mechanism for the rural populace to convert agricultural surplus into coin. These coins, moreover, were intrinsically high-value, the gold in particular (one *solidus* might be more than a peasant's annual income).[127] Given the disparities of resources and surplus between peasants and large landowners we may expect differing strategies for the payment of taxes. The larger landholders will have been assessed at amounts requiring whole units of coin. The smaller taxpayers on the other hand may at times have been grouped into a collective and it was the latter that was assessed for tax; for instance this was the attested method for the payment of the *aurum tironicum* (the recruit tax).[128] It became the case that the larger landowners increasingly took over the payment of the tax due from their tenants (at a cost to the tenant), so the tenant would pay tax and rental together direct to his landlord. We have seen (p. 9) how much of the annual produce this could amount to, so it is not surprising that in some areas peasants became essentially the bondsmen of their landlords. There is a stream of imperial legislation concerning itself with this latter process in the east: it is perfectly possible that the same taxation system produced similar results in the west.

How then was surplus turned into coin or bullion? Simple market transactions in the towns would not have sufficed, the volume of surplus would have overwhelmed the artisan productive capacity; moreover these transactions need not necessarily have involved coin. The answer which the literary sources give us is that the main customer for such produce was the state itself, needing supplies over and above that raised in taxation. These sources (*cf.* p. 9) point to the huge volume of goods bought in by the state in return for cash, particularly at forts, towns and stations of the *cursus publicus*. In the sources the state figures as the single largest consumer for agricultural produce. Thus the producers had a market, they were able to obtain coin, and the demand created by the state over and above that already created by taxation would further stimulate production, especially since this production brought a tangible return which that removed through taxation did not. In addition there may have been a class which approximated to the 'factor' of eighteenth- and nineteenth-century Britain, merchants who made their living by buying commodities in bulk in return for coin and selling them on at a profit. In the case of the late Roman empire obvious consumers for such produce would again be the state and private consumers, or the supplies could be stored against a time of shortage for greater profit. Evidence for such persons is difficult to find in the written sources. For the literary authors this may have been because such people were not fit subject for comment. But both in the literary sources and in the legislation there are references to grain-merchants and others profiteering in time of famine, this most famously in the preamble to Diocletian's Edict on Maximum Prices at the turn of the third and fourth centuries. People in such a position in the chain of supply and demand would appear to be the sort we seek. The *nummularii* or their equivalents may also be relevant here. The legislation makes it clear that they bought gold and silver from individuals for bronze, and the state recovered it from them, also in bronze. Thus the *nummularii* regularly had access to quantities of coin in all three metals. It is possible that they acted as general money-changers, and that what we see in the legislation is only a part of their activities, the part that interested the legislators. In the laws the *nummularii* seem to have a restricted geographical distribution,[129] but the authorities' need to recover gold and silver was empire-wide. *Nummularii* or their equivalents and factors would provide the mechanism for the conversion of agricultural surplus into coin. Such evidence as we have for *nummularii*, commodity-merchants and the operations of the tax system all point to the towns as the place where such transactions occurred. If this was so, then the operations of the tax system would have afforded the main economic activity in the towns. This distinguished Roman towns from the more familiar mediaeval towns which did not have such a regular and demanding tax-system operating through them.

Archaeologically we cannot really expect too much, since it was not the purpose of any participant in the chain that grain or animals or coin should become archaeologically visible through loss. Nonetheless there are a couple of possible avenues of approach. One is that on occasion bought surplus would have to be stored. Thus the granaries and store-buildings which have been found attached to some town houses at 'large' towns might be for such purposes. The trouble is that they might also be for official storage (*cf.* p. 49) or simply for the storage of produce to be consumed by the household. A well-known feature of late Romano-British towns is the quantity of coin (almost all of low-value bronze) found at them. This may betoken the presence of *nummularii* or their equivalents, but it is not demonstrable. This question will be referred to in the general discussion of coinage below (*cf.* p. 91).

Finally in this section on the implications for towns of the fiscal system we must also note the sources of gold and silver available. One was the circulating 'pool' of precious-metal coin and plate derived from the earlier economic history and activity of the island. By 300 this must have been considerable but is now unquantifiable. The second is the payments made during the fourth century to the army and officials and for other state requirements and projects. A third may have been the *nummularii*, who generally feature in the legislation only insofar as they acquire gold and silver for the state, but this does not seem to have been the limit of their money-changing.

This brings us to the second of our major topics, the commercial aspects of towns in the fourth century. Here it will be appropriate to consider both the 'large' and the 'small' towns since they both had parts to play. It is perhaps worth remarking here that though the 'small' towns had only a minor part to play in the civil and legal administration, they may have been more significant in the fiscal cycle as places where coin could be obtained, even if it had to be surrendered at the *civitas*-capital. Commercial activity may be crudely divided into two unequal and unequally-distributed types. One was the provision of 'higher-order' goods and services, essentially those that were costly and of which only a limited number could be afforded. Mosaics are a good example of the sort of goods with which we are dealing here, being specialised and costly. The services are those provided by expensive 'professionals' such as doctors, lawyers, academics and other such social parasites. On general grounds they might be expected to be concentrated at the 'large' towns, since it was there that the landowning classes who could afford their goods and services had their town houses, and it was there that the wider populace had to go at certain times for administrative and tax purposes, purposes which themselves often entailed the need for professional services. Such evidence as we have matches the theory; analysis of fourth-century mosaics in Britain has identified a number of regional 'schools', based at Cirencester, Dorchester (Dorset), Water Newton (by far the largest 'small' town) and quite possibly York.[130] The little epigraphic evidence we have for professionals,[131] though it is mainly early in date, does focus on the towns.

Much more numerous and significant is the evidence for 'lower-order' activity, the day-to-day production and/or distribution of everyday goods such as leatherwork, metalwork, pottery, textiles and woodwork. This applies not only to the 'large' towns but also to the 'small', where the buildings known from excavation or aerial photography are overwhelmingly of artisan type. Three main categories of evidence may be used to demonstrate the presence of artisans and the rôle of towns as market centres: building-types; evidence for manufacture; and the distributions of finished products. As we have already seen (p. 64) the characteristic artisan building in Romano-British towns was the strip-building.[131] Often this had an area at the front devoid of evidence for manufacture, and this is often interpreted as the selling area, with goods displayed there for those passing along the street. In the rear portions there were often ovens and hearth-bases, attesting to heat-using processes. There was also often waste material, most usually iron slag. As well as strip-buildings simpler (sometimes very simple) rectangular buildings are found, which also yield hearths, ovens, slag and other such evidence for artisan processes. The strip-building in particular is a building-type virtually confined to sites conventionally regarded as towns, and absent from rural sites such as villas, though it does also appear at *vici*, the civil settlements outside forts, which had a quasi-urban nature and function.[132]

What is the evidence for the extent of production and redistribution at late Roman towns in Britain, and how does this compare with earlier periods? Here we are seriously hindered by the shortage of published, large-scale excavations which allow us to compare areas both within and across centuries. For the 'large' towns two of the most useful may paradoxically be those where because of the early date and underdeveloped methods of excavation the evidence is most problematical — Caerwent and Silchester. Their great advantage is that we have substantial areas of the town plan. At Caerwent the overall plan[133] is of an east-west through-road lined with strip-buildings and one or two public buildings such as the forum/basilica and the baths. This location

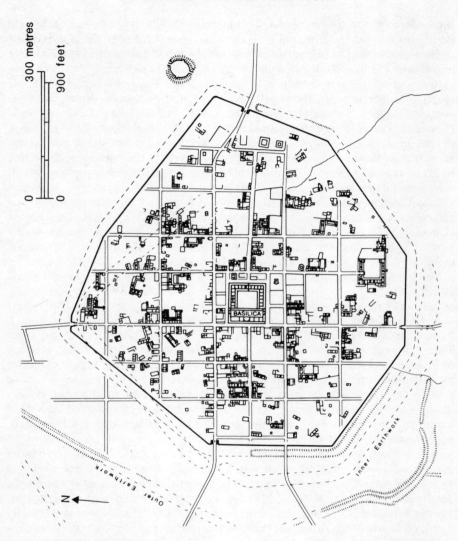

Fig. 19 Silchester general plan

for commercial properties makes sense in terms of ease of access to the premises for the customer, in terms of concentrating commercial premises close to each other and in terms of taking advantage of through-traffic on the main road. It is similar to the modern High or Main Street. The original excavations[134] suggested that these premises were in use during the fourth century, and re-excavation of one of the buildings showed that the stone version was late Roman. The original excavators at Caerwent seem to have concerned themselves principally with the stone buildings, and the new excavations have consistently shown stone private buildings to be late. It may therefore be that the familiar published plan of Caerwent[135] with its strip-buildings along the main east-west street and town houses to north and south is essentially a representation of the town in its fourth-century state. A similar situation seems to be developing for Silchester. Again there is a well-known plan (fig. 19)[136] which shows strip-buildings concentrating along either side of the main east-west road, with large town houses taking up much of the rest of the area within the defences. The original excavations recovered fourth-century material from many structures, but the stratigraphic position of this material is seldom clear. The new excavations in the town allied with analysis of the original photographic record suggest that usually the Victorian excavators dug down to the top of the surviving deposits and then stopped. Many of these were fourth-century. Some of the town houses contain fourth-century mosaics. All in all the bulk of the buildings shown on the general plan are more likely than not to be fourth-century. Of more modern excavations we have already encountered Verulamium, where in Insula XIV along the Watling Street frontage we have the six strip-buildings built in the late third century and occupied well into the fourth. Smaller-scale excavations at 'large' towns such as Cirencester,[137] Exeter,[138] Winchester[139] or Wroxeter[140] also show fourth-century strip-buildings and commercial properties, often along the main streets.

To compare the level of commercial activity in the towns of the fourth century with that for earlier periods is very much more difficult because of the lack of modern excavation on a large enough scale. Again Verulamium Insula XIV must be cited. There, as we have seen, the six late third-century strip-buildings replaced twelve burnt down c. 155. At Cirencester (Admiral's Walk),[141] excavation revealed traces of both second- and fourth-century commercial buildings, and the fourth-century ones were fewer in number. These are very tentative indications, but they may suggest that there were fewer manufacturing premises in the 'large' towns in the fourth as compared with the second century. Trading, of course, does not have to take place in permanent structures; a market place or open space will do.

The second criterion we listed, the presence of evidence for manufacture, is a problematical one. In the first place many manufacturing processes need not leave archaeological traces; it is mainly the heat-using processes that do, in the form of hearths and oven-bases. Secondly, even where one does have such evidence it is difficult to identify the process being carried out, because few leave distinctive archaeological traces; the most common being slag from iron-working, which is well-nigh ubiquitous. Also, because the finished product was made to be sold it does not remain at the point of production, so it is difficult to identify particular sites as the point of origin for particular classes of artefact. Nevertheless the archaeological record consistently describes fourth-century hearths, ovens, vat-bases and the waste from production.[142]

That goods were being traded from the towns is clear. We have already encountered the evidence that towns were the bases for mosaicists. For day-to-day commodities the most useful evidence is that furnished by pottery. This is not the place to pre-empt the more general discussion of the information on late Roman Britain afforded by pottery (*cf.* p. 85), but a few points may be made. The first is that for the large-scale fine ware industries of fourth-century Britain there is good evidence that the towns played an important part in their distribution. The same is probably true of the local coarse wares, though as yet they are more difficult to document. This evidence derives from the amount and variety of fine wares found at towns as opposed to rural sites, from the concentration of fine ware distribution in and around towns and from what we know in general of coarse ware distributions.

The evidence from building types, from the presence of industrial activities and from the distributions of finished goods argues that fourth-century towns were centres of production and distribution. In this they differ from rural sites where there may be industrial processes for immediate needs, but which do not show the concentration on production and distribution or that they were centres of distribution. One further point worth making is that at Silchester a rough calculation of the area occupied by the artisan zone along the main east-west street and some subsidiary groups of such buildings comes out at *c.* 8 ha. (20 acres), an area similar to that of many 'small' towns. This suggests that for the 'lower order' production and redistribution the 'large' and 'small' towns may in that sense be taken together, and may have formed a uniform network over the south and east of Britain.

One of the other functions at both 'large' and 'small' towns was the third of our major criteria: accommodation. It is generally assumed that strip-buildings were not only places of work but also the home of the artisan and his family; they lived over the shop, (fig. 20). At the 'small' towns there is nowhere else where the inhabitants of the town could reasonably have lived. At the 'large' towns too there were significant areas taken up with such buildings, and there too they presumably housed those working in the various industries. At these towns there were also the town houses which we have argued were an increasingly important component of the late urban landscape. It is exceedingly difficult to form any estimate of how many people may have lived in these buildings. This is because we are hard put to it to identify the functions of most of the rooms; are they 'living rooms', or reception rooms, or sleeping accommodation or what? Most of them merely show the archaeologist the bland and uninformative face of a tessellated or other uniform floor surface. One may surmise that they would have housed the owner and his family, and given that they were expressions of wealth and that it was customary in the late Roman world for the wealthy to be accompanied by a retinue of servants and attendants, then we may surmise their presence also. Many of the owners of such properties would have been of the curial

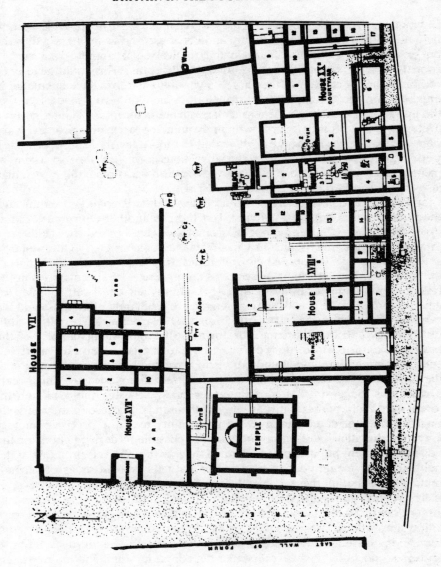

Fig. 20 'Strip-buildings', Caerwent

class, so the purpose of these houses would have been to provide accommodation for the head of the family and his household as he attended to the business of the *civitas*, or participated in the social round which such a congeries of the well-to-do would undoubtedly entail. This could have been seasonal; the population of the 'large' towns may therefore have fluctuated in numbers and social composition through the year. We have already seen that the literary evidence from the curial classes of fourth-century Gaul displays a preference for country over town; in Britain the archaeological evidence suggests that it was in the rural villas that the more lavish displays of wealth were manifested rather than in the town houses (*cf.* p. 108), so a similar picture of a country-based aristocracy, resident on occasion in the towns, may also be appropriate for fourth-century Britain.

So far we have been considering the towns of late Roman Britain through the buildings that housed the living. But there is another enormous, under-exploited source of information: the cemeteries that housed the dead. At a number of 'large' towns such as Cirencester,[143] Colchester,[144] Dorchester[145] and Winchester,[146] extensive new cemeteries were laid out in the early part of the fourth century. At all of these towns there were several cemeteries in the fourth century, but at none of them has more than one been sampled by modern methods.[147] The allocation of large areas of land to burial use and the evidence for careful lay-out of the burial areas are consonant with a still-functioning central authority in the town. So far only small samples of the known areas of fourth-century burial at these towns have been excavated, but even so these have yielded hundreds of close-packed burials. Extrapolation to the likely areas of cemetery, derived from casual discoveries and small-scale excavations, suggests that at Dorchester or Winchester the total fourth-century cemetery population runs into the thousands. Because of the relatively small number of dated samples and uncertainty over the precise cemetery limits and the density of burials it is not yet possible to derive figures for the size of the parent population. A figure in the low thousands is probably of the right order of magnitude. In comparison with the known areas of second-century burials at all these towns, the fourth-century cemeteries are extensive. It has been remarked that at Winchester the fourth-century cemeteries are larger than those for the other three centuries combined. But we must beware of too simplistic an approach to these data. There seems to have been a major change in attitudes to the disposal of the dead in the third and fourth centuries, most obviously expressed in the adoption of inhumation in preference to cremation. Thus simply to compare the second and the fourth centuries may in this case not be to compare like with like. Nevertheless the point remains that the late cemeteries at the large towns are extensive and betoken a considerable population.

For the 'small' towns our information is inadequate, due to an almost total lack of excavation. But nineteenth-century records of the disturbance of extensive, late cemeteries at Alcester[148] and Irchester[149] make it clear that this class of towns also could have had extensive burial grounds, with the population which that implies. In addition at the 'small' towns there was a tradition of less formal burial areas, such as at the backs of properties on the edges of the town, as well as in cemeteries, as for instance at Ilchester.[150] As at the 'large' towns it would appear that the cemetery evidence for the 'small' towns testifies to a continuing urban population of some density. One further point needs to be made about the urban population in late Roman Britain. It is accepted that the population of the towns of mediaeval England was not self-sustaining; the documentation shows regular migration from the country to the towns, which thus, other things being equal, maintain their population levels. There is no reason to think that the situation was different in the Roman period. Such migration would of course mean that much of the rural population had social as well as economic links with the towns.

What, in sum, may we say about the towns of late Roman Britain? They clearly remained centres of population, of economic activity, of social resort, and of administrative and other public functions. The morphology of the towns, their building types, the range of activities in them and the size of the population were all quantitatively and qualitatively different from those of the various types of rural settlement. At the 'large' towns the basic public amenities such as the streets and the water supply were maintained. The more grandiose public structures bequeathed by the civic pride of the second century had mixed fortunes, but there was no widespread neglect or demolition of them. As for private buildings, it would seem that there were two principal areas. Along the main through road(s), and often prolonged outside the gates, were areas of artisan buildings, their occupants engaged in the production and distribution of finished items, mainly to the local rural populace. Away from these built-up commercial frontages the majority of the area within the defences was taken up by towns houses standing within large properties. By comparison with the second century there had been changes. On the artisan side there appear to have been fewer strip buildings in the fourth century than in the second, but there are many more town houses. Overall there was probably a diminution in the level of commercial activity — though whether this represents decline, or a settling-back from a precocious early growth is a moot point. On the other hand, the late towns see a far greater investment by members of the landed classes in the form of their town houses, though this involves a lower building density. A case can be made for the population density of late towns having been lower than early ones, but as yet this is an impression rather than a quantifiable statement. The cemetery evidence nonetheless demonstrates population levels higher than for any other type of settlement in late Roman Britain. At the 'small' towns the evidence is again for a continuing nucleation of population heavily engaged in non-agricultural pursuits, principally production and distribution, again for the market afforded by the local rural populace. This analysis clearly does not accord with the view that towns in late Roman Britain were administrative shells; the evidence currently available simply does not concur with such a position. Nor can these towns successfully be characterised as places of conspicuous consumption and monumental display, contributing little or nothing to the overall economic well-being of their area.[151] It does on the other hand suggest that the changes in the physical and social composition of the 'large' towns may have been more far-reaching than others have allowed.

Clearly we have here a marked contrast with the situation in the fourth-century towns of Gaul (*cf.* pp. 24–7). There the differences between the early and late *civitas*-capitals were far more striking, particularly in respect of the physical contraction of these settlements, than we have just examined for Britain. These Gallic towns certainly retained their administrative functions and of course were centres for taxation. It is possible, though, that they retained more of their manufacturing and distributive functions than has so far been generally allowed. But they do not seem to have been centres for population, especially of the landed classes, in the way that we have noted that their British counterparts were. The 'small' towns of central and northern Gaul seem to have fared even worse than the 'large', and certainly were not a match for those in late Roman Britain. As we shall see, the picture to be gained of the countryside in late Roman Britain is also more expansive and prosperous than that for the centre and north of late Roman Gaul. That the two areas should apparently differ so much must in part be attributable to the differing incidence and impact of the troubles of the third century, and shows how regions of the Roman Empire could vary one from another even within the overall framework of the state and its institutions.

There was one important and interesting apparent exception to the general pattern for the 'large' towns in the late period: the largest of them all, London. In the fourth century London was the seat of the *vicarius* of the Britains, of the *consularis* of Maxima Caesariensis, of the *rationalis* of the financial administration of the diocese, of the *praepositus* of the diocesan *thesaurus*, and of the staffs and households of all these gentlemen. To judge by the analogies of important administrative centres on the continent, such as Arles, this should have ensured the town a relatively high level of prosperity and activity. But the archaeological evidence shows far less activity in the London of the fourth century than of the second. Can this seeming paradox be resolved? London had developed thanks to its favourable trading position. Lying opposite the mouths of the Rhine it had joined the list of places such as Arles, Lyon, Trier and Cologne which had benefited mightily from their position on the state-occasioned supply route from the Mediterranean to the armies on the Rhine and in Britain. At the Boudiccan revolt in 61, less than two decades after the conquest, it was already famous for its traders and commerce. In the second century its position as the principal port of entry into Britain was attested by the construction of massive quays and water-fronts,[152] and the quantities of samian and amphorae traded through its docklands.[153] To the rear of this there was a burgeoning town of close-packed, timber-framed strip-buildings, processing this trade and adding to it by the manufacture of goods. Probably around the turn of the first and second centuries this thriving centre became the residence of the governor of Britain. But late in the second century the long-distance trade networks of the western empire began to falter, the Rhône-Rhine axis atrophied, and with this the lif-blood of commercial London began to dry up.[154] Great timber quays continued to be constructed[155] into the early third century and the land walls were built enclosing 132 ha. (330 acres), comfortably the largest area in Britain,[156] but this seems rather to have reflected past experience than present reality. To the rear the busy commercial quarters fell silent, the timber buildings were demolished, were not replaced and became covered with 'dark earth' (*cf*. p. 147). London's agricultural hinterland could not take up the slack paid out by the demise of the town's trade. So the settlement the archaeologist encounters in the fourth century is profoundly different from that of the second. There were some monumental buildings surviving from earlier days such as the massive forum-basilica complex and the governor's palace.[157] In the early fourth century the circuit of defences was completed by the construction of walls along the river front, re-using stonework from earlier monuments and impeding access to and from the waterfront.[158] Yet this indicates that London was still thought to be worth defending. What was being defended? The late Roman structures that are known within the defences tend to be large, stone-founded town houses set at a distance from each other.[159] A similar situation may be seen across the river in the suburb of Southwark.[160] Presumably these are in large measure the residences of all the administrative staff to whom we have already referred. The productive and trading capacity of London was a shadow of its former self. It may be that at London we have a very pronounced version of what we have seen at the other 'large' towns. In the second century it developed as the greatest mercantile centre of the island, and its decline was correspondingly great. In the late period its administrative pre-eminence caused its buildings to serve principally that function and those functionaries, to an extent greater than that associated with the landed aristocracy at the other 'large' towns. Roman London, both early and late, could be characterised as an exaggerated version of trends visible in the other 'large' towns of Britain.

In our consideration of London we noted the importance of long-distance trade to the fortunes of the town, and further treatment of the topic is needed. In the second century there had been regular, large-scale movement of goods from the Continent into Britain. This we have already encountered, and seen that the main vehicle for this was the need to supply the army with grain and Mediterranean products such as olive oil and wine. Parasitic on this was trade in manufactured goods such as glass, metalwork and pottery. In addition, huge quantities of samian, the fine red-gloss tableware from central Gaul, were shipped to Britain, apparently for its own sake rather than along with supplies. The first half of the third century saw both the final collapse of the samian industry[161] and the decline of the established long-distance trade patterns.[162] The archaeological picture of trade between Britain and the Continent in the late Roman period is very different (fig. 21). In the south-east, especially on sites around the Thames estuary, there is some pottery from the Argonne region of northern Gaul and a little from the Rhineland, principally Mayen ware.[163] This latter could be an expression of the shipping of grain from Britain to the Rhineland (*cf*. p. 33). In central southern Britain there is a small quantity of *céramique à l'éponge* from Aquitania.[164] This Continental pottery differs markedly from that of the second century in its tiny amounts and geographically restricted distribution. Other Continental imports there still were, principally glass, but this was a luxury, not a bulk commodity. In return there is only a smattering of British pottery on the

Fig. 21 Find-spots of imported pottery

Continent, mainly from sites along the Channel coasts of Gaul.[165] Again this is small beer. Fourth-century Britain seems to conform to the pattern visible for the north-western provinces in general, whereby long-distance movement of goods was uncommon, and the emphasis was on regional and local distribution. Even the British grain shipments to the Rhine do not seem to have engendered the parasitic trade visible in the second century.

Pottery

To stay with consideration of pottery, we may now use it to examine further the nature of manufacture and trade in late Roman Britain. As so often in archaeological studies, pottery has to stand proxy for a host of industries simply because it survives where their products do not. And not only does it simply survive; late Roman pottery in Britain is ubiquitous and found in large amounts. It has therefore been the object of study over many years, with the result that we now know far more about it than about any other industry in the diocese. Traditionally, pottery has been used as a means of dating, since its occurrence on coin-dated sites allows the relative sequence of its typological development to be linked with the absolute calendar dates derived from the coins. Another use has been the study of pottery distribution. A number of kiln-sites are known, and petrological examination of the clay fabrics allows some wares to be assigned to general areas of production, even if the precise kiln-sites are undiscovered. More recently, pottery has been used as an aid to the functional examination of sites or parts of sites. Here we shall concern ourselves with two aspects: one is the evidence of the production sites for the organisation and scale of manufacturing industry; the other is analysis of the distribution patterns to determine the mechanisms and places of 'trade'. By the second century there were three main elements in the pottery repertoire of Roman Britain. First, there were the imported wares, principally samian, which came to the province in huge quantities, but also fine wares from the Rhineland and amphorae from the Mediterranean. Second, there were the fine wares of British manufacture, pottery of a high standard of technical competence and finish, often decorated. This was widely traded from the large manufacturing centres such as Colchester, Mancetter and the lower Nene Valley. As well as being widespread across the sites of the region around the kilns, these industries also show the effect of military demand, being commonly found on military sites in northern Britain, giving rise to a bi-partite distribution pattern. This militarily-induced distribution was a smaller-scale analogue of the Rhône-Rhine axis. The third element was the so-called coarse wares. These were wares which, while technically competent, lacked the conscious superiority and decoration of the fine wares and are assumed to have been for utilitarian purposes such as cooking. Usually these were fired in a reducing kiln, giving a grey surface to the pottery, the ever-present 'grey wares'. What little we know of the manufacture and distribution of these wares suggests that they were locally produced for sale at the nearest market town.[166] Unprepossessing though they generally are, they nonetheless represent the bulk of pottery from Romano-British sites.

The third century witnessed a number of changes in the pottery industries of Britain. The most obvious was the demise of samian and the consequent opening of an important gap in the fine-ware repertoire. Another was the decline of many of the second-century industries and the rise of a number of new, regional fine-ware producers. The two were to an extent linked, since an important part of the output of some of the new centres was red colour-coated vessels. Of the second-century producers, the only one to have retained its share of the market was the Nene Valley (which now took to producing red-slipped wares). All the other fine-ware industries declined into relative insignificance. In the mid-third century two of the new industries emerged, in the New Forest[167] and in Oxfordshire.[168] The New Forest had no local predecessor. In Oxfordshire there had been a modest industry principally concerned with the production of *mortaria* (heavy mixing-bowls studded on the inner surface with grit for grinding foodstuffs). The sudden efflorescence of both these industries may represent a deliberate plantation of potters. There was also an industry producing imitation samian around Much Hadham in Hertfordshire.[169] Two others of the regionally-distributed industries of the fourth century are difficult to categorise simply as fine-ware producers. One is the extensive grey-ware industry of Alice Holt/Farnham on the Hampshire/Surrey border.[170] This managed to capture the London market as well as more local sites. To an extent it may be compared with the black-burnished ware industries which had developed in the second century around Poole Harbour and the Thames estuary.[171] These had produced unlovely, hand-made pots which had nevertheless achieved wide distribution, especially again in the military north. The Poole Harbour industry (BB1) was still active, though with a reduced distribution, in the fourth century. In the north was the Crambeck/Malton industry, near the fort of Malton to the east of York.[172] This produced a range of forms in a parchment ware, an off-white fabric, sturdy rather than fine, sometimes decorated with red-brown paint motifs. It rose to be the dominant fabric on sites north of the Humber, both civil and military. These industries produced huge quantities of their characteristic wares (and sometimes grey wares also as in the New Forest), which were widely distributed and are commonly found on sites within their hinterland. But they co-existed with a still important local coarse ware industry. For instance, it has been calculated[173] for the Saxon Shore fort at Portchester that 75 per cent of the grey wares (forming the largest single group of pottery from the site) came from kilns within a 16-km. (ten-mile) radius of the fort. Yet no kiln is known from that area. This is an indication of the difficulties still confronting us in analysing the most common category of pottery on late Roman sites in Britain.

Though the locations of many of the fine-ware production sites are known, (fig. 22) such excavation as there has been has tended to concentrate on the kilns themselves rather than the ancillary workshops, drying-sheds, clay dumps and so on. Certain conclusions may nonetheless be drawn. In the Nene Valley, the New Forest and Oxfordshire the kilns excavated have been either

Fig. 22 Location of major pottery industries in Britain

single or in small groups, suggesting an organisation centred on the individual
potter or group of potters rather than a rigorously centralised and directed
factory system. This is supported by the overall distribution of the kilns of
these industries, which is straggling and intermittent, covering several square
miles, rather than nucleated and circumscribed. Excavation on kilns of the
Oxfordshire industry at the Churchill Hospital on the eastern side of modern
Oxford[174] revealed a certain amount about the ancillary structures and
features. As well as the kilns, there was a feature interpreted as a drying-floor
constructed in exactly the same way as a T-shaped corn-drier of the type
common on Romano-British rural sites and there interpreted as being for the
drying or parching of grain.[175] Also present were fragments of querns, which
in the context of a pottery site could have been used for grinding the
trituration grits of mortaria, but otherwise could equally well be used for
grinding grain. This ambiguity in possible uses of these things has led to the
suggestion that potting was not a year-round profession but rather a skill
possessed by members of the agricultural community and exercised at the
slacker times of the agricultural year. The pottery so produced could even be
seen as a form of cash-crop.[176] Such a situation would parallel what is known
of the better-documented English mediaeval pottery industry and in other
times and areas where potters and the agricultural population were closely
associated.[177] It would also mean that potters could integrate efficiently with
the woodland management cycles for fuel and materials for kiln-building. The
picture from these fine-ware industries is therefore one of individualistic,
seasonal production, though of course with a measure of standardisation of
output. Though the output of a single kiln or kiln-group might not amount to
much, cumulatively and over time the production of these industries was
enormous. None of the available evidence from other industries contradicts
this picture, and it is very likely to be the system operating amongst the small-
scale, coarse-ware producers. Whether this is also true for other rural-based
industries such as metal-winning and working we cannot as yet say, but it is
not unlikely. What it does appear to contrast with is the picture that we have
for urban artisans, who are assumed to have been in residence and operation
the year round. But the point of a town-based artisan is that he is available as
and when people want him, otherwise they will look elsewhere. The scale and
organisation of these pottery industries is also congruent with evidence from
elsewhere in the Roman empire and from modern pre-industrial societies.[178]

The distribution patterns of Romano-British pottery have been the object
of intense study. They can be approached in two basic ways. Either the
distribution from a production site may be studied to see where its products
got to, in what quantities and how; or it can be studied from the point of view
of a consuming site: where was the pottery coming from and in what
proportions? Usually this is pursued on a chronological axis to assess changes
through time. These studies have necessarily concentrated on distinctive
fabrics whose sources are known; therefore it has principally been the fine
wares that have been looked at (fig. 23). A study of the distribution of the
various fabrics produced at the New Forest kilns[179] showed that there was a
differential between the relatively restricted travel from source of the grey

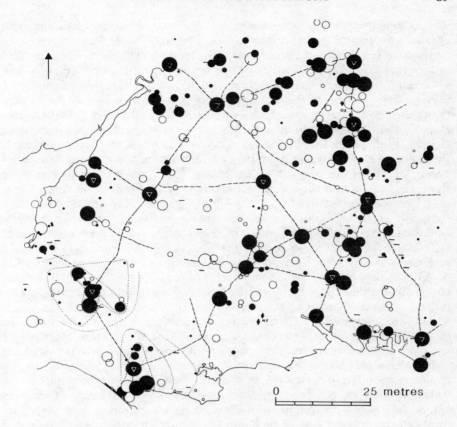

Key. Percentage of fine ware in total assemblage.
Filled circles   Open circles

≥ 19

15–18   ≥ 41

13–14   31–40

11–12   21–30

9–10   16–20
7–8   11–15
5–6   6–10
3–4   1–5
1–2

Filled circles = assemblages including featureless coarse-ware body-sherds.

Open circles = assemblages without featureless coarse-ware body-sherds.

Triangles = walled towns.

Lozenges = kilns in the New Forest and Oxford areas.

Horizontal bars = contemporary assemblages without fine wares.

Fig. 23 Distribution of fine wares in southern Britain

wares, compared with a greater spread of the red colour-coated fabrics, and greatest of all of the purple-coated wares. This must be the result not only of consumer preference but also of a response by the distributors, since they did not bother to take the coarse wares far afield. The distribution of the Oxfordshire products has also been analysed. One conclusion is that the military bias so clear in the second century is far less evident in the fourth. Gone are the bi-partite distributions in the south and in the military north. Instead the Oxfordshire industry has a regional distribution in southern Britain. Within that distribution fall many of the forts of the Saxon Shore and they received considerable quantities of Oxfordshire ware, more than other classes of site in the area other than towns.[180] Although those forts outside the main distribution area were not specially sought out, nonetheless there may have been input from the army supply system. This would require the bulk movement of goods, and thus create a volume transport system. Middlemen needing to move goods such as pottery would take advantage of this system at little or no cost to themselves. On a large scale the grain shipments to Rome and elsewhere made possible the widespread distribution of ARSW; on a small scale the movement of supplies for the army in Britain could have made possible much widespread distribution of comparable pottery, such as that from Oxfordshire.

Another feature of the distribution of Oxfordshire wares was the influence of water transport; that is to say the Thames. Those sites within easy reach of the river and its estuary received significantly more Oxfordshire pottery than those which had to be reached overland.[181] This is an illustration of the commonplace that in pre-industrial societies such as the Roman empire water transport is always cheaper, with less risk of breakage. But even within areas where the wares were commonly available there was differing representation. Study of the proportions of fine wares at fourth-century sites in Sussex[182] shows that they occurred mainly at the *civitas*-capital of Chichester, the 'small' town of Pulborough and the Saxon Shore fort of Pevensey; and to a much lesser extent on rural sites. To the west of the main area of distribution of New Forest and Oxfordshire wares similar discrimination can also be detected.[183] In the area of the modern counties of Avon, Dorset, Gloucestershire and Somerset, mapping of the distribution and percentages of these wares shows that they were much more common on the sites of Gloucester, Bath, Sea Mills, Charterhouse-on-Mendip, Ilchester and Dorchester. To reach all of these, Oxfordshire wares would have to leave the Thames at Cirencester to be transported overland down the Cotswold scarp. They could then either travel down the Fosse Way and its branches, or the Severn estuary and its affluents. The New Forest products would have had to travel overland across Salisbury Plain, except for the route to Dorchester down the Hampshire Avon and up the Dorset Stour. The sites listed above are all towns of one sort or another. It is they that were the targets of this distribution, and it was the villas and rural sites in their catchment areas that this pottery reached, but not further afield. Certain common features may be noted. The first is that the on-cost of transport and handling involved in getting the pottery from the Thames or the New Forest was thought worth it.

The second is that it was the towns that were targeted, suggesting that they were still market centres to and from which the pottery could be traded. How was this trade organised? A common assumption is that it was a direct producer–consumer relationship; the potters arranged for the transport of their wares, perhaps themselves accompanying them.[184] This would have been a waste of the potters' time, and anyway not all potters are good tradesmen. Much more likely is that it was organised by middlemen (*negotiatores*) who identified potential markets, brought the products to them and made a percentage out of the transaction. What we know of the distributions of the fine-ware producers accords well with such a model.

One feature of the Alice Holt/Farnham, Much Hadham, New Forest and Oxfordshire kilns which is held to distinguish them from their second-century counterparts is their rural rather than urban location. The Crambeck industry was essentially similar despite the proximity of the Malton fort. This has been seen as representing a rural rather than an urban basis for the economy of late Roman Britain, but it can also be pointed out that the New Forest kilns were well-placed for access to the *civitas*-capitals of Chichester, Dorchester, Silchester and Winchester with their associated 'small' towns. The Oxfordshire kilns lay between the 'small' towns of Alchester and Dorchester-on-Thames, and midway between the 'large' towns of Cirencester and Verulamium. Thus a rural location may still have been geared to an urban marketing strategy.

Because of the problems in provenancing grey wares, little work has been done on their distributions, especially for the fourth century. Examination of the distributions of comparable first- and second-century wares has shown patterns characteristic of the products of rural kilns having been marketed through nearby towns. The distributions centred on, and fell off with distance from, the towns rather than the kiln-sites.[185] But there were some other fourth-century coarse-ware distributions which are not so readily explicable in terms of town-centred trade. For instance, some of the coarse-ware products of the Churchill Hospital kilns referred to above had a distribution which did not conform at all with that of their fine-ware cousins. They were not present at the local 'small' towns of Alchester and Dorchester-on-Thames, and their distribution was unfocused and purely rural.[186] Here a direct producer–consumer relationship is one possible explanation. This could also turn out to have been the case for some other coarse wares, such as the grog-tempered fabrics (tempered with crushed pottery) of central southern Britain. There would, therefore, appear to have been a distribution system which was not mediated through towns, alongside that which was. At present the town-centred one is more visible in the archaeological record, but this may be because work has concentrated on the more easily recognised fine-wares rather than the more difficult and unprepossessing grey wares. More work on the latter may alter the balance between the two modes of distribution.

Coins and hoards

An aid to the marketing of pottery, particularly in the urban context, will have been the large volume of low-value, bronze coinage in circulation suitable for such trivial, day-to-day transactions. But though these low-value, copper-alloy coins remind us of our own low-value, copper-alloy coins, and we often think of them as fulfilling the same functions, it is not as simple as that; we have already seen (p. 11) that they were struck for a very different purpose connected with the needs of the state rather than of the individual. Moreover there are also the precious-metal coins to consider. Nonetheless, recent research does mean that we can begin to say some things about the meaning of coin finds from late Roman Britain.

To begin with we must establish some ground rules about how coins enter the archaeological record. First of all, the archaeologist most commonly encounters coins either in the form of hoards, or as individual coins from an excavation or survey ('site finds'). Given a pool of coins in circulation, there will be selection processes operating towards the loss or the retention of a particular coin. In the late Roman tri-metallic system (gold, silver, bronze) there will have been a clear preference for retention of gold and silver coins, because of their intrinsic value; because of their face value (which may not be the same thing); and because of the premium on them for their rôle in the revenue cycle. This preference often reveals itself in the form of hoards. Conversely, site-finds will be biased against precious-metal coins, since the objective was to keep these, not lose them. Even the commonly-used words 'lose/loss' beg questions. It is often assumed that the coins found on settlement sites (but possibly not religious sites and cemeteries) are an expression of casual and random coin-loss. In itself coin-loss is a two-stage process: first there is the dropping (or whatever) of the coin; there is then its non-recovery. Neither of these stages needs to be random. Modern experience tells us that it is all too possible to lose coins by chance, but it is also possible to dispose of them for a purpose: deliberate discard. For the late Roman period one cause of such discarding could have been demonetisation. This happened to coins of the usurper Magnentius in 354 and appears to have affected still-circulating coins of the House of Constantine.[187] Thus a peak in site-finds of these coins may tell us nothing about the site, only about numismatic factors. Whether this also happened to coins of legitimate emperors is more problematical.[188] Non-recovery can be random. It may be due to the owner being unware of the loss in the first place, or, even if he is, being unable to locate or recover the coin. Non-recovery can also be non-random. The coin may be known to have been dropped and be recoverable, but the owner does not choose to recover it. This is most often because the coin is literally not worth it. This is deliberate non-recovery. This will obviously be a function of value; it may also be a function of size — a large coin is easier to spot and recover. Size and value are often linked and this is the case in the late Roman bronze coinage. Thus there will be preferential 'loss' of smaller coins. In the discussion below reference will be made to 'loss' for the sake of brevity and convenience, but the caveats entered above should be borne in mind and will on occasion be referred to.

Further complicating the interpretation of the coins from late Roman Britain is the fact that coin supply to the diocese was not regular either in its frequency or in its volume. This was a result of coin being struck for official purposes and shipped to Britain as and when it was officially felt necessary. Thus there were peaks and troughs in overall supply. These have been characterised for the bronze coinage, but not yet for the gold and silver. For the first two decades of the fourth century coin-loss was low. This was the *floruit* of the Diocletianic *follis* — a large, valuable coin with a silver-enriched surface. In the 320s and 330s this coin declined to being a small, bronze coin and was commonly lost. A trough in supply occurred in the late 330s and early 340s until the emission from 348 of a huge coinage celebrating the eleven-hundredth anniversary of the City of Rome. In the 350s there was a slump in the supply of imperial coin, combined with the effects of the edict demoneti-sing the coinage of Magnentius, and apparently affecting already-circulating coins of the House of Constantine. This produced an acute shortage of bronze coinage in Britain which was not reversed until the huge issues of the House of Valentinian from 364 to 378. From 378 to 388 there was another trough in supply, with bronze again being supplied in quantity from 388 until the reorganisation of the western mints in 395 saw the near-cessation of the production of bronze other than at Rome. No bronze minted after 402 entered the diocese. This means that rises and falls in the number of coins on a site in the fourth century cannot simply be translated into rises and falls in the economic or social status of that site. If these rises and falls conform with the pattern described above, then the site is merely reflecting the pattern of available coinage. Only if the proportion of coins from a site for a particular period of issue (for instance 364–78) is significantly different (at least one standard deviation either way) from the norm for all sites should it excite attention. So far such episodes are rare and may often be explained in terms of factors peculiar to the site.

Having sketched in some of the more evident problems and variables affecting coin-loss on late Roman sites in Britain, we may now turn to what they can tell us. Two aspects of coin-lists are usually considered in an attempt to wring information out of them; one is the behaviour of the individual site, the second is the behaviour of numbers of sites to see if groupings may be established. For reasons of space the first cannot concern us here unless an individual site has something particular to tell us. The second is of interest, since it has been established that, numismatically, different groups of sites behave differently, and these numismatic groups correspond with archaeologically-identifiable groups. The broad groupings are 'large' towns on the one hand; with 'small' towns, rural sites and religious sites on the other; though these latter are not a homogeneous group. In the first place 'large' towns tend to yield more coins than other classes of site. This can be seen in simple terms by comparing the figures published for a range of types of site.[189] But this is too simple. What we need to make these figures truly comparable is figures on the sizes of site: certainly the area excavated in square metres, probably the volume excavated in cubic metres. A survey of the former has yet to be undertaken, a survey of the latter would at present be nearly impossible because of inadequate data on the depth of excavations as opposed to their other two dimensions. Nonetheless it remains true that rural sites which yield in excess of a hundred coins from excavations covering up to two acres are a minority, whilst excavations in the 'large' towns commonly yield several hundred from similar areas. This suggests that at the latter bronze coins were far more commonly used and available for loss. More sophisticated analyses have been undertaken of the coins from a number of sites, concentrating particularly on fourth-century coins which are present in large enough numbers at enough sites to allow for quantification and statistically-significant results.[190] These analyses study the percentages of the total coin list for a site represented by the various periods of issue and also compare across periods (particularly the percentages for the years 256–96 and 330–402). Again the 'large' towns come out as a discrete and homogeneous group. The 'small' towns are more variable in their results, though there is little overlap with the range of values for the 'large' towns. They do, though, share with the 'large' towns the tendency towards larger coin lists than those of rural sites in the fourth century.

Though rural sites generally have fewer coins of the fourth century in absolute numbers than town sites, this was nevertheless the century for which there is the highest loss at such sites, particularly villas. Some of these sites, however, have very large coin-lists: those at Barnsley Park and Frocester Court run to 900 and more than 700 respectively. How far this is the result of large-scale, modern excavations and how far it is due to factors affecting the sites in the Roman period has yet to be examined. At farmsteads the overall numbers remain very low, usually under fifty. At rural sites in the north coins are the exception rather than the rule. Overall, rural sites share in the pattern for the towns, with the largest numbers being lost in the fourth century, suggesting that bronze coins were becoming more available in that century. This was presumably because for the first time there was a low-value coinage circulating widely. There seems to be a generalised correlation with the socio-economic status of rural sites, with the more 'romanised' ones, principally villas, showing the greatest integration into a money-using economy.

Religious sites might be expected to show variation because of the use of coins for different purposes from the usual, for instance as votive offerings. There are some deposits which are clearly exceptional and this may be put down to their circumstances of deposition. One is the collection of some 12,000 coins of all centuries of the Roman period recovered from the excavation of the sacred spring at Bath.[191] Such a place, a threshold between this world and the underworld and wreathed in steam, was an obvious site for placatory or intercessory offerings. A similar deposit of coins was excavated in the last century at Coventina's Well[192] outside the Hadrian's Wall fort of Carrawburgh. Of course the bulk of these coins were earlier than the fourth century, but the presence of fourth-century coins shows that at these sites they were still being used for special, religious purposes. Another site which has yielded coins which may be linked with religious observance was the great fourth-century temple-complex at Lydney[193] on the north side of the Severn estuary. There were found large numbers of tiny, bronze coins (*minimissimi* — fifty to cover an old halfpenny or modern twopenny piece) copying mid-fourth-century prototypes. These were far too small to be of any practical use, and their presence on a temple site may suggest that they had some token, votive use. But apart from these special deposits or types of coin, the coin-loss pattern at temple sites seems at present to be similar to that at other rural sites.[194]

Given the purposes for which coins were minted and paid out, one class of site where one might expect coins to be relatively common is forts. But in fact this is not the case and there are clear discrepancies between the coin-lists from forts on Hadrian's Wall and those from the forts of the Saxon Shore. In the north the Wall forts are famous (or notorious) for the lack of coins found at them. Hardly any has yielded a number of coins on which statistically-valid comments may be based. Indeed it has proved necessary to aggregate the coins from a number of sites to try to give us an idea of coin-loss patterns in the area.[195] By contrast excavations on the Saxon Shore have produced much larger numbers of coins from these sites — Burgh Castle, 1,180 (including hoards); Lympne, 304 (limited trenching); Portchester, 603 — and Saxon Shore forts were only occupied for about half the length of time that forts on the Wall were. These numbers resemble more closely those to be expected from town sites in the south, whereas the northern forts share in the general numismatic poverty of their region. It seems at least possible that again we are seeing military sites behaving in concert with the overall behaviour of their regions rather than in a specifically military fashion.

In general, then, bronze coins in the fourth century would seem to have been circulating in greater numbers and on a wider range of sites than was the case for most of the first three centuries. Towns in particular saw great numbers being lost, both absolutely and relative both to their own earlier history and to the contemporary experience of rural sites. How is this to be regarded? One avenue of approach is the uses which the state had for coin. It is possible that here we are seeing the operation of the tax system, with bronze coins used for the purchase of gold and silver being lost preferentially at the sites through which the tax system operated: towns. The more common view (based on modern practice) is that these coins had served their turn in the state revenue system and were now being used as a medium for everyday commercial transactions. Under this interpretation the absolute and relative quantities of coins from towns show their pivotal place in a developing monetised market economy.

One category of coins which we have not yet discussed may lend weight to the commercial rather than the taxation hypothesis; this is copies. From the later third to the later fourth century, whenever there was a shortfall in the supply of bronze from the imperial mints there was an outbreak of local counterfeiting in Britain (and to a lesser extent northern Gaul, but not commonly in southern Gaul or Italy).[196] The first great outpouring was in the last third of the third century with the production of 'barbarous radiates', imitating the issues of the Gallic Empire and central emperors such as Gallienus (260–8) and Claudius II Gothicus (268–70). The next major episode of copying was in the late 330s and early 340s (commonly copying *Gloria Exercitus* issues of the House of Constantine). The biggest spate of copying in the fourth century took place in the late 350s and early 360s between the demonetisation after the suppression of Magnentius and the appearance of the huge issues of the House of Valentinian. These copies usually imitated the imperial issues celebrating the eleven hundredth anniversary of the City of Rome and bearing the reverse legend *Fel(icium) Temp(orum) Reparatio* (the return of happier times).[197] Though these often started out as reasonably close to their models in point of weight and style, many of the later ones were very small and crude (we have already mentioned the extreme example of the *minimissimi* from Lydney). The trough in supply from 378 to 388 did not cause significant copying; it is possible that the preceding issues of the House of Valentinian were so numerous that they tided the financial system over. After 395 there is no copying either and this is significant given the counterfeitings of the previous hundred years and more. Its significance will be assessed in the next chapter (p. 140). A major problem with these counterfeits is who used them and for what? As with the *Fel Temp Reparatio* copies, some would have passed muster as regular issues, but most would not. They cannot therefore have been used for official purposes because the staff of the *rationalis* or the *nummularii* would have spotted them. The penalties for counterfeiting were designed to be deterrent. The copies must, therefore, have been for more local use. They are mostly found in the south, and that is where they seem to have been made.[198] This suggests that they were a civilian rather than a military phenomenon, and the simplest answer would seem to be that they were produced and used as small change, and passed muster because people wanted or needed them to. To return to the original point, this would lend weight to the view that site-finds of bronze coins are generally an indicator of commercial activity.

Two final caveats need to be entered on the topic of site finds. One is that they represent an unknowable fraction of the total circulating pool of coins of all types, and so may not be a representative sample upon which to base generalising comments. They tell us about themselves, but not necessarily anything about the overall level and nature of numismatic activity at a site. The second is that it is dangerous to predicate interpretation concerning the site as a whole on this one class of objects in isolation. It is a truth universally acknowledged amongst archaeologists that to interpret sites or cultures on the basis of one settlement- or structure- or artefact-type, ignoring the other available data, is a short-cut to misinterpretation.

So far we have been dealing with site finds, virtually synonymous with bronze coins. It is now time to give some consideration to hoards, (fig. 24). A hoard is a means of keeping something safe until it is opportune to recover it. The reasons for putting together and concealing a hoard may vary. The commonest form of hoard is a value hoard, one put together and concealed to safeguard objects of intrinsic or other value. Hoards of gold and/or silver objects (such as coins) are an obvious example of this type. But as with site finds there are more reasons for hoarding coins. One not uncommonly encountered is what may be termed a 'de-valued' hoard. This consists of coins which have been demonetised or are at least no longer acceptable currency. This applies particularly to non-precious-metal coinage, since precious-metal coinage can always be converted back to gold or silver. But though 'bronze' coins of the Gallic Empire, for example, had a proportion of silver this was

Fourth-century plate/jewellery hoards
Gold/silver coin hoards, A.D. 380+

Traprain Law

Balinrees

Corbridge

Whorlton

Biddulph

Water Newton

Thetford

Mildenhall

Balline

Great Horwood

Canterbury

0   50   100   150 kilometres
0 20 40 60 80 100 miles

Fig. 24 Fourth-century hoards

too low (<5 per cent) to make its recovery worthwhile. Such hoards were therefore put together and concealed in the hope that the coins would again become negotiable. In a way they are a value hoard, but the value is potential rather than actual. Similarly, there can be various reasons occasioning the deposition of a hoard. The one most usually envisaged is because of the perceived threat of military instability, often a barbarian invasion; but the Roman army on campaign against internal or external enemies was probably just as much of a threat to property. On the other hand hoards could be a means of safe-keeping for a society with no real banking system. The 'de-valued' hoard of the type mentioned above would also have to be kept somewhere. One further general point is that today we deal with those hoards which were not recovered — and the ones that have been found at that. These have been referred to as 'unsuccessful' hoards, the argument being that hoards were not only designed for safe-keeping, but also for recovery. If it was not recovered it has somehow 'failed'. This assumes that hoards actually are to be recovered, but for instance in the case of the 'de-valued' hoard their recovery is conditional upon their re-valuation; if the latter does not occur neither does the former. Moreover a hoard cannot recover itself; if its owner is not in a position to do so then the hoard can only remain concealed, so the implicit judgement of 'unsuccessful' is inappropriate. But as with site finds this does suggest that known hoards represent a biased sample of an unknowable original parent body consisting of all hoards.

In fourth-century Britain there were hoards of bronze coins, of gold and/or silver coins, of silver plate and of gold and/or silver objects. Coins often constituted a part of the latter two types of hoard. As yet there is no discernible chronological or geographical patterning in the distribution of hoards of bronze coin, though those of Magnentius may prove to be more than usually numerous. For the precious-metal coins the situation is basically similar until the late fourth century. Then large numbers of coins of the House of Theodosius were taken out of circulation for hoarding, though when they actually got into the ground is another matter. These are more fully discussed in the next chapter (p. 139).

A particular feature of British hoarding in the late Roman period is the number of hoards of plate and other valuables. This is a phenomenon not observed on the Continent. These hoards seem to fall into two broad categories, depending on whether they were buried inside or outside the borders of the diocese. Within the borders the best-known hoards are those of silver plate, usually buried intact. The most famous is the huge hoard recovered from Mildenhall, Suffolk in 1942. This consisted of thirty-four items, of which half were pieces of plate and the other half ladles and spoons. The Great Dish is 60 cms. (two feet) in diameter and weighs 8256 gms (18lb.2oz.). The date of deposition for this hoard is given as c. 360, but this rests on a very flimsy chain of associations.[199] The other hoard discovered in modern times is that found in 1975 at Water Newton.[200] This consisted of nine items of plate along with nineteen other items, all bar one also of silver. The chief interest of this hoard is that it is explicitly Christian (cf. p. 127). Antiquarian records make it clear that there have been other such finds, for instance at Corbridge[201] (of which the sole survivor is the Corbridge *lanx*) and at Whorlton, Yorkshire.[202] Silver plate hoards are not the only hoards of plate known from late Roman Britain; there are several of pewter (poor man's silver),[203] and there was a huge hoard of bronze found in the last century at Knaresborough, Yorkshire of which only a few pieces remain. More recently a hoard of bronze vessels was recovered from Irchester,[204] so plate hoards may have been a more generalised phenomenon. Slightly different are the hoards consisting of a mixture of coins with pieces of plate and/or items of personal adornment. These are known from Canterbury,[205] Great Horwood, Buckinghamshire,[206] and Biddulph[207] and Great Wincle,[208] both in Cheshire. Finally and spectacularly there is the hoard of gold jewellery, precious stones and silver spoons found at Thetford[209] in 1979 (Pl. 8). Some of the latter were inscribed with the name of the deity Faunus, and so probably formed a temple treasure. Of the jewellery some was unused, as were some of the stones, suggesting a jeweller's hoard. All of these hoards represent a considerable store of wealth in terms of weight of precious metals. But for none of them is the precise archaeological context of their burial known. Nor is the occasion for their burial. The Canterbury and Thetford hoards may be dated on numismatic and stylistic grounds respectively to the turn of the fourth and fifth centuries. The Water Newton hoard contained no vessels characteristic of the fifth century. The date of the Mildenhall plate remains uncertain. One must also distinguish between the date at which the objects in a hoard were made, the date at which a hoard was assembled, and the date at which it was deposited. None of these three needs to be the same. Given that there was a spate of hoard-deposition of precious metal coinage in the first part of the fifth century (*cf.* p. 139), would this be a context for the burial of other hoards? In the number of its hoards Britain stands out from the Continent. There are major hoards of plate from Kaiseraugst[210] in Switzerland, from the Esquiline[211] in Rome, from Carthage[212] and there is a hoard from Ténès[213] in Algeria. There are also individual pieces such as the *missorium* of Theodosius I in Spain (Pl. 2).[214] But these are very widely spread compared to the examples from Britain. There must have been some very wealthy people in late Roman Britain to afford this plate and jewellery.

The other main group of hoards found in the British Isles, but outside the imperial frontier, is of the type known as *hacksilber* — cut silver. The common characteristic of these hoards, which distinguishes them from the type we have just been discussing, is that the items of plate are not complete but cut up and often folded. The best-known is the hoard from the large hillfort of Traprain Law[215] south-east of modern Edinburgh. From Ireland come hoards from Balline[216] and Ballinrees.[217] Such hoards used to be thought of as the proceeds of successful raiding on the coastal settlements of Britain and Gaul. But re-examination of them has shown that some of the packages of gold and silver correspond in weight to Roman pounds or to fractions or multiples thereof. It now seems more likely that these treasures represent gifts of coin and plate from the Roman authorities, and came out of their precious-metal revenues. They should probably be seen as subventions to friendly rulers or attempts to buy off unfriendly ones.

The countryside

The industry which underpinned all the activities which we have been examining so far was of course agriculture, and it is this which we must now consider. The countryside was the area in which the great majority of the inhabitants of Roman Britain lived and moved and had their being. Studies of modern pre-industrial societies suggest that the agriculturally non-productive such as the army, the urban population, administrators and others would not have made up more than about 10 per cent of the total population. But it is when we try to examine the agriculture and rural settlement that we encounter our most serious problems with the evidence. On the one hand hundreds of sites have been the subject of excavations and there are thousands of sites known from aerial and field survey; but on the other the nature of the excavations and the analysis of the evidence have been very partial. Excavation has until recently concentrated on the villa, the most typically Roman of rural sites, but one which as we shall see was in a minority relative to the entire range of rural settlement. Moreover even the excavations of villas have tended to concentrate on the dwelling-house and its mosaics and hypocausts, rather than on the agricultural buildings and the evidence for the farming which actually provided the finance for the villa. Excavation of farmsteads has been limited, much of it taking place in the north where adverse soil conditions have vitiated the survival of much of the evidence. In the south it is only recently that analogous settlements have been recognised to be an important component of the settlement pattern, and afforded a reasonable measure of excavation. In all, this means that though there are hundreds of sites in the literature, few of them are very useful for the examination of the sorts of problems which now interest us, such as the nature of the agricultural régime or the social structure and relationships of rural sites. All that can be offered here is a preliminary and often impressionistic sketch.

To begin with basics. Such evidence as has emerged in recent years from the study of faunal remains of the period, particularly the more environmentally-sensitive classes such as beetles and snails, suggests that the climate of late Roman Britain was at least as favourable as that of modern Britain. The presence of some species of beetle, for instance at York,[218] whose present-day distribution is predominantly to the south of Britain may mean that the climate was somewhat warmer than at present. Given the inherent suitability of the soils of most of lowland Britain for agriculture, this would have ensured the agricultural base for the feeding of the population, for the acquisition and display of wealth and for the satisfaction of the demands made upon the rural economy by the requirements of the state. If the climate was appreciably better than today's, then the upland areas of Britain would have benefited most from a longer growing season for arable agriculture and perhaps more extensive upland pastures for summer grazing. Certainly there are systems of Roman-period field boundaries in areas now marginal, and the remains of Roman settlements in now uninhabited uplands in Wales. The reverse of this coin, though, is that when the post-Roman climatic deterioration set in,[219] it

Fig. 25 Rural sites mentioned in text

would be these areas that suffered disproportionately since they had been only just above the threshold of viability.

Over most of Roman Britain the predominant agricultural régime was mixed arable and pastoral, or at least individual sites yield evidence for both animals and crops. In most major respects the system was not introduced by the Romans, but followed lines laid down in the earlier part of the Iron Age, and to a great extent the millennium comprising the Iron Age and Roman Britain may be seen as an agrarian continuum, with major changes only occurring in the post-Roman period.[220] The Iron Age had seen intensification of forest clearance, particularly in the north. This was probably in part brought about by the pressures of a continuing increase in population through later prehistory. But it was also in part the result of the introduction of the iron-shod plough and of new strains of crops. The former allowed the working of heavier soils previously less exploited, the latter were more tolerant of such soils and yielded well if the necessary effort was put in. Such an expansion in the potential for crop production could in turn support further population increase. The deforestation continued through the Roman period, more especially in the north where there was more forest remaining and there was the necessary economic stimulus, much of it from the army.[221] This can be seen both in the pollen record, showing the decline of tree pollen and the rise of grasses and other species of open ground, and in the increased alluviation in northern river valleys as soil was eroded off the deforested hillslopes.[222] By the fourth century the percentage of the landscape still wooded was probably roughly comparable with that of today. This would of course have meant that surviving areas of woodland would have been an important economic resource. Roman Britain consumed annually vast quantities of timber for construction, industry and heating. Each of these needed different species and different ages of wood, so coppicing and management of woodland would have been essential.

The technology of agriculture remained fairly constant from that developed by the later Iron Age. The only innovations currently ascribed to the Roman period[223] are the coulter (a knife placed vertically in front of the ploughshare to cut the root-mat) and an early form of asymmetric share. The latter was an important development as rather than repeatedly scratching the top of the soil it would help undercut the roots of weeds, particularly of perennials and would turn the soil over. So far coulters and asymmetric shares have only been found at some more romanised sites of the third and fourth centuries.

The principal crops grown were those established in the earlier part of the Iron Age. The main wheat cultivated was spelt, largely replacing the earlier emmer in lowland areas, though spelt was less common and emmer more so on upland sites. There is evidence also for the presence of breadwheat, high-yielding but requiring a large energy input, though the heyday of breadwheat was the mediaeval period. As well as wheat, barley and oats formed a siginficant part of the cereal repertoire. Besides grains evidence has been found for the cultivation of legumes such as peas, beans, lucerne and vetch. These fix nitrogen in the soil, helping preserve its fertility. As such they are components of many of the classic crop-rotation sequences, but whether there was actually such a system in Roman Britain we do not know; the presence on the same site of cereals and legumes does not of itself prove rotation. They could also be used for animal feed and for 'green' manuring, ploughing in the plants to enrich the soil. In addition seeds and pollen have been found attesting the growing of vegetables and herbs, from cabbage and cucumber to coriander. These would have been relishes to enliven the staple grain diet. Market-gardening may have been an important activity in the vicinity of towns, proximity minimising the problems of perishability.

The range of animals raised in Roman Britain had, like the crops, been broadly established by the end of the Iron Age.[224] In terms of numbers of bones found the dominant species were cattle, sheep and pigs. Alongside these there is evidence for dog, goat, horse and domestic fowl, not all of them necessarily kept as potential food.[225] There are many pitfalls for the unwary in the study of animal bones, and some of the more noteworthy deserve to be mentioned here. First, simple numbers and percentages of bones of the various species from a site can be misleading. One problem is that of recovery: on the one hand base-poor soils tend to destroy bone which entails an over-representation of large bones from large species; on the other, until recently archaeological retrieval strategies were not designed to recover small bones such as fish, where they survived. Secondly, even on a site with good preservation the percentage of bone from a species may differ radically from what that represents in terms of meat; one Iron-Age sheep yielded only 14 per cent of the meat of one Iron-Age cow. Thirdly, animals were not necessarily kept principally for their meat; in life they can yield important by-products such as blood, manure, milk and wool, as well as acting as a wealth-store. Fourthly, a distinction must also be drawn, particularly in a period such as the Roman with a strongly-articulated trading system, between producing and consuming sites (such as forts or towns); the bone assemblages from each may be quite different. Finally here we may observe that the total bone assemblage from a site, however subtly analysed, is unlikely to yield information crucial to the people at the time; how often meat was eaten, from what animal and by whom — in other words, what the contribution of meat was to the individual's diet.

This said, some general observations may nonetheless be made about the management of stock and patterns of consumption. The one major species where the Roman period arguably saw the introduction of a new, larger strain was cattle.[226] Otherwise there was a trend through the period towards larger sheep, but so gradual as to suggest improvement by selective breeding rather than the introduction of new breeds. Analysis of bones to determine the age at death of animals enables us to build up a general picture of the stock management practices prevalent in Roman Britain. For cattle there were two main peaks of mortality; one in the first year of life, the other in maturity. The first peak was probably in part the effect of juvenile mortality, but also of killing for meat and of the culling of unwanted animals such as supernumerary males. The keeping of large numbers into maturity indicates that they were valued more for their blood, milk or traction power than for their meat. At death they would have yielded hides and workable bone as well as stewing steak. A similar mortality pattern has been observed in sheep, suggesting again that juveniles were killed for meat and for stock management and that the remaining animals were kept primarily for their wool and to an extent their milk. Pigs, a much less important component of the faunal assemblage but one requiring little looking after, were mainly killed in the first two years after birth, presumably for meat. All these animals, but especially cattle and sheep, not only had utilitarian value but also acted as a wealth-store for their owners. In many agrarian societies large social transactions such as bride-price are traditionally rendered in the form of animals, even where coin is available.

Analysis of the differences between producing and consuming sites has not yet been able to progress very far for lack of data. But the Saxon Shore fort of Portchester[227] and the *civitas*-capital of Exeter[228] have both yielded pre-dominantly mature rather than juvenile cattle and sheep, so they may have been required principally for their by-products such as milk and energy rather than for meat. Another possibility is that they were only driven to the consuming sites after energy, milk or whatever had been extracted at the producing site. For Portchester the workings of the taxation in kind system may reasonably be invoked and thus suggest that the cattle there were for meat and leather at least. Another recent approach to the study of bone assemblages has been to examine the proportions of species represented at different types of site.[229] In the early Roman period, 'romanised' sites such as forts, towns and villas exhibited a different pattern from other classes of site, with a preference for cattle as opposed to sheep. Military sites were particularly distinctive. In the later period the distinction between military and civilian sites had largely disappeared (something we have already encountered in other contexts), though this is less so in the north. The assumption is that what we are seeing reflected here is dietary preference, with 'romanised' and 'indigenous' types, but given what we have already said about the other uses for animals this assumption should not be made too readily. Nevertheless there was a clear change both chronologically and by status of sites in the animals killed through the Roman period, and this was presumably in large measure due to imported tastes or practices.

There are several strands of evidence now pointing to intensification of rural settlement and land-use during the Roman period, culminating in the pattern observable in the fourth century. Surveys in areas such as Northamptonshire[230] or the Gloucestershire Cotswolds[231] have shown large numbers of sites producing fourth-century pottery, in the former case with a density of about one site per half square kilometre. This is considerably greater than in the second century. These sites have mainly been identified by field survey, so we know little about their nature — the lack of building débris at most of them suggests that they were farmsteads rather than villas. It may be objected that since the late Roman levels were the ones nearest the modern surface they would be the ones most liable to disturbance and thus fourth-century material would be disproportionately represented. But any site occupied from, say, the second century to the fourth will have residual second-century pottery in its fourth-century layers. So if a site only yields fourth-century pottery there is a strong case for its only having been fourth-century. On the other hand there are few datable sites which have not yielded fourth-century pottery. Overall the picture is of a peak in rural population in the later as compared with the earlier Roman period. It is less easy to make meaningful comparisons with other periods since, for instance, Iron Age or early Anglo-Saxon sites do not yield the quantities of pottery characteristic of Romano-British sites and are thus difficult to locate. Of course it must not be imagined that the sort of site-density mentioned above can be extrapolated to cover the entire Romano-British countryside. For instance, in the modern county of Bedfordshire[232] sites are common on the alluvial soils of the river valleys, but very rare on the heavy claylands. Another strand of argument pointing to intensive use of the landscape is the number of Roman-period systems of land-division in areas of marginal agricultural suitability or utility, such as some of the gritstone uplands in the Pennines[233] or on the sides of steep chalk downs in southern Britain.[234] That these areas needed to be brought into use indicates a need to exploit all available land. A more detailed and systematic programme of research in the upper Thames valley[235] linked with a detailed programme of research on the environmental evidence provides another case-study. In broad terms the preferred area of settlement in the valley from Neolithic times on was the second gravel terrace. This afforded the optimum conditions in the area of an easily-worked and productive soil with good, though not excessive, drainage. Other zones in the valley, such as the damper valley floor, could be used for pasture. In the Roman period settlements occurred in profusion along the second terrace, but also on the lower, wetter first terrace and the alluvium of the flood-plain. There is also more evidence for use of these areas for other purposes as well as settlement. Thus again the Roman period seems to have seen the need to exploit all available land to the full, even if it was not prime agricultural land. In the immediately post-Roman period these Thames valley areas fell back out of use and post-Roman settlement retrenched onto the second terrace, implying that the increased exploitation of the Roman period was peculiar to that period and due to stimuli operating within it. This detailed study of a relatively small area confirms the general impression gained from overall area surveys.

The causes for this pressure on the land are imperfectly understood. The reasons normally advanced are the imperatives of taxation, of other state requirements, of the need to feed the urban population, of the desire to avail oneself of the goods and services on offer in the towns and of a steadily increasing population. All bar the last of these were to a greater or lesser extent the effect of inclusion within the Roman empire with its accompanying political, social and economic constraints and conventions.

To turn to the rural settlements themselves: here we must beware of being overwhelmed by bits of evidence from a long list of partially-excavated sites. Our concern here will be to identify the pattern and overall hierarchy of rural settlement; to try to articulate the types of site socially and economically and to relate them in the same sorts of ways to the populations and functions of the towns. This is again an attempt to define what was characteristic about the Romano-British countryside, and what contribution inclusion within the empire made, both then to the life and now to the archaeology of the countryside.

The normal pattern of rural settlement in Roman Britain was a dispersed one, farmsteads and villas spread across the countryside, rather than the population being nucleated into settlements such as the villages familiar from much of later mediaeval England. Currently rural sites are categorised by a coarse two-fold division into 'villas' and 'farmsteads', the essential difference between the two being that the former displayed at least some elements with a 'romanised' plan or architectural idiom, whereas the latter did not. It should be noted that this is a categorisation based solely on building style; it says nothing about the agricultural regimes or land-holdings. It may well have been that these were similar at both villas and farmsteads. In broad terms villas were a phenomenon of the south and east of the diocese, the great majority lying south-east of a line from the Severn to the Dee to the Humber. North-west of that line, in the 'highland' zone, the dominant settlement type was the farmstead, but this type was also numerically dominant in the south-east, it just has not been afforded as much attention as the villa. By the fourth century there were probably the best part of a thousand villas in Britain. They were not evenly distributed across the south-eastern parts of the island. There were concentrations along the Jurassic ridge around the towns of Ilchester, Bath and Cirencester, in the south Midlands and in Northamptonshire, particularly around Water Newton. There were other concentrations around Winchester and Rochester. On the other hand there were few in the west Midlands, and none in the Fens, the Weald or on Salisbury Plain. It has been suggested that the Fens were an imperial estate. The Weald may still have carried forest, and the soils of Salisbury Plain had probably been near-exhausted in prehistory. Another situation where villas were rare was on the gravel terraces of major river systems, for instance the Thames. This is less easy to explain, since as we have seen some of these areas are very favourable for agriculture. It may be that having been intensively settled from early prehistory the tenurial subdivision of the area did not permit of the aggregation of sufficient land to support a villa. By contrast the Cotswolds near the headwaters of the Thames are classic villa country, but they may have had a rather different agricultural and tenurial history. Quality of soil was clearly an important factor in the presence or absence of villas. A map of the villas in the Winchester area[236] clearly shows a preference for the soils over the chalk and the gault clays and an equally marked aversion to the quaternary sands and gravels of the Hampshire Basin and the Kennet valley. Overall the pattern of villa distribution showed a close correlation with the presence of towns, suggesting that the two were two sides of the coin of the romanisation of the economy. The towns provided the market for the surplus of the estates and the craftsmen and specialists to build the villa and lay the mosaics. The villa estate used the market and specialists of the town and thereby contributed to their livelihood. Why certain towns attracted clusters of villas whereas others did not is not yet resolved. This may be to do with agricultural resource, and/or social factors (cf. p. 80).

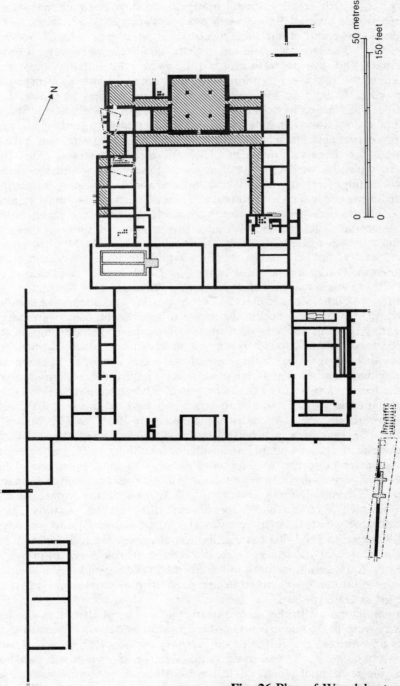

Fig. 26 Plan of Woodchester

By the fourth century wide variations had developed in the scale and complexity of overall plan and internal appointments of Romano-British villas. At one end stood such palace-villas as Bignor[237] or Woodchester (fig. 26).[238] The latter was laid out in three axially-aligned courts. Round the innermost and smallest were grouped the principal residential appartments, including the massive reception or dining room (*triclinium*) which needed four pillars to hold up the ceiling-span and had the largest mosaic known north of the Alps on its floor — one of a number of mosaics at the site. Near the main room was what appears to have been a sculpture gallery. The middle court was part agricultural and part residential, including what may have been a house for the estate manager. The outermost and largest court (about which, typically, we know the least) was presumably where the principal farm-buildings were situated. Such a concentration and display of wealth was in the league of great continental establishments such as Montmaurin, and the owner of Woodchester might well have made the property qualification for the senatorial order (though Britain seems to have been one of those areas of the empire without a strong senatorial tradition). Not as grand as Woodchester, but still indicating considerable wealth, were such villas as Chedworth,[239] Keynsham,[240] Littlecote[241] or North Leigh[242] and many others. Again there was separation of domestic and agricultural areas, and the former comprised buildings of architectural sophistication and decorative lavishness. At Keynsham, for instance, at the angles of a porticoed court were pavilions consisting of a central polygonal space defined by rooms opening off it. At Littlecote in the mid-fourth century a suite of rooms was constructed, of which the largest was a three-apsed room (a triconch) opening off a rectangular chamber. The superstructure must have involved semi-domes and a raised central vessel. On the floor was an elaborate mosaic (Pl. 7). Even villas with less overall pretension could still have features of architectural elaboration, such as the centrally-planned bath-suites at Holcombe[243] or Lufton.[244] There was a broad class of villas displaying the comforts of hypocausts, mosaics and painted walls and ceilings, with the agricultural dependencies at a remove. Numerically this was the largest group. Some villas were very small, little more than romanised cottages, such as Barnack,[245] a row of rooms along a corridor, with a well at the front. A simple categorisation[246] of fourth-century villas into three classes: A (those showing considerable wealth); B (the comfortable middle ground) and, by implication, the rest, showed that the distribution of classes A and B in broad terms paralleled that of villas in general, with the main concentration in the West Country. Such variations both in the overall incidence and in the location of wealthy villas can be observed in many continental provinces, and we have noted it in Gaul (p. 30).

In comparison with the second century the villas of Britain in the fourth century were more numerous and there was more display of wealth in their plans and furnishings. In the second century mosaics had been basically an urban phenomenon,[247] and town houses were on the whole more elaborate than villa residential blocks.[248] In the fourth century, town houses, though comfortable, do not show the size or complexity of the larger villas. Many

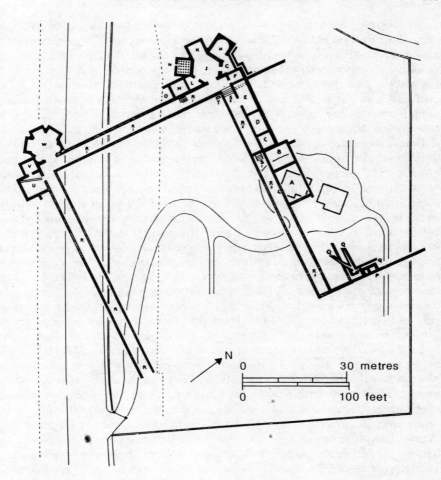

Fig. 27 Plan of Keynsham

more fourth-century mosaics were being laid at villas than in the towns.[249] All this points to it being the villas on which the élite was spending its money and at which it displayed its wealth. It suggests that in late Roman Britain the *curiales* were principally based on their country estates, and reinforces the suggestion that town houses may only have been in seasonal use. This archaeological evidence from Britain coincides with the literary evidence from Gaul, where men such as Ausonius and Sulpicius Severus lived on their country estates, only visiting the town as and when appropriate.

Before considering the rest of the rural settlement pattern it is worth looking at one aspect of the villas in more detail; the mosaics. We have already (p. 75) encountered fourth-century mosaics as a luxury item with a town-centred distribution; what concerns us here is their content, particularly the representation of human and divine beings.[249] Two of the late Roman 'schools' of mosaicists operating in Britain had distinctive repertoires of such figured mosaics. The Corinian 'school' (based at Cirencester) produced a number of mosaics (including the Great Pavement at Woodchester) showing Orpheus. In the late Roman empire Orpheus was one of a number of saviour deities who, by having himself overcome death, held out to his devotees the chance that they might do the same. Another saviour god, Christ, was depicted on a mosaic of the Durnovarian 'school' (based at Dorchester) at the villa of Hinton St Mary (Pl. 6).[250] He was shown as a beardless young man in the style common in the late empire, and with the chi-rho (a Christian symbol formed from the first two letters, χ and ρ, of Christ's name in Greek) behind his head. The chi-rho also appears on a mosaic from the same 'school' at Frampton villa. Both mosaics also showed the Greek demi-god Bellerophon mounted on Pegasus and slaying the Chimaera. A strikingly pagan motif one might think, but it could also have been read as the triumph of good over evil or life over death in a thoroughly Christian fashion. Orpheus appeared on a number of other mosaics across late Roman Britain, such as that in the triconch at Littlecote. Another eastern cult was represented by the mosaic at Thruxton showing Bacchus; and another, more esoteric still, on that from Brading, showing the cockerel-headed Abraxas. At Low Ham there was a mosaic showing scenes from Virgil's *Aeneid*. At Rudston the fourth-century motif of a victor in his chariot made its appearance. What all these and almost all other figured mosaics from Roman Britain (and not just of the fourth century) had in common was that their subject-matter was inspired by the myths, legends and religions of the classical Mediterranean world, and not of the Celtic world. One must search a long way in Britain to find any mosaics of the latter. The evidence, obviously far more fragmentary, of the wall paintings[251] goes along with this classicising preference. The Romano-British upper classes evidently regarded themselves as assimilated to the classical tradition in culture, aesthetics and religion, at least as far as public display was concerned.

It is now recognised that the great majority of the rural population of late Roman Britain lived not in the villas but in sites whose overall plan and whose building-types owed little to Roman influence; the farmsteads. In the south-western peninsula, in Wales, and in England north of York they enjoyed an almost unchallenged monopoly. The principal structural type was the round house, either wholly in timber or with stone footings. In dimensions and appearance this had not changed since the Iron Age. Most farmsteads consisted of at least three or four of these buildings, sometimes freestanding, sometimes conjoined. Some were certainly used as dwellings, but others were probably used for specialist purposes such as weaving, or as animal stalls when the need arose. Some settlements contained numbers of structures in double figures, and in remoter parts of the diocese some Iron Age hillforts seem to have still been in use or to have been brought back into use, for instance those at Garn Boduan and Tre'r Ceiri in north-western Wales.[252] These latter obviously had defensive, or at least enclosure, walls, and many lower-lying settlements were also enclosed, though not necessarily for defence against human predation. The agricultural economy of the farmsteads would obviously have been heavily influenced by resources and climate. Work on the environmental evidence from sites in north-eastern England has shown that farmsteads on the good soils of the coastal plain and river valleys of the modern counties of Durham and Northumberland were engaged in mixed arable/pastoral agriculture. But settlements on the poorer, upland soils overwhelmingly yield evidence for cattle-raising, which was both more suited to their natural resources and which had a ready market in the garrisons along the Wall and in its hinterland.[253] Similar distinctions must also have obtained in Wales with its marked variations in topography and soils.[254] On the analogy of mediaeval and modern practice, it is likely that many upland sites were only occupied seasonally for the summer pasture, pre-figuring the later *hafod* and *hendre* system.

Analogous settlements are now seen to have been the numerically (if not necessarily economically or socially) dominant settlement type in the south and east of the diocese also; more numerous, certainly, than the villas. As yet they have not been afforded the attention they deserve because of concentration of effort on the villas. Only a small number of them have been examined, and that usually very partially. In addition to 'classic' farmstead sites there were a number of other categories of rural site in the south and east. Some were nucleated settlements consisting of simple rectangular buildings. In Somerset there were settlements such as Bradley Hill (fig. 28)[255] and Catsgore;[256] the former consisting of three simple, rectangular, stone-founded buildings in a Roman style, the latter of a string of such buildings. In Hampshire there was the settlement at Chalton (fig. 29),[257] which consisted of simple, timber structures in small plots ranged along a trackway. Similar settlements existed further to the west, on Salisbury Plain, at places such as Chisenbury Warren.[258] Though Bradley Hill and Catsgore displayed a romanised architectural idiom they were not villas, for they lacked the principal residence characteristic of villas. Instead they, and architecturally simpler sites such as Chalton, were nucleated settlements, perhaps somewhat akin to the later hamlet. Aerial survey in such areas as the Cotswolds, and field survey in Northamptonshire and Essex, have shown that farmsteads and other such settlements are common, lying around and between villas and right up to the defences of towns.

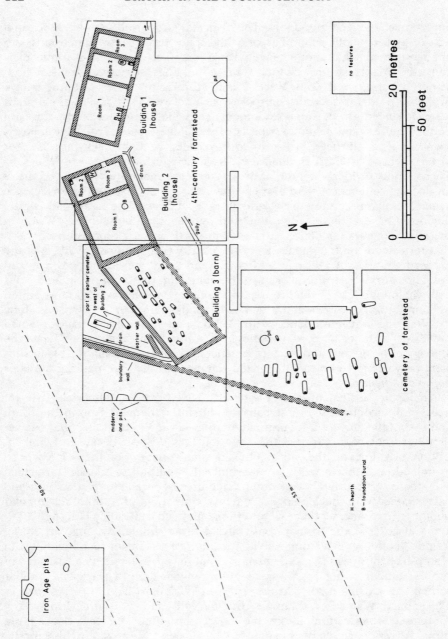

Fig. 28 Plan of Bradley Hill

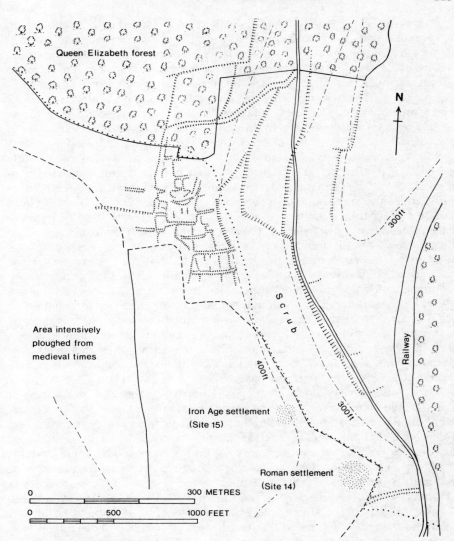

Fig. 29 Plan of Chalton

One of the important questions that this raises is the relationship between villa and farmstead. Were they mutually exclusive, economically and socially, or was there a measure of interdependence? It also raises the question of the nature of estates and land apportionment in Roman Britain. From the Roman literary sources it is clear that a wealthy landowner could own property in many places. This was certainly the case with the great senatorial families, and a member of one of them, Melania the Younger, is specifically recorded as having had possessions in Britain. A similar situation obtained with the provincial aristocracies, for instance the Pontii Leontii of Aquitaine. This would have led to a single landowner having had a multiplicity of discrete properties. It is uncertain whether a property consisted simply of an area of land all owned by the landholder. It could itself have been fragmented over different soil-types to build up a complementary pattern of resources for both arable and pastoral activities. It may be that property consisted of rights to certain resources, for instance upland grazing, which were not in single ownership. The Roman literary sources also assume that an estate was worked by a tied colonate or, less probably, slaves. The nature of the dependency of a *colonus* upon his *dominus* (master) is not fully understood. Clearly it could and did on occasion mean that the *colonus* was essentially a chattel of his master. But given that *coloni* were originally (and remained in legal theory) free men, we may envisage a situation where the dependence was expressed through an obligation to labour or other service on the master's behalf. The *colonus* may thus have retained a measure of independence, perhaps even some land. One other feature of Roman estates is that they were not necessarily expected to pass *en bloc* to a single heir.

The Celtic sources[259] (admittedly post-Roman), on the other hand, suggest that partible inheritance was the norm for these people. Under this system the landholding instead of descending intact through the generations would be split equally between the heirs. Theoretically this could be taken to an absurd extreme. Social relations such as marriage must somehow have controlled this tendency. This could, though, have been one reason why individuals were reduced to the status of *colonus* as their property ended up too small to be viable. It may also suggest one reason why villas were absent from some areas. Villas imply a reasonable level of resources, if only to build and maintain them. In an area with a long history of partible inheritance it may have been that the tenurial landscape was too fragmentary to permit of the accumulation of the resources necessary for a villa. One of our sources for Celtic practice, the Llandaff charters of the late sixth century on (*cf.* p. 187), also displays a feature common to such late Roman and late-Roman-derived (Vulgar Latin) property law. This is the confusion between *possessio* and *dominium* — legal title and overall lordship.

All these factors will have made land ownership in late Roman Britain a lot more complex than appears from a simple consideration of the archaeological distribution maps. It must be the case that many farmsteads were in some way dependent on the local villa. It may be that they lay on the estate of the villa and were the dwellings of the estate's labourers or *coloni*. It is noticeable that very few villas have any provision for housing a labour force. Alternatively the farmsteads may technically have been tenurially independent, though their occupants paid rent or owed labour service to the villa-owner. Such an arrangement would be in line with what the Classical sources tell us of the structure of Celtic society. Combined with the possibility of partible inheritance amongst the more Celtic elements of the population, this may explain why so many remained at the farmstead level. It may also mean that an estate was not simply a tract of land, but also a network of social obligations and responsibilities. Thus production could have been organised through social relations as well as expropriative ownership. This would have meant a social reality far removed from the archaeological dichotomy between villa and farmstead.

This must also warn us against acceptance of models for the operation of the Romano-British countryside which oppose romanised villas with native farmstead. Currently much debate about the Romano-British countryside is conducted explicitly or implicitly along these lines. Villas, along with towns and other 'Roman' sites, are seen as expressions of a Mediterranean-derived economy and society that worked over and alongside, but separate from, a continuing indigenous tradition of subsistence agriculture represented by the farmsteads. The relationship was essentially exploitative, and social relations moved only one way in the hierarchy. Obviously villas and towns were manifestations of and dependent on Roman institutions; that is a central tenet of this book. Equally clearly the archaeological evidence is that the farmsteads were little touched by Roman material culture, but this can degenerate into an exaggerated opposition of the two. In fact, of course, the rural population was economically, demographically, socially and culturally bound into the Roman framework, and influence from the wider Roman world percolated down to it, visibly or invisibly, wanted or unwanted, through the local hierarchy.

Economically, the Roman land tax and other impositions, along with the need to pay rent and other dues, will have conditioned the agricultural strategies of these people. It was not simply a subsistence matter of producing enough to feed one's family and have the seed-corn and animals for the following year. There had to be production over and above that level. In crude terms this will have meant an expansion of production, and we have seen that there is ample evidence for this from the Roman period. More subtly it will have caused the adoption and adaptation of strategies the better to fulfil the demands laid upon the rural populace. We may see this in the concentration on cattle-raising in the north-east. This was an effect of and relied on the continuing demands of the state and its greatest organ, the army. There was also the presence of the towns with their goods and services, from the utilitarian for which the peasantry had a recurring need, to the luxury for which it did not. This would again stimulate production, not only of staple crops but also of more unusual ones such as fruit and herbs. It would also provide access to tools and techniques which would themselves make possible innovation in the agricultural régime. The towns were also a demographic link, for as we have seen they needed a regular influx from the country to maintain their population levels. Thus many, if not all, country-dwellers in the south-east will have had kin or social relationships with town-dwellers. Moreover, given the dispersed nature of rural settlement, towns would have been particularly important as channels for the spread of news and ideas. In the north and the west the army had long been locally recruited, and would have afforded an avenue of escape from the toil of life on the land. Such horizontal social links with the people in the towns and the army would have been augmented by vertical links up the social hierarchy and the reciprocal social obligations that characterised such links. Thus 'Roman' and 'native' interlocked in many spheres of activity. Though the peasantry was undoubtedly exploited by the landowners and authorities alike for the surpluses whose extraction enabled their continued existence, it also received cultural and material input in return. To modern notions of profit and loss the traffic may, rightly, look one-sided, but it was not one-way. To impose a bi-polar divide on this discussion oversimplifies and misleads. We should not be entirely dependent on the presence of round houses or the absence of fine wares for our perception of the state of the rural population. To have to say this is in large extent to re-invent the wheel, for such conclusions are a commonplace of the study of better-documented pre-industrial agrarian societies.

Religion

One area of life (and death) in which the arrival of the Roman empire had stimulated change at all levels of society was religion. In the fourth century Britain was still predominantly a non-Christian island, but with an influential and growing Christian minority. The study of religion in the island in this period has, with a few exceptions,[260] been dominated by the related questions of the extent of Christianity and the effect of Christianity on the pagan religions. The historical and archaeological records have been searched for possible pieces of evidence for Christianity, and paganism has been seen as essentially on the defensive from the beginning of the fourth century on, with a brief respite under Julian the Apostate (361–3), but suffering increasingly repressive legislation from the time of Gratian (375–83) onwards. The fact that Julian spent the entirety of his short reign in the east of the empire where he was markedly unsuccessful in reviving paganism is usually passed over. Here, by contrast, we shall certainly be concerned with Christianity in late Roman Britain because of its importance for the immediately succeeding period, but first we must afford some consideration to the non-Christian religions.

To study any religion it is necessary to have access to its beliefs, how they were expressed and the value- and behaviour-systems it enjoined, for those are the central concerns of any religious system and of its participants. In the case of a religion which is no longer extant that means we must have reliable written evidence, for religion is a conceptual rather than a concrete entity and the abstract is better conveyed in words than in things. Things of course had their uses, but only within a conceptual framework; their significance to a devotee is not usually intrinsically manifest or fully comprehensible. To take a

1 Medallion from Beaurains, Arras. The obverse showing a forceful Constantius I, the reverse the relief of London in 296 (cf. p. 17).

2 Silver *missorium* showing Theodosius I seated between Valentinian II and Arcadius, with Honorius in front (cf. p. 99).

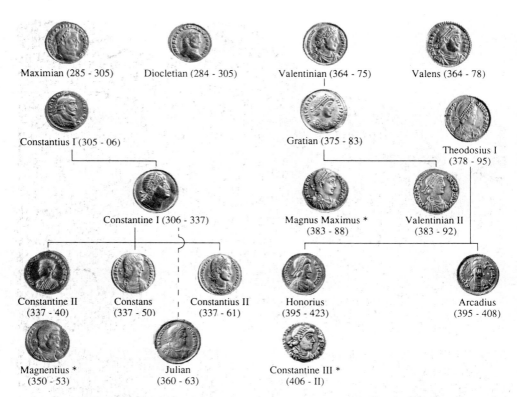

Maximian (285 - 305) Diocletian (284 - 305) Valentinian (364 - 75) Valens (364 - 78)

Constantius I (305 - 06) Gratian (375 - 83) Theodosius I (378 - 95)

Constantine I (306 - 337) Magnus Maximus * (383 - 88) Valentinian II (383 - 92)

Constantine II (337 - 40) Constans (337 - 50) Constantius II (337 - 61) Honorius (395 - 423) Arcadius (395 - 408)

Magnentius * (350 - 53) Julian (360 - 63) Constantine III * (406 - II)

3 Coins of the principal emperors and usurpers (*) relating to late Roman Britain.

4 *top right* The late Roman walls at Le Mans showing the patterned facing (cf. p. 24).

5 *bottom right* The Saxon Shore fort at Portchester, with the medieval castle and priory lurking in opposite corners of the Roman defences (cf. p. 53).

6 The mosaic from Hinton St Mary, Dorset, with the probable representation of Christ (cf. p. 110).

7 The mosaic from Littlecote, Wiltshire, showing Orpheus. Note the elaboration of the plan of the room (cf. p. 108).

8 Gold buckle from the Thetford treasure. The classicising style of
the figure, the beaded edge and the decoration of the loop are all
characteristically fourth-century (cf. p. 99).

9 The forum-basilica at Silchester (looking south), showing the fourth-century industrial activity (cf. p. 71).

10 The baths-basilica at Wroxeter with the rubble platforms of the post-Roman timber buildings (cf. p. 152).

11 The temple precinct at Bath with the successive remetallings interleaved with accumulations of earth. The whole sealed by the destruction of the Roman buildings (cf. p. 155).

hackneyed example: if one presented the proverbial archaeologist from Mars, ignorant of Christianity, with the ground-plan of Canterbury Cathedral how much could he learn from that about the beliefs and history of the Christian religion? The answer, of course, is nothing of any significance. The material remains have a tale to tell, but if the written sources are not there to give us the ears to hear, then it will be faint and distorted. All the religions for which we have evidence in late Roman Britain have serious deficiencies in either their written and/or their material remains.

For ease of discussion the cults in Roman Britain are usually grouped under three broad headings: the official cults of the Roman state; the indigenous Celtic cults; the eastern or mystery religions. The state cults had two aspects to them. On the one hand their deities did undoubtedly inspire personal worship and devotion in the individual; but also, because of their distribution throughout the empire they had had the effect of cementing the loyalty of a far-flung empire through the worship of the Roman pantheon of gods, of the reigning emperor and his house and partly through concepts such as *Concordia* or *Disciplina*. In Britain these had been particularly practised by the army (it is from the north that most of the epigraphic evidence for the state cults comes), and in the main towns. But with the conversion of Constantine I to Christianity many of the manifestations of these cults fell into disfavour, with the exception of those concerned with loyalty to the ruling house. In Britain, as in many parts of the empire, this was coupled with a poverty of epigraphic expression in the fourth century, so we have little evidence for these cults in the diocese.

The most numerous cults, and those which presumably appealed to the bulk of the populace of the island, were the Celtic ones, derived, as we assume were their devotees, from Iron Age antecedents. Here we have the problem of an abundance of material evidence but a poverty of literary sources, since they were suppressed or altered as Christianity gained the upper hand. The literary sources either pre- or post-date the Roman period in Britain and relate to Gaul or Wales and Ireland. Pre-dating the Roman conquest of Britain there were the accounts in writers such as Poseidonios of Apamaea[261] or Julius Caesar. Both of these described what they saw of the Celts from a Classical standpoint, and the latter for very self-serving purposes. From mediaeval Wales and Ireland came the myth-cycles such as the *Mabinogion* or the *Táin Bó Cuálgne*, but they were late and from a different cultural milieu, one, amongst other things, already Christianised. They therefore give us clues as to what in the supernatural was important to the Celts (such as springs, heads, the number three) and to how the Celts viewed their gods and heroes, but they cannot be related directly to the material remains from Romano-British religious sites. From the Roman period we do have the written evidence from inscriptions. Though setting up inscriptions was a Roman graft onto Celtic practice, this material can offer useful insights, for instance, the name or epithet of the deity may be revealing, such as *Rigonemetos* (King of the Sacred Grove). We may be able from appeals or thanks on inscriptions to learn the areas in which the divinity was held to be efficacious. Or there was the practice of *interpretatio Romana*, by which the name of a Celtic deity was

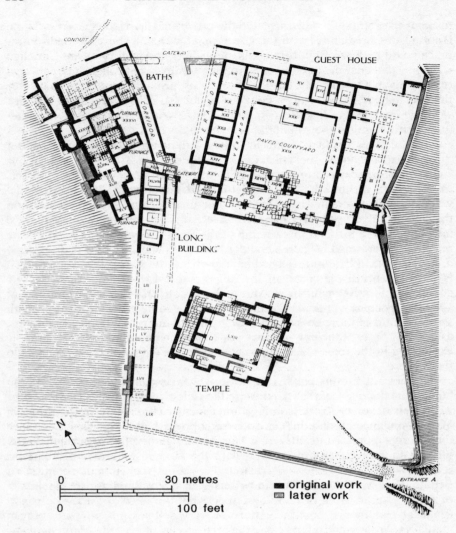

Fig. 30 Plan of Lydney

conjoined with that of a classical one sharing similar properties, for instance *Mars Rigonemetos*. But again for the fourth century there is a desperate dearth of religious, as of other, inscriptions. There is one exception, and this is the considerable number of lead curse sheets (*defixiones*) which have been discovered in the last decade, with the large group from Bath recently published.[262] The majority of these were appeals to the goddess Sulis Minerva to exact retribution from a person or persons who had wronged the worshipper. The matters were usually fairly trivial, such as the theft of personal possessions; nevertheless they afford a fascinating window into the world of the individual Romano-Briton.

This leaves us with the material remains of buildings, sculpture, objects, and of course without a knowledge of the system of belief these range from the ambiguous to the incomprehensible. The most common form of building was the Romano-Celtic temple (so-called).[263] This usually consisted of a square within a square or a polygon within a polygon. The inner vessel was the *cella* which housed the cult statue or totem or whatever, and would have risen above the level of the surrounding ambulatory to provide clerestorey lighting. These temples were small, they were designed for the statue and for the ministrations of the priesthood, not for congregational worship. Many, if not most, of such temples lay within an open space which could have been used to accommodate crowds of worshippers on particular occasions and festivals. Temples tended to stand alone within their *temene* (precincts), though at some such as Coleshill there were ancillary structures within the boundary wall. More elaborate were the complexes at sites such as Lydney[264] and Uley.[265] At the former a large and elaborate Romano-Celtic temple (though still only the size of a small mediaeval parish church) lay surrounded by an open area. Against the walls of the *temenos* were a long range of rooms (perhaps shops), a bath-house and a large courtyard building. This latter may simply have been a hostel for pilgrims, but the excavator suggested that it might have had a religious dimension as an *abaton*, a place for the divination of dreams. In general temples were common over the southern and eastern parts of Britain. Some clearly succeeded Iron Age places of worship, some were at natural sites such as springs, and others were new foundations of the Roman period, for instance the many temples in the towns. The overall correspondence between the distribution of temples and that of towns and villas can be no accident. It is another indication that it was the south and east of the island that were most heavily imbued with romanised attitudes as expressed in buildings.

It has been shown that during the course of the fourth century there was an overall decrease in the number of temples in Britain.[266] Analysis of this chronologically and by whether the temples were rural or urban has thrown up interesting evidence. All types of temple seem to have peaked numerically about 300. Thereafter rural temples show some decline. But it is urban temples which show the most marked decline, especially in the second half of the century. This has previously been attributed to the activities of zealous Christians, but it does parallel the general decline in the number of buildings to be seen more generally in both town and country. Moreover, as we shall see, the mystery religions tend to be urban and aristocratic in their appeal, so it may be that these were attracting worshippers in the towns at the expense of the traditional cults.

These eastern or mystery religions, usually of east Mediterranean or western Asiatic origins, by the fourth century essentially offered to the initiate personal salvation in the afterlife in return for adherence to the cult and its precepts in this life. Usually the divinity concerned had himself conquered death and thus could hold out to a follower the hope that he or she could do the same. These religions were exclusivist in their operations. Very often membership was restricted to, for instance, males or the freeborn. Neither did they actively proselytise. The principal cults represented in Britain[267] were those of Mithras and Bacchus/Dionysos, and there is evidence also for worship of Cybele and Atys, Isis, Sarapis and *Sol Invictus* (the Unconquered Sun). Last, and ultimately most successful, came Christianity. Much of our evidence for these cults pre-dates the fourth century; nevertheless it is clear that they continued into that century. Their temples tend, not unnaturally, to be small and are often difficult to identify. Widest-spread and most readily identifiable to us were the *Mithraea*, the temples to Mithras. These consisted of an aisled chamber for the initiates with an apse at one end for the altars and the representation of the god, and at the other end a narthex (porch running the width of the building) probably for initiation ceremonies. Mithraism had always been popular in the army, and it is at forts that the majority of *Mithraea* in Britain were sited. Some of these, such as the one at Carrawburgh[268] on the Wall, came to a sudden end in the fourth century. Again Christians are usually blamed, but on no real evidence. The largest *Mithraeum* in the island, that by the Walbrook in London,[269] may also have passed out of use, or out of Mithraic hands, in the fourth century. At some point a hoard of marble sculpture of Mithraic and Bacchic significance was concealed.[270]

Rather more difficult to classify is the evidence for the god Orpheus. The evidence for Orpheus in fourth-century Britain comes principally from the mosaics on which he is depicted. We have already noted that Orphic mosaics were a stock-in-trade of the Corinian 'school' of mosaicists, but representations of the deity were by no means restricted to the mosaics of this 'school'. There was the mosaic in the triconch at Littlecote, and others up into the east Midlands. These mosaics lay in the rooms interpreted as the principal reception room of these villas, but they would have been large enough to double as a place of worship for a group of devotees. But this is rather slender evidence on which to base an argument for a cult like that of Mithras. Evidence from elsewhere in the empire suggests that Orpheus was a popular subject for floor mosaics as, for instance, were the Four Seasons, and the representation of Orpheus may have had no more religious significance than they did. Most known shrines and mosaics of the various mystery religions were at towns or villas. This accords with the other evidence for the assimilation of Mediterranean norms and ideals by the upper classes in late Roman Britain.

In many essentials Christianity conformed with the other mystery religions, but it also displayed several important differences. It was open to all, regardless of gender or status. Where other cults were exclusivist it proselytised actively. Instead of the tolerance and tendency to syncretism typical of other cults, it was actively hostile to beliefs and practices other than its own. Whereas other cults had little in the way of hierarchy over and above that within individual communities, Christianity had a strict, universal, hierarchical system. Add to this in the fourth century the enormous benefits of imperial favour and patronage, and the conditions were present for Christianity's rise to dominance at the expense of other religions. Since history is written by the victors, we know a fair amount about the beliefs and attitudes of late Roman Christianity, though the physical evidence varies widely in quantity and quality.

The organisation of and evidence for the Church in fourth-century Britain in many respects parallels that for central and northern Gaul. The first substantive reference to organised Christianity in Britain is the list of delegations attending the Council of Arles in 314 (*cf.* p. 35). In two places Athanasius[271] claims that bishops from Britain were present at the great councils of Nicaea (modern Iznik, Turkey) in 325 and Serdica (modern Sofia, Bulgaria) in 343. But as the records of these councils mention few bishops west of Italy, it may be that the mention of Britain was for the sake of geographical comprehensiveness in support of Athanasius' arguments rather than a strict record of fact. British bishops were undoubtedly present at the Council of Ariminium (modern Rimini, Italy) in 359/60. Constantius II had ordered that state hospitality was to be given to any bishop who desired it. Almost all the bishops refused, not wanting to be beholden to the emperor at a controversial council. But three from Britain accepted through poverty, which has been taken as a symptom of the poverty of the Church of late Roman Britain. This is to read the relevant passage of Sulpicius Severus through an insular magnifying-glass. As a good ascetic and disciple of Martin of Tours, Sulpicius was much exercised by the sight of worldly bishops. The three bishops from Britain were held up as an example of holy poverty and thus a stick with which to belabour prelates too much concerned with the things of this world, such as Sulpicius' own bishop, Gavidius. Nothing should be deduced from this passage either about the wealth of the sees of the three bishops or about the state of the Church in Britain overall. At the end of the fourth century Victricius of Rouen came over to Britain at the invitation of the Church. Some have thought that this was to combat the Pelagian heresy (*cf.* p. 128) in the heresiarch's native land, but since Pelagius' theological career had not yet got under way this seems a little fanciful. There was presumably some internal dispute within the Church in Britain which needed an arbiter. Taken together these scattered references show that there was a functioning ecclesiastical hierarchy in place in late Roman Britain. The list of delegations at the Council of Arles suggests that it was the metropolitan churches that were represented. We may thus also expect bishops for the *civitas*-capitals, at least in theory, though the example of Belgica (p. 35) must make us chary of assuming that they always existed in practice.

Archaeological evidence for Christianity in Britain is at present sparse (as indeed it is over much of Gaul), though growing gradually. There are four

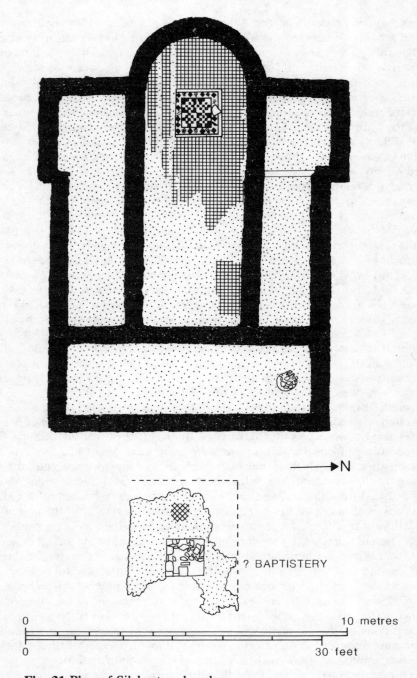

? BAPTISTERY

0   10 metres

0   30 feet

Fig. 31 Plan of Silchester church

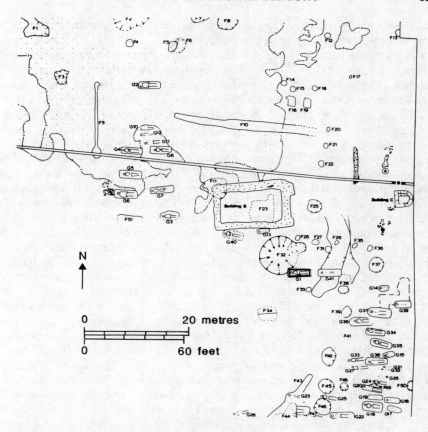

Fig. 32 Plan of Icklingham church

main classes of evidence: likely church buildings; villas with evidence for Christianity; cemeteries and cemetery churches; objects. The best-known candidate for a church building is that outside the south-eastern part of the forum at Silchester (fig. 31).[273] It was a small apsidal building with aisles and a narthex. The apse faced westwards. Outside the eastern end was a square foundation with a central base and soak-away. The usual interpretation is that this was a church, in essence an immensely scaled-down version of the great Constantinian basilicas such as Old St Peter's, Rome. According to this interpretation the square, eastern structure would be a baptistery. In the early church baptism was a sacrament administered by bishops to adult candidates (catechumens) by affusion; that is, the candidate was standing and the officiant poured water over his or her head. Baptisteries in this position were a commonplace in the early church, and still survive in some churches with late Roman antecedents, such as the Duomo at Florence. Thus the Silchester buildings would make sense in terms of a Christian church. But it has been pointed out[274] that there is no positive proof that the Silchester building was Christian. It could have been the shrine of some other mystery religion or other private group. These interpretations likewise lack positive proof. At present the idea of a church seems the least worst interpretation. If this was the *titulus* of the bishop of Silchester it can hardly argue for a large or wealthy congregation. Another church with a font has been excavated on the edge of the undefended 'small' town at Icklingham (fig. 32).[275] The font consisted of a horseshoe-shaped, brick-built structure within which the catechumen would stand, with the officiant on a little step in the interior. This lay to the east of and on axis with a small, rectangular building which may have been a church. Associated with these there was a cemetery of some forty inhumations on the same alignment as the church, only two of which had any grave-goods. To the north of the 'church' were found at different times two large, circular, lead tanks bearing the chi-rho (*cf.* p. 128). Another built font, resembling those from some forts on the Rhine frontier, is known from inside the north-western angle of the Saxon Shore fort at Richborough,[276] though no certain church building has been located in association with it. Large military establishments could and did have their own bishops in the late Roman period. Apart from cemetery churches that is the tally of archaeologically-demonstrated churches or likely churches from fourth-century Britain.

A number of villas have yielded evidence for Christian observance. The best-known is that at Lullingstone.[277] There the wall-plaster from a fourth-century remodelling of part of the villa was preserved when, at the decay of the structure, it fell off the walls into a basement room. A suite of rooms at one end of the main residence had been divided off from the rest of the building and made into a private chapel and annexes. Access was from outside the building, and as there was no direct communication with the residential quarters it could have served the estate workers too. The long walls of the rectangular room had been decorated with figures in the characteristic *orans* (praying) position of the early church (with arms outstretched and hands upraised), standing between pillars. The end wall of the room was dominated by a painted chi-rho within a wreath. Had the plaster not by happy chance survived, there is no way we would have known that here was a Christian chapel. To how many other chapels, Christian or pagan, has time been less favourable? We have already (p. 110) encountered the mosaic at the villa of Hinton St Mary with its head of Christ, and the stylistically-linked pavement at nearby Frampton with a chi-rho. At both villas the mosaics floored apsidal rooms with rectangular ante-chambers. Could these have been private chapels with provision for catechumens?

Recognising Christian cemeteries is not as easy as it might be, as often one has to rely on a concatenation of negatives rather than on any positive evidence. Moreover, it is clear that many late Roman, non-Christian religions practised burial rites very similar to the Christian, and from which the Christian rites themselves in large part probably derived. A Christian burial should have been aligned east–west with the head to the west and have had no grave-goods. Neither of these practices was peculiar to Christianity in the late Antique religion. There was a general preference for inhumation over cremation, and the east–west alignment could be influenced by causes as various as a devotion to the Unconquered Sun or the topography and boundaries of the cemetery. Nor did a burial have to have grave-goods to be pagan. At present there are but three cemeteries in Britain which can be argued with a fair degree of conviction to have been Christian: Icklingham; Poundbury, Dorchester; Butt Road, Colchester. The association of the Icklingham burials with the probable church, and their general alignment and lack of grave-goods, make them almost certainly Christian.

At Poundbury (fig. 33)[278] a large part of one of the fourth-century burial areas of Dorchester has been excavated, with over a thousand graves having been examined. The vast majority were aligned east–west, were in simple, wooden coffins and had no grave-goods. Some burials were in more expensive stone or lead-lined coffins; these were usually clustered together. Other foci were provided by a number of rectangular, semi-subterranean mausolea, one of which had robed figures painted on the walls. The few grave-goods that there were were generally associated with the burials of juveniles, and one was a coin of Magnentius pierced for suspension so that the chi-rho on the reverse (but not the imperial portrait on the obverse) would hang upright. In general great care had been taken to see that later burials did not intersect with and disturb earlier ones. The cemetery also avoided a burial-ground containing north-south inhumations with grave-goods. This may be seen as avoidance of a manifestly pagan burial-ground. The care over not disturbing earlier burials may have been a reflection of the early church's literal belief in the line of the Creed formulated at the Council of Nicaea: '*et exspecto resurrectionem mortuorum*' — 'and I look for the resurrection of the dead'. The chi-rho on the coin and the otherwise general lack of grave-goods would fit with a Christian interpretation. Again we do not have proof positive, but Christianity is the explanation which best fits the data. The main phase of the Butt Road, Colchester[279] cemetery had overall similarities to the Poundbury cemetery in layout, lack of grave-goods and the provision of mausolea. The cemetery was also associated with a long, apsidal building aligned east–west which had probably contained two burials. This may well have been a

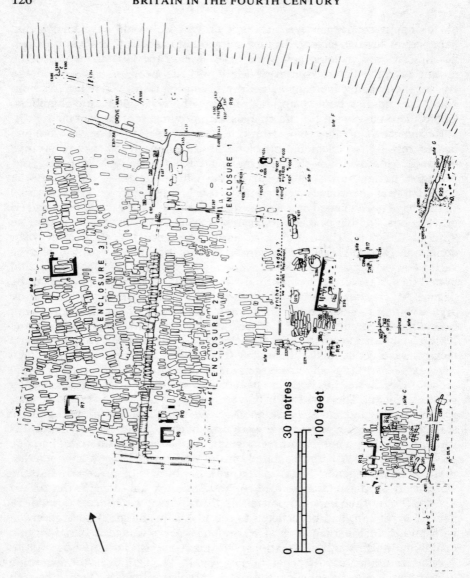

Fig. 33 Plan of Poundbury cemetery

martyrium or *cella memoriae*. Both Poundbury and Butt Road originally ran to hundreds of burials in the course of the fourth century. If these derived solely from the populations of the towns to which they were attached, then the Christian communities there must have been numerous. Alternatively, it may be that the town burial-ground served the wider Christian community in the area, including the rural Christian population. After all, the Frampton and Hinton St Mary villas were not far from Poundbury. Either way they are a more impressive testament to the strength of the new religion than was the Silchester church.

Cemetery churches are a type of site which has been eagerly sought in Britain in the past couple of decades, sometimes with more determination than prudence. They have been seen as an important way in which Roman Britain and Anglo-Saxon England could be linked, after the manner of places such as Bonn or Xanten (p. 36). But given what has been established in Chapter 2 (p. 38) about their paucity in fourth- as opposed to fifth-century Gaul and the Rhineland, and given that they were a manifestation of the cult of the saints which only became widespread in northern Gaul in the early fifth century, we must take a less sanguine view of their likely presence in fourth-century Britain. Undoubtedly the best candidate on circumstantial grounds for a late Roman cemetery church with succeeding mediaeval settlement on the continental model is Verulamium/St Albans.[280] On the literary side the story of the *passio* (martyrdom) of Alban can be traced back to late antiquity and is topographically largely accurate. For the early fifth century a shrine of Alban was visited in 429 by bishops Germanus of Auxerre and Lupus of Troyes (*cf.* p. 162). It would be perverse to doubt that it was the one at Verulamium that was meant. On topographical grounds, the mediaeval and modern abbey lies on a hill outside the south-eastern side of Verulamium in an area of known late Roman burial. Such a siting for a *martyrium* on the site of the *passio* or a *cella memoriae* on the site of the saint's burial would parallel that at Bonn or Xanten. The late Saxon and mediaeval town of St Albans grew up around the abbey rather than on the site of Verulamium, again paralleling Bonn and Xanten. Given such evidence the presence of a late Roman cemetery church here is more likely than not. In the preceding paragraph we noted that the building associated with the Butt Road cemetery was a strong candidate also for having been a cemetery church. It did not have a mediaeval successor, and Anglo-Saxon and mediaeval Colchester lay within the Roman town walls. The mausolea at both Butt Road and Poundbury are reminiscent of those on the continent, not only at Bonn or Xanten, but also at Cologne or Trier. Such structures seem to have been more characteristic of fourth-century Christian cemeteries in the north-west of the empire than were churches.

Christian objects are known from a variety of sites and in a variety of materials. The most spectacular is the Water Newton hoard,[281] found in 1975 within the defences of this 'small' (the term here is particularly unapt) town. It consisted of nine complete vessels or parts of vessels, eighteen triangular votive silver plaques, a gold disc and some fragments. Four of the vessels and ten of the plaques bore the chi-rho, often with Alpha and Omega (the beginning and the end). Two vessels and a plaque were inscribed, one of the vessel inscriptions having an almost liturgical ring to it. The hoard is clearly Christian, even if the votive plaques were derived from a well-known pagan type — such evidence shows that even Christianity was not immune to the lure of syncretism. The hoard presumably belonged to a church or community. Other pieces of Christian silver are known, such as the (lost) *lanx* from Risley Park[282] which bore the chi-rho and the name of a bishop — Exsuperius. Individual pieces in hoards such as those from Canterbury and Mildenhall also bore the chi-rho, though it is more doubtful whether this means that those hoards were specifically Christian. Another definite class of object often bearing the chi-rho was the circular lead tanks now known from a dozen or more sites, principally in East Anglia and the south Midlands.[283] These were clearly designed to hold liquid, and have often been found in or near wells and rivers. It has been suggested that they may have acted as fonts or as vessels for ritual ablution. Apart from these classes or groups of material, there is a scatter of individual objects of Christian significance, such as potsherds inscribed with the chi-rho, across Britain. What the island at present lacks is any examples of the Christian epitaphs of the type developing on the Continent in the fourth century. This may just be a reflection of the general epigraphic poverty of late Roman Britain.

In general, then, the picture of Christianity in fourth-century Britain accords well with what we know of the religion in northern Gaul at the same time. There was a hierarchy, almost certainly in parallel with that of the civil administration. The bulk of the evidence comes from urban and aristocratic contexts. It might be objected that the Christianity of the poorer classes may have been less materially durable. But the known distribution coincides both with that for the other mystery religions in particular and for the romanised élite in general. It also accords with the picture we have from the literary and archaeological evidence for the incidence of Christianity in late Roman Gaul. So Christianity in late Roman Britain seems to have accorded well with what might have been expected from the Continental evidence.

Finally, early in the fifth century Britain fostered a first-rate heresy: Pelagianism. Pelagius was born and brought up in Britain, but it must be admitted that he received his higher education on the Continent, and did his most influential work at Rome. He taught that through prayer and good works man could accumulate sufficient heavenly credit to ensure salvation. He was opposed by a far greater thinker, Augustine bishop of Hippo, who argued that ever since the fall of Adam and Eve mankind has been innately flawed, and however good (or bad) a man might be it was only through the operation of divine grace (*gratia*) that he could achieve salvation. The linked doctrines of Original Sin and Divine Grace were to carry the argument and become the orthodox position of the catholic Church.

Britain and the Continent

Lastly and briefly we must step back from a purely British analysis of the state of affairs in the fourth century and examine how the diocese compared with its neighbours across the Channel. We may divide the evidence into two classes. On the one hand there were those areas of the diocese's life directly responsive to the demands of the state, and on the other there were those which, while influenced by the demands of the state, were more autonomous in their activities and responses. In the first category were such aspects as the army and the civil and financial administration of the diocese; these all show great overall similarity to the situation elsewhere in the western parts of the empire and, except in points of detail, Britain was an unexceptional part of the empire's structure. In addition, an institution which mimicked the state hierarchy and was to become ever more closely identified with the imperial system, the Church, also shows broad similarities between Britain and the continent.

On the other hand, there were areas of clear divergence and difference, generally to be found in the civil aspects of the diocese where the state had no interest in imposing uniformity. The most obvious aspects here were the towns and the villas. In late Roman Britain both the 'large' and the 'small' towns seem to have retained far more vitality than their Gallic counterparts. The British 'large' towns maintained the extended defensive circuits typical of the second century, and within those circuits were the buildings of both a commercial, artisan class and of the landowning *curiales*. The Gallic *civitas*-capitals, though, were much reduced in area from their second-century extent and had at their cores small, heavily defended enclosures. Though the state of these towns may not have been as diminished as is often thought, they do not compare with the Roman-British examples. The contrast seems more marked in the 'small' towns, where those of late Roman Britain had again maintained their size and functions, whereas many of those of northern Gaul had ceased to exist, and the rest were shadows of their second-century selves. One must be careful of extending the grim picture of northern Gaulish towns to the entirety of Gaul; the south seems to have fared far better, but nevertheless the towns of late Roman Britain seem to have been significantly larger, more prosperous and with a different social structure from those of their nearest neighbours across the Channel.

The same seems to have been broadly true of rural settlement. In Britain the full hierarchy of villas and of other types of rural settlement had been maintained through from the second into the fourth century, but over much of northern and central Gaul villas were a rarity in the fourth century. At present it is very difficult to define the pattern and hierarchy of late Roman rural settlement in these areas, but it may have owed a lot more to indigenous factors than to an imported, Mediterranean ideal. Both the literary and the archaeological evidence again make it clear that there was a change further to the south and south-west, in Provence and Aquitaine, where something approximating more to the British pattern may have continued.

It is clear that for northern and central Gaul the second half of the third century had been a time of crisis and change in a way it had not been for Britain or for southern Gaul. This must have related to the barbarian invasions of the period. Initially simply destructive, in the longer term they seem to have precipitated major changes in the settlement and possibly the society of the north and centre. The differences visible from Hadrian's Wall to the Pyrenees demonstrate the point that within the over-arching structure of the state, local resources, history and circumstance gave rise to differing local responses to those structures and the demands they made. That Britain should be both like and unlike other areas of the western empire is only to be expected.

FOUR

The Passing of Roman Britain: 380–430

In the late fourth century the Roman empire and its civilisation held intact. Mistress of the known world, Rome still had immense resources and the prestige of the civilisation which had dominated the Mediterranean basin and much of Europe for half a millennium. Yet by the middle of the fifth century most of her European and African possessions were effectively under the control of barbarian peoples, and Rome's attempts to reassert her authority were becoming increasingly futile. Britain was no exception; in the late fourth century she was still a diocese of the empire with the administration, the economy and the society fashioned by three hundred years of Roman rule still firmly in place. But by the middle of the fifth century Britain was no longer ruled from Rome, and all the apparatus of Roman civilisation and values was in pieces. In this chapter we shall examine not only the varied evidence for what was going on, but we shall try to order it so as to bring out *why* it was happening. The upper point of the date bracket has been chosen for two reasons; the first is that it approximately coincides with an observable change in the archaeological record. The second is that it makes the point that the ending of Roman Britain was rooted within the Roman period and must be seen within the framework of the demise of the western part of the empire, and certainly not only attributed to the *deus ex machina* of Germanic invasion.

A considerable body of evidence is now accumulating to suggest that the last quarter of the fourth century saw a marked recession in activity in Roman Britain. This is most clearly visible in such areas as the towns, the villas and the pottery industry and will presumably be traceable in other spheres in due course. In the towns the evidence is of two main sorts, sometimes with both occurring at the same town. The first is the abandonment and non-replacement of buildings. The second is a decline in the maintenance and quality of both public amenities and private residences. We may start again with the work at Verulamium. In the previous chapter (p. 66) we saw how by the middle of the fourth century the Watling Street frontage was built up with strip-buildings, and that away from the arterial street there was ample provision of well-appointed town houses. In the latter part of the century occupation receded.[1] The date of the abandonment of the Insula XIV strip-buildings cannot be fixed with any certainty because of post-Roman disturbances to their uppermost layers, but there was a marked lack of coins of the Houses of Valentinian and Theodosius from the area compared with the other parts of the excavation. Insulae XX, XXI, XXVIII all saw town houses abandoned in the course of the second half of the fourth century. To set against this there was the construction of a new strip building in Insula XIV (XIV,3), overlying a coin of Valentinian I, and subsequently extended, in Insula XXII there was a sequence of demolition and replacement in this period (XXII,1), and most famously in Insula XXVII a new, large town-house was built in the last quarter of the century (XXVII,2). Nevertheless, by c. 380 the number of buildings in the excavated area was down by at least half compared with the level of fifty years previously. And not only were buildings being abandoned, they were not being replaced, either on the same site or elsewhere in the vicinity. We have already noted (p. 68) that abandonment of single sites need not be significant because of apparent fluidity in the availability of property, but here we have a large number of sites falling out of use and not being reused later. A similar pattern may be detected at other 'large' towns, for instance at Chichester,[2] where excavations on a number of buildings in the north-western quadrant of the town showed town houses and the public baths in decline in the last quarter of the fourth century, and surprisingly for a large Romano-British urban site no coins of the House of Theodosius from the area. Similar evidence for abandonment and non-replacement of buildings in the second half of the fourth century may also be cited from Colchester[3] and Exeter.[4] Again there are new constructions to set against these at towns such as Cirencester[5] and Winchester,[6] but at the latter there are also cases of abandonment. At present the picture is patchy and difficult to quantify for lack of detailed publication, but it does suggest that numbers of buildings were being abandoned and not replaced in the latter part of the fourth century in a number of major centres. Related to this was an observable decline in standards at several 'large' towns. For instance at Canterbury[7] excavations in the area of the public baths showed that in the later fourth century some large buildings of the early part of that century became little more than shells, with their interiors colonised by timber structures. At the same time the public sewer system was breaking down, with blockages occurring and consequent backing-up and flooding of the foul water. Round about 400 timber buildings started to encroach on the street itself. Similar decay in the maintenance of the streets and drains has been observed in central Winchester,[8] where the latest metallings were of markedly inferior quality and again timber buildings encroached on the carriageways. But these metallings and structures, however much they represent a decline in standards, also represent a continuation of population. It appears that it was at this time that the baths-basilica at Wroxeter was systematically demolished.[9]

Similar evidence is now accumulating for the 'small' towns also. At Brampton, Ilchester, Kenchester and Water Newton there is evidence either that the extra-mural areas of occupation were contracting in the later part of the fourth century, or that occupation was becoming less intense without an actual contraction.[10] There are others, though, such as Alcester or Catterick, where the evidence points the other way, and of course for the majority we cannot as yet be sure. The evidence for contraction again takes the form of buildings abandoned and not replaced and of drains silting up and pits being filled in, associated with coins of the House of Valentinian. New buildings and features were rare or absent.

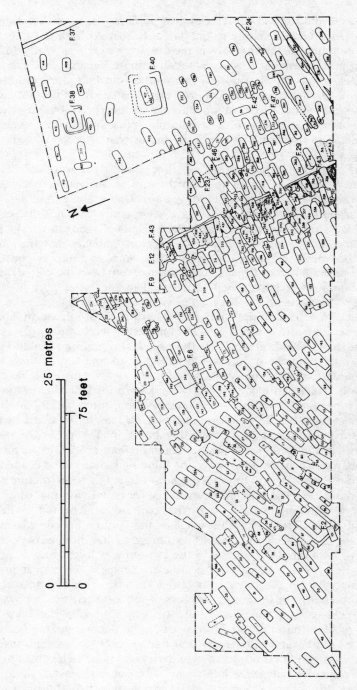

Fig. 34 Plan of Lankhills cemetery

The excavated urban cemeteries also point in the same direction, though this evidence relates mainly to the 'large' towns. At both Lankhills (fig. 34) and Poundbury the latest graves in the cemetery were less neatly dug then the earlier, and often shallower. Wooden coffins became less common. At Lankhills the established burial rites of the fourth century mutated into a wider and less uniform variety of practices. The late fourth century at this site was also characterised by the appearance of the rite of burying decapitated bodies, one in association with a cenotaph. Some sort of social stress seems to be reflected in the variability in burial site as well as in the overall decline in standards.

Villas also seem to have been in decline. First, there were no villas built *de novo* in the last quarter of the fourth century, nor were there any major extensions or refurbishings of existing ones. Dating the end of occupation of villas can be difficult since, as we have seen, coins were not that common at most sites, so the absence of particular periods of the coinage (for instance, the House of Theodosius) cannot be taken to indicate that the site was no longer occupied. Nonetheless some villas, such as those in the Chilgrove valley[11] to the north of Chichester, do seem from both the coin evidence and the stratigraphy to have been abandoned in the latter part of the fourth century. The same also holds for the villas at Gadebridge[12] in the Chilterns and Barnsley Park[13] to the east of Cirencester. To use the term 'abandoned' may be to overstate the case, since it implies the end of the villa as a whole. All that is really indicated is that the principal romanised buildings were no longer in use and the owner would have had to find some other, less plush accommodation; the villa as a functioning estate may still have been in operation. Much more common is the evidence for a decline in the standard of upkeep of villa buildings, a phenomenon often described by earlier workers as 'squatter occupation'. In this there may have been a reduction in the number of rooms in the building being inhabited, as for instance at Latimer[14] in the Chilterns. Another common feature was the turning over of previously well-appointed areas of the building to messy and crude activities. For instance, rooms with mosaics might have seen the construction of hearths on the mosaic, or there might be evidence for metal-working, or a mosaic or tessellated floor might have been covered by one of beaten earth with the accumulation of rubbish. This suggests that utilitarian considerations had ousted those of leisure and taste. It also suggests that there were no longer the means to maintain the building in the style to which its owners had become accustomed; or that there were no longer the specialist craftsmen available (presumably from the towns), or both. The date at which this occurred is often uncertain. The term 'squatter occupation' often carries implications that it was post-Roman camping-out in the decaying villa buildings, perhaps therefore fifth century. But in most cases the decline in standards was not separated stratigraphically from what had gone before, suggesting no great lapse of time, and that this changed activity was nonetheless part of the main Roman sequence, albeit the latest part. Thus some at least of these sites may have seen this decline in area occupied and in standards of occupation during the later fourth century.

Another class of site which shows no new examples in the late fourth century and a significant decline in the number of existing examples before the end of that century is temples, both urban and rural. This has often been interpreted as evidence for the growing influence of Christianity, and the consequent closure of pagan places of worship on religious grounds. We have already seen (p. 128) that the evidence for Christianity being sufficiently widespread and organised at this date for such demonstrations is unconvincing. Instead temples seem to have been declining in parallel with an overall decline of all classes of civilian building during the latter part of the century.[15]

It is not only buildings that show evidence for change and decay in the later fourth century; so also does the best-known of the British industries, pottery. Analysis of the typological development of two of the major late, fine-ware industries, the New Forest[16] and Oxfordshire,[17] shows that the last third of the fourth century saw significant trends. For the Oxfordshire industry, essentially the range of forms and decoration established in the 360s continued without significant variation down to the end of the industry in the earlier part of the fifth century. For the New Forest the evidence is for decline in the second half of the century, both in the overall volume of production and in the range of fabrics and decorative styles. Another feature of the later history of the giant fine-ware producers in the south is the extension of their market both geographically and in terms of market share. For instance, Oxfordshire wares started to appear more commonly in sites accessible from the Thames estuary in Essex and Kent, where they had previously not been common. They even made their presence felt in the heartland of the Nene Valley industry. Moreover, their percentage of the total assemblage from sites rose. The interesting suggestion has been made[18] that the reason behind this expansion was a static market. In such a situation the only way to maintain or improve overall output would have been greater market penetration. The reverse of this is of course that smaller, local producers would have been squeezed. The evidence both from the industries themselves and from their markets suggests, therefore, that the late fourth century was a period of stagnation at best, probably of overall decline.

As yet our knowledge of other industries and aspects of late Roman Britain is not precisely enough quantified for us to be able to judge. We have, though, already noted the absence of counterfeiting of bronze coin during the trough in supply from 378 to 388. It may well be that the issues of the House of Valentinian had been so huge that they satisfied the market, but it could be that the coin-using economy was already in recession. It certainly was twenty years later, when not only did all supply of coin from the imperial mints cease, but also there was no counterfeiting to make up the shortage in supply (cf. p. 140).

Overall then, such evidence as we have indicates that the late fourth century was certainly not a time of expansion. It is hard to argue that it was a period of steady-state maintenance of levels of activity established earlier in the century. Much more plausible is the notion that the overall levels of the most visibly romanised sectors of the economy and culture were in decline.

There is no evidence for a decline in the population or the productivity of the land; what was being affected was the economic superstructure dependent on that agricultural basis. It was the towns, the villas, the large-scale industries that were in trouble. Since we have argued that these were a manifestation of the romanised economic system then it suggests that that system was itself in decline. How and why this should have come about is as yet unclear. The structures of the state were still in place and the revenue cycle was therefore still essential to them. Was there a declining ability or willingness to continue to shoulder the burden, leading to diminishing revenue returns? This would make sense as a prelude to the breakdown which occurred early in the next century. One important point is that this decline may well not have been peculiar to Britain. There is now some evidence from sites and industries in northern Gaul and the Rhineland[19] for a similar episode of decline in quantity and quality. If this is so, then Britain must be viewed against the Continental background. This does not make the reasons any clearer, but it suggests that something was going awry with the Roman system in this entire region of the empire; an impression supported by the parallelism between Britain and northern Gaul in the early fifth century (p. 160). It may be that the demands of maintaining the Roman state and civilisation were overtaxing the resources, of co-operation as much as of grain and coin, of the region. One other point to note is that ever since the publication of Edward Gibbon's great work,[20] decline and fall have been inextricably linked, and therefore this late fourth-century decline is seen as the harbinger of the fall in the fifth century. We must be alive to this mental conditioning. Is it possible that the changes of the late fourth century were simply a realignment, overtaken by the events of the fifth century? It is a possibility, but given the way in which the events of the later fourth century dovetail so neatly with those of the early fifth, and given the way in which the archaeological sequence runs through from the one to the other without break, it seems more likely that the decline of the late fourth century was indeed a prelude and contributory factor to the fall of the early fifth.

By chance some of the historical events contemporary with that fall are preserved for us. In the first decade of the fifth century Britain again figures in the historical sources. In 406 the army in the diocese elevated three successive claimants to the imperial purple: Marcus, Gratian and Constantine. The first two each survived only a matter of months, Constantine, elevated *ob solam speciem nominis* (on the strength solely of his name)[21] — it was exactly a hundred years since Constantine I had been proclaimed at York — lasted longer, due to external events. On the last night of December 406 a horde of Alamanni, Burgundiones, Vandals and others crossed the frozen waters of the Rhine in the area of Mainz. This was to prove the end of the Roman frontier on the Rhine, and the barbarians raided far and wide into the interior of Gaul. The army in Britain was fearful for its communications with the central parts of the empire and forced Constantine III (as he is usually known) to mount an expedition to Gaul to try to restore the situation. In this he was only moderately successful over four years, until he was besieged at Arles in 411 by the forces of the vigorous new Roman commander in the west, the patrician Constantius, captured and executed. During the rule of Constantine III we hear something of what was passing in Britain. Somewhere around 409 'the people of Britain, taking up arms and exposing themselves to danger on their own behalf, liberated the cities from threatening barbarians; and all Armorica and the other provinces of Gaul, imitating the Britons, liberated themselves in the same way; they threw out the Roman officials and within their power set up their own order'.[22] In 410 the emperor Honorius wrote to the cities (*poleis*) of Britain telling them to defend themselves.[23] Also for 410 or 411 we are told that Britain was laid waste by a Saxon incursion.[24] Taken together these sources give a superficially coherent picture of a diocese under threat because of the withdrawal of troops by Constantine III struggling for its own survival and ejecting the representatives of the illegal régime. Honorius' letter (or Rescript) both *de facto* signalled the end of Roman ability to intervene in the affairs of the island, and suggests that the municipalities were the only surviving authority after the ejection of Constantine III's officials. The idea of Britain setting up a new, post-imperial order of things has proved very attractive to some. We thus are given external threat, imperial impotence and Britain having to go it alone: the end of Roman Britain.

As so often in Romano-British studies, the fragmentary historical sources have been taken too much at face value and too much credence given to nuances to be wrung from the precise wording. What were these sources? There were two principal historians: Orosius and Zosimus. Orosius was a Spaniard writing in the early fifth century. His *Historia Adversus Paganos* (History Condemning the Pagans) is a reputable source for some of the activities of Constantine III on the Continent, but has nothing to say about the internal affairs of Britain. These latter are principally to be found in the work of Zosimus, written in the eastern empire at the turn of the fifth and sixth centuries. Given Zosimus' chronological and geographical distance from the events he was describing he is not a first-hand source. He was, in fact, an excerptor, précis-ing the works of earlier authors to provide an easily-assimilated historical digest. For the events of the early fifth century he was dependent on the work of Olympiodorus of Thebes. The few fragments of Olympiodorus which survive command respect for his powers as a historian. When and if Zosimus transmitted him accurately there is no problem. But if the transmission is over-compressed or corrupt, or Zosimus did not understand or care about an episode, then there is a clear danger of garbling. Zosimus is our source for two of the crucial episodes: the fighting and revolt of 409, and the Rescript of Honorius in 410. The former is generally agreed to be a passage where Zosimus has over-compressed events. This is clear from the description of events in Gaul which does not tally with what is known from other sources. This must prejudice the usefulness of this passage as a detailed description of events in Britain. It certainly means that the passage cannot be taken as a starting-point for a reconstruction of what was going on. The so-called Rescript of Honorius has also been the subject of criticism.[25] It has been pointed out that the chapter of Zosimus in which this occurs is otherwise concerned with events in Italy centring around Alaric's movements before the Sack of Rome; the reference to Britain is sandwiched between discussion of affairs in northern Italy and in Liguria. Following a suggestion which has been made before but usually ignored, it has been proposed that either Zosimus or one of the manuscript's copyists misread or mistranscribed *Brettannia* for *Brettia* or *Brittia*, acceptable Greek spellings for Bruttium (now Calabria) in southern Italy. If this emendation is accepted then the passage refers to Italy, which is the subject of the chapter, and not to Britain at all. This seems a reasonable piece of textual criticism, but it has been vigorously disputed,[26] on the grounds of the eminence of the scholars who have preferred the *Brettannia* reading rather than on textual grounds. The reference to the devastation of Britain by Saxons in 410 or 411 comes from the Gallic Chronicle of 452. Such Chronicles were composed from the fifth century on as continuations of the great Chronicle set down by St Jerome. This one was set down in 452 (hence the name), apparently in southern Gaul.[27] It is thus not first-hand information for 410/11, and must lie under suspicion of projecting back into the early part of the century the state of affairs prevailing in the late fifth century. All in all there are reasonable grounds for regarding all these references to Britain in the years around 410 as suspect. Though one would not wish to stifle debate on the matter, equally one would not wish to use these passages as the cornerstone for the study of this period.

But if one returns, nevertheless, to the events surrounding the usurpation by Constantine III, and more particularly the aftermath of his fall, there is a great deal of the first importance to be deduced. Perhaps most important is what did not happen, and the consequences this had for Britain. In brief, there is no evidence that the civil, financial and military administrations of the diocese were continued or replaced after the fall of Constantine III. Those of a contrary disposition may argue that this is simply an argument from silence: no source actually documents such a discontinuity; it is just that none mentions further officials and there were after all plenty of gaps in the fourth-century lists for Britain. This is to be over-critical, however; the silence of the sources is unanimous and deafening. If one must have a single date for the end of Roman rule in Britain then 411 is it. The Romans seem to have surrendered their hold on the island not for any very positive reason, but because the chaos north of the Alps at the time caused Britain to be neglected in a fit of absence of mind.

The most crucial result of this for the question of how and why Roman Britain ceased to exist was the removal of the revenue/payment cycle and its associated activities. That it was removed can be positively demonstrated by the absence of new coins being shipped to Britain. The latest issues of gold from Britain are those of Arcadius and Honorius minted in the first decade of the fifth century, and those of Constantine III. The issues of the later part of the reign of Honorius are not found in Britain.[28] The same seems to hold good for silver. The only problem here is three coins with the reverse *Vrbs Roma* of the Trier mint. These are usually dated *c.* 420, but they have recently been re-classified as counterfeit coins, mixing the obverse of Honorius with a reverse type from earlier coins.[29] For bronze the latest issues are those of

395–402 from the mint of Rome. The issue of 404 on has not been found on British sites. Interestingly, Constantine III does not appear to have felt the need to strike bronze. This evidence is unequivocal. Coins were a *sine qua non* of the revenue/expenditure cycle of the state, but after 411 were no longer being supplied to Britain. If the state was no longer providing coins to the diocese of the Britains then that diocese no longer formed a part of the empire.

But there is more to it than that. There are features of the end of coin-use peculiar to Britain, and there are the implications for the withdrawal of the revenue/expenditure cycle for the whole economy to be considered. One feature of the latest period of coin in Britain is the large number of hoards of gold and/or silver coins found in the island. A recent survey[30] of these hoards enumerated sixty-one of them; some more have been reported since. The three hoards from Southsea (Hampshire), East Harptree (Gloucestershire) and North Mendip (Somerset) contained 1167, 1485 and 2045 coins respectively, but these are exceptional; the general run of hoards numbers between one hundred and three hundred coins, with several under a hundred. This episode of hoard-deposition is a phenomenon not to be observed on the Continent. Nor is a common feature of the coins (especially the silver *siliquae*) in the hoards, that the edges of the coins have been clipped; a means of obtaining silver.[31] During the fourth century a number of imperial prohibitions of the practice had been issued, threatening trangressors with the death penalty. Given that the coins would regularly come to the notice of the authorities for tax, these edicts were effective and there is hardly any evidence for clipping before the end of the fourth century. But in the hoards under discussion here clipping was rife. This indicates that the Roman authorities were no longer in a position to prevent it. The minting dates of the latest coins in the hoards are of the first decade of the fifth century. This, of course, gives us only a *terminus post quem* for the clipping and the hoarding. Two pieces of evidence suggest that the hoards were deposited not too long after the beginning of the fifth century. The first is that in some hoards, such as that from Canterbury, the coins were associated with other Roman objects datable to the late fourth and early fifth centuries. The second is that in no case is there an object of post-Roman-British or of Anglo-Saxon manufacture in the hoards. Compared with the paucity of precious-metal coin hoards of the fourth century from Britain these hoards represent a major episode of deposition. Nor should coin hoards be considered in isolation. We have just mentioned the Canterbury hoard; the Thetford hoard too is dated to the early fifth century. It may be that there was an episode of value-hoard deposition, and if so, one might wonder whether some of the poorly-dated late Roman hoards such as that from Mildenhall may not belong here also. The circumstances of and reasons for the deposition of these hoards are at present unknowable, but that this happened indicates a period of sufficient uncertainty for these valuables to have been felt to be at risk. As we shall see the first half of the fifth century was a time of tremendous upheaval, social and economic as much as military, and this may well provide an overall context for the phenomenon, even if the specific circumstances remain obscure. One final point on these hoards is that their existence shows that despite the best efforts of the fiscal authorities there were quantities of gold and silver coins in circulation, more than site-finds and earlier hoards might lead us to believe.

Turning to the bronze coinage, there is a significant absence. As we have already seen (p. 95), when in the fourth century there were periods of low supply from the imperial mints there were corresponding outbreaks of counterfeiting. After the cessation of official supply of bronze coinage from 402 there was no counterfeiting to speak of; Roman Britain evidently no longer felt the need for quantities of low-value coinage to be in circulation. In the previous chapter (p. 96) it was argued that copying was an epipheno-menon of the commercial rather than the official use of coinage; the copies were used for day-to-day transactions. Since the counterfeits were of bronze and there was a great deal of bronze in existence in late Roman Britain, not just as coins but also as a whole range of objects, there was no practical obstacle to producing counterfeit coins if they were wanted or needed. The disappearance of the need for such coinage must therefore indicate, according to our assessment of the cause of counterfeiting, that the town-centred, coin-using commercial system characteristic of the fourth century was no longer functioning. This would have had important repercussions for such industries as the giant fine-ware potteries, whose distribution was predicated on such an economy. It would also gravely affect the romanised strata of rural society which had participated in and benefited from the urbanised economy. Exchange will not have ceased, but it had to revert to non-coin-using modes, and so presumably became re-embedded in social relations of exchange rather than mediated through an independent, monetised system.

So the opening of the fifth century saw the rapid running-down of the fourth-century economic system as formed by the mechanisms of the late Roman state. Because the coins we do have only give us a *terminus post quem* for this running-down it is very difficult to say how long it took, but we shall argue below (p. 144) that the great majority of the evidence suggests that the great majority of the Roman features of Roman Britain (towns, villas etc.) had passed out of use by *c.* 430, that is to say in the course of about one generation. Thus it would have been a relatively short, fairly sharp shock.

What was happening to the coinage is also informative about the dis-location of the wider economic regime. If no gold or silver coins were being shipped into Britain then the state was no longer paying its servants. The single largest and most important group of these was what was left of the army. Cease paying soldiers and the soldiers will in due course cease to be soldiers: the same applies to any administrators who might still have been left. But state expenditure was only one side of the coin; the other was taxation. If the specie into which the taxpayers needed to convert their surplus in order for it to be acceptable to the authorities was no longer being made available, it can only mean that tax was no longer being imposed. A more vivid testament to Rome's cession of rule in Britain could not be devised.

It could be argued that the system of taxation was maintained for a time by bodies within Britain. On the Continent it was, with varying degrees of (in)competence, by the Germanic successor-states. For Britain the Anglo-Saxons were not at that time in any position to attempt such a thing. Local authorities or rulers in Britain could have tried to maintain the land tax and its revenue; either the curial class operating through the mechanisms of Roman local administration, or local strong-men within their sphere of power. If this did happen it did not lead to any new coin being issued as it did on the Continent. It could, though, have been operated entirely in kind. At present we have no evidence for anything of this sort, certainly none that can be seen influencing the archaeological record after the disappearance of the full Roman system. If such local taxation did occur it was short-lived and localised, in no way replacing the universal Roman system. At present there is no evidence for it, so it cannot affect our overall argument.

The effect of the disappearance of the demands for revenue and the associated means of meeting these demands will have been profound for the civil population. Overall there was the removal of a major stimulus to production, particularly agricultural production. Added to this there was the demise of state purchase and the purchasing needs of the military, both units and individuals. The conditions would thus have existed for a major economic retrenchment. For the towns the consequences would have been just as catastrophic, if not more so. In Chapter 1 (p. 9) we established the likelihood that revenue-generated exchange and trade was the largest engine of the late Roman economy, and that they were mediated through the towns. In Chapter 3 (p. 73) we considered the implications of this for the towns of late Roman Britain, and suggested that it was central to their economic structure. Disrupt it and the towns would be seriously or terminally undermined. Given the pivotal place of towns in the romanised society and economy of Britain, serious disruption to them would have reverberated through the whole structure of Roman Britain. It is now our business to examine the various aspects of fifth-century Roman Britain and work through the consequences of this disruption.

This process will inevitably be based on the archaeological evidence, so first we must examine an archaeological consequence of the cessation of the coin-supply: massive problems in the dating of sites. Just at the point when the breakdown of the old order and the transition to a new makes chronological calibration and accuracy critical, we are deprived of our main dating mediums. Clearly, with no coins coming into Britain from the first decade of the fifth century the latest site-finds will be bronze issues of 388–402, which can only afford us a *terminus post quem*. What is at present unknowable is how long bronze coins continued to circulate after 402: presumably to 411 at least since the structures of the state were still in place. Thereafter they will probably have become worthless in financial terms as well as intrinsically, for the evidence is that the financial system had broken down. They probably passed out of circulation quickly; the current estimate is by *c.* 420.[32] In addition it is coins that are used by archaeologists to date the typological and stylistic development of the pottery which is the other main dating tool for the Roman period. From the opening of the fifth century there is no independent means of dating pottery. Add to this the observation that in the late fourth century the typological development of much Romano-British pottery seems to have stagnated, and the problems became worse. Theoretically, a pottery assemblage of 370 could be virtually indistinguishable from one from the end of the pottery industries somewhere in the early fifth century. Physical methods of dating such as radiocarbon are usually of little help in dating events at this period, since the standard deviation (the date limits within which the given radiocarbon date has a 66 per cent chance of falling) is normally too wide to be helpful. We are left with sequential or relative dating. A given sequence of deposits should through the fourth century see the introduction of new issues of coin and types of pottery. If the sequence continues to accumulate after the introduction into it of the latest pottery and coin types (particularly for the latter the issues of 388–402), then that part of the sequence must date within the fifth century. In that late part of the sequence the only coins will be those up to 402, but they will now be 'residual', that is appearing in deposits formed after the end of the coins' currency. The same will apply to the pottery. We shall meet with individual examples of such sequences where the problems of the dating can be further dealt with. The essential point is that from the beginning of the fifth century accurate dating is no longer possible.

We must look now at the various major categories of site which we discussed in the last chapter as being characteristic of late Roman Britain; the nature and chronology of their disappearance and the reasons for it. We shall look at the army and military sites, the towns, the pottery industries and the countryside. The evidence suggests that the history of the Roman army in Britain ended not with a bang but a whimper. The force that Constantine III took with him to Gaul in 407 presumably consisted of the comitatensian troops of the *comes Britanniarum*. After the defeat at Arles in 411 they will not have been returned. This was partly because, as we have seen, the Roman state was no longer interested in reasserting its power in Britain, and also because the patrician Constantius would have had better uses for them there. This would have denuded Britain of a vital strategic component of her defences and left only the *limitanei* on the Wall and the Saxon Shore. When the imperial authorities stopped paying them their response can easily be imagined. There is the instructive tale from the province of Noricum Ripense on the Upper Danube, contained in the early sixth-century Life of St Severinus.[33] In 452 the saint came to the province where there were scarcely any *limitanei* still in garrison. The reason for this is explicitly stated: in the old days they had been paid. That had ceased and soldiers sent to Italy to try to get pay had been murdered *en route* by barbarians. In consequence the troops had ceased to serve, apart from a few, very small formations which went in fear of the barbarian forces. A similar scenario for the disappearance of the British *limitanei* is only too probable.

The archaeological evidence from the *limitaneus* forts of Hadrian's Wall and its hinterland, and of the Saxon Shore, is compatible with such a view. In the north, though coins are rare, there are some of Magnus Maximus and the House of Theodosius.[34] This gives the lie to the theory that the events of 367 saw the end of occupation on the Wall. At some forts such as Housesteads[35] and Vindolanda[36] the rubble from the collapse of the buildings overlies the late fourth-century deposits, suggesting that occupation did not continue far into the fifth century. At Binchester[37] the occupation sequence continued after the introduction of the latest coins, and of pottery types from the Crambeck kilns, but there is a marked change in the nature of the occupation, with military structures being put to new, non-military purposes, so it is questionable whether there was continuing, full-time, professional military occupation. Elsewhere the evidence is poor, but no strong case has been made for the occupation at Wall and associated forts continuing much past 400.

The circumstances surrounding the ending of the Saxon Shore system are also obscure due to the lack of large-scale, modern excavation. The one excavation of this type, at Portchester,[38] revealed that in the late fourth century occupation was declining both in intensity and in orderliness. After 400 there is little archaeological evidence from the site. There was a *grubenhaus* (a building over a scoop, a type associated with Anglo-Saxon settlements here and on the Continent) with a sherd of Anglo-Saxon pottery of the first half of the fifth century and a brooch of the second half of that century in the fill of the scoop. There was also a well with an iron purse-mount/strike-a-light of the second half of the century three feet up in its fill. Both the features cut through the latest Roman deposits, and there is nothing in their relationship to the Roman lay-out and features to suggest any connection between the two periods. At present the evidence from Portchester would not contradict a break in occupation in the first half of the fifth century.

The extensive excavations at Richborough between the wars were unfortunately not sufficiently discriminating in their method to tell us much about the latest history of the fort.[39] There is, though, one considerable peculiarity there. Of the huge number of coins, 56,000, recovered in the excavations, some 20,000 or 45 per cent were of bronze minted 395–402[40] — more than are known of this period from all the other excavated Roman sites in Britain put together. How these came to be at the site is a problem and a puzzle. As they are uniformly distributed in the topsoil and in the latest Roman deposits it is unlikely that the theory that they come from a number of hoards not recognised upon excavation will hold up. They must therefore represent some form of 'loss'. We have already seen (p. 92) how treacherous a term 'loss' can be. It could be that there was massive deliberate discard after the coins became effectively worthless. If so, this again points to the demise of the financial system and a market economy, otherwise the coins could have retained some value. But this still begs the question why they were present at Richborough in such overwhelming numbers in the first place.

The other forts of the Saxon Shore are even less informative. From Burgh Castle came a hoard of glass vessels of the early fifth century, but no indication of occupation later than that, until the foundation of the monastic community in the seventh century.[41] Lympne[42] may have been abandoned as early as the middle of the fourth century. One piece of evidence can be discarded, and that is the tiles from Pevensey bearing the stamp HON AVG ANDRIA which were thought to indicate reconstruction under the Augustus

Honorius at Pevensey (*Anderida*) at the turn of the fourth and fifth centuries. These have now been shown[43] to be twentieth-century fakes, perhaps by some of the same men also responsible for the Piltdown Man hoax. The evidence from the Saxon Shore forts, as with that from Hadrian's Wall and its hinterland, would allow us to argue that none of them was held far into the fifth century, according with our model for what happened to the *limitanei*.

Military weakness was not of itself sufficient to bring about the ending of Roman Britain; it needed somebody to exploit that weakness, and that does not seem to have been happening to any great extent in the first third of the fifth century at least. Far more disruptive was the collapse of the towns, and consequent upon that collapse the disappearance of the romanised economy and the society and culture that depended on that economic underpinning. That the towns of Roman Britain ceased to fulfill the functions that they had in the fourth century somewhere in the first half of the fifth century is now generally agreed. How and why and when this came about has, on the other hand, been the subject of general disagreement over the last twenty years.[44] To an extent this is a reflection of the difficulties of the evidence; but it is also the fault of two of the ways in which that evidence has been studied and structured. One is the tendency to examine particular sites or towns rather than to look for general models and processes. The second is that the whole problem of the end of towns has got inextricably bound up with the question of the degree of continuity between Roman Britain and Anglo-Saxon England — a question usually addressed by those whose expertise lies in the early mediaeval rather than the late Roman period. The basic assumption has been in favour of a degree of continuity, and this has led to emphasis being laid on individual sites with a sequence which extends well into the fifth century at the expense of the remainder of known sites — the majority. This has in its turn reinforced the dominance of the single site/town approach. It has also encouraged the insular, British approach to the study. The question of continuity is further treated in Chapter 6.

Here we shall develop instead the arguments advanced in Chapters 1 and 3 about the nature of late Roman towns in Britain, and how the dislocation of the Roman administration and economy led to the end of those towns. To start with let us consider the fate of the 'large' towns, and begin by constructing a model of the effects of the aftermath of the events (or rather, non-events) of 411. In Chapter 3 (p. 73) it was argued that the single largest economic activity in these towns was concerned with the state revenue cycle, especially the conversion of agricultural surplus into the coin necessary to pay a significant proportion of the tax levy. In addition to their role in the fiscal administration these towns also retained a role as local administrative centres. They were also centres of manufacture and distribution and (at least seasonally) of residence of the landed aristocracy, the *curiales*. These latter, both when they were in town and on their country estates, were patrons of the urban artisans and professionals. So too was the rest of the rural populace, the peasantry, who both consumed the finished goods and the services of the towns and in return supported the urban population. We have also seen that there is growing evidence that the towns were already in significant physical and economic decline before 411. The towns were therefore already weakened, and that is why when the hammer-blow of the end of the taxation system fell it proved fatal. Odd as it may sound to modern ears, the removal of taxation was disastrous. With its end came the end of the largest volume economic and financial transaction at the towns. With it came the end of the supply of the low-value coinage which had encouraged the market-oriented economy of the fourth century, though the use of that medium of exchange seems also already to have been in decline. The end of the civil and financial administration also meant the end of a major reason for the *curiales* to participate in the urban economy and society, and consequently the diminution of their patronage. We have already seen that the literary evidence for the western empire in general and the archaeological evidence for Britain in particular both suggest a predisposition to a rural- rather than an urban-based way of life amongst the landowning classes, for social as well as economic reasons. The disappearance of the tax system would also have affected the peasantry, since it would have lifted that burden or stimulus from their shoulders. Even the most grasping of landlords could not long exact surplus for the payment of taxes which he no longer had to render. We shall deal with the overall picture of the effects of this on rural settlement and economy in due course, but what must concern us here is that there is widespread evidence for retrenchment and the passing-out of use of areas which had been in production in the fourth century. This decline in rural production can only have adversely affected the surpluses available to be turned into urban goods and services. As these goods and services fell away, the rural populace would feel even less need for the towns, engendering a self-perpetuating cycle of both urban and rural material decline. Finally, we have also noted that demographically these towns were unlikely to have been self-sustaining; they needed consistent rural immigration to maintain their population levels. When the towns were perceptibly in decline and were no longer offering attractions or even a secure livelihood to the rural populace, that immigration would dry up, and irreversible population decline would be the inevitable result. Put all these factors and processes together and we have a model for how the economy and population of the 'large' towns would decline to a point where they were below the threshold of viability. It is clear that such a decline could occur over a relatively short time-span, of the order, say, of a generation.

To test this model we must turn to the archaeological evidence. There is evidence from a number of towns that defences were being refurbished or strengthened at the end of the Roman period. These towns were Caerwent,[45] Kenchester[46] and London.[47] At London the eastern end of the riverside wall (now within the boundaries of the Tower of London) was realigned at a date very close to 400. That the defences of the diocesan capital should continue to be maintained at this date should occasion no surprise. Rather different are the cases of Caerwent and Kenchester, where the south and west gates respectively were blocked. The date at which this was done is in neither case ascertainable; sometime late in the Roman period is the best that can be said. There is evidence for the blocking of gates at other Roman towns such as Colchester (Duncan's gate)[48] and Lincoln (the north and south gates of the upper *colonia*),[49] but at these towns there is the possibility that this was done in the mediaeval period. By contrast, when the superstructure of the south gate at Winchester[50] collapsed in the late fourth century there is no evidence for the gate being re-built, and traffic passed through the hole in the defences over the surface of the superstructure rubble. Gate-blocking is a more decisive action than simple refurbishment. By interdicting or impeding access from the countryside it shows a perception of threat. What this threat was we do not know. Traditionally it would have been said to be the Anglo-Saxons, but the date for these blockings could be earlier than that at which the Saxons were a threat; moreover we have no evidence that the Saxons were able to mount an effective attack on defences — the evidence of other barbarian peoples against Roman defences at the time rather suggests the reverse. Another possibility is that there was internal unrest. At present this can only be a hypothesis. It is also possible that these measures were a reaction to a generalised perception of a decline in security rather than to any specific threat. It is also important to remember that town defences, any defences, were only of any use so long as there were sufficient military personnel or townspeople to man them. Once these had gone in the early fifth century then no defences, however magnificent, would be of much use.

Within the defences of the 'large' towns the evidence overall conforms to a consistent pattern. Some buildings had passed out of use and not been replaced before the end of the fourth century. At the majority of sites which were still occupied at the end of the fourth century there is little stratigraphic build-up after the introduction of the latest coins of the House of Theodosius. In this latest phase there is often evidence for drains and sewers no longer being maintained, and for pits and wells being filled-in with no later ones dug. These deposits are then sealed by the rubble of the collapse of buildings and/ or the 'dark earth'. This latter is a deposit now known from several towns; its nature is still imperfectly understood, but it is generally agreed that its appearance betokens abandonment. It is dicussed further in a moment. Thus the evidence from the majority of sites is that they were abandoned not long after the latest Roman coins to reach Britain became current. It is difficult to assign a precise date, and there will have been variation from site to site, but somewhere in the first third of the fifth century should comprehend the great majority of abandonment dates. This accords with the evidence from the cemeteries and with the evidence of artefacts, no Roman-style objects apparently being produced later than *c.* 420–30. It is also supported by the evidence of the few sites which did continue in use later, for what distinguishes these from the general run of sites is that their stratigraphy did continue to develop.

Let us examine these various classes of evidence in more detail. The evidence for the ending of 'large' towns in the early fifth century has recently been reviewed[51] in general terms, and this has confirmed that the generality of sites do not continue long after 400. To catalogue all the evidence from the various towns here would be tedious and otiose, but a few examples may suffice. To return again to Verulamium, of the thirteen or so buildings excavated, in whole or in part, only two show any evidence for use later than

c. 410–20. One, Insula XIV Building 3,[52] it is suggested was abandoned c. 430+, the end of our suggested overall date-range for abandonment. The other, Insula XXVII, Building 2, is one of the few town sites in Roman Britain with a longer history, and is further discussed below. At other towns such as Chichester,[53] Cirencester,[54] Colchester,[55] Exeter,[56] Lincoln[57] and York,[58] the evidence from modern excavations is consistently that buildings were abandoned in the early fifth century. These conclusions were arrived at independently by a number of excavators.

As well as the evidence of decay and rubble deposits overlying the latest fourth/fifth-century deposits there is the 'dark earth' referred to above. This is a deposit which has been observed at a number of towns and is of great significance in the question of the end of the towns. The 'dark earth' has been encountered at Canterbury, Gloucester, Lincoln, London and Southwark, and Winchester, with analogous earth deposits at Cirencester and Exeter. The common characteristics are that it immediately overlies the latest Roman deposits; that it contains only Roman artefacts, though some mediaeval material may appear at the top of the profile; that there are no traces of structures or surfaces within it. Investigation of the physical and chemical structure of the 'dark earth' and of the processes of its formation is still at a very preliminary stage. Even to assume that these visually-similar deposits are in fact broadly the same for different sites within a single town may be risky, let alone to make that assumption for more than one town. At present this is a working hypothesis. Analysis of 'dark earth' from London[59] showed it to be a poorly-sorted, circum-neutral, clayey earth, with plentiful inclusions of pottery and other artefacts, bone, shell and flecks of charcoal, which last gave it its characteristic colour. Analysis of pollen from the deposit showed a suite of plants characteristic of waste ground. The internal structure of some 'dark earth' suggests that it may have been dumped; more often it appears to have accumulated gradually. The present material and mode of formation remain uncertain, but a suggestion may be advanced here. The majority of buildings in late Romano-British towns were timber-framed (usually on stone sill-walls) with clay or wattle-and-daub infill panels. The collapse and decay of these would cause a suitable parent material for the formation of the 'dark earth'. In addition, as with any derelict site, colonisation by plants would be immediate. Initially colonisation would be by grasses, herbs and weeds; gradually scrub would take over, and eventually trees. The pollen record referred to above is in line with this. The annual cycle of the growth and decay of the plants would contribute further to the mass of the deposit and would modify the existing soil. Accidental summer fires might contribute charcoal. Other modifying agents, as with all developing soils, would include the weather and the activities of earthworms.[60] Some sites with 'dark earth' may have been ploughed. If so, then this would seem a reasonable use for such areas of overgrown ground. Whether the 'dark earth' was deliberately created for such a purpose is more doubtful. One drawback of ploughing for the interpretation of these deposits is that it would have churned up the soil and destroyed its profile, thus making study of its origins and development very difficult. At all sites bar London the dating evidence is that the 'dark earth' overlies buildings abandoned in the later fourth and early fifth centuries. At London it appeared as early as the late second century, but that can be connected with the particular development of that town (*cf.* p. 82). If this picture for the cause and nature of the 'dark earth' is anywhere near the truth, then we may envisage the sites of Romano-British towns in the fifth century as largely consisting of acres of tumbled buildings gradually disappearing under weeds and scrub and surrounded by the mute circuit of the town walls; as eloquent a testament of abandonment as any provided nowadays by bomb sites or industrial wasteland.

Outside those walls the evidence from the cemeteries points to the same conclusion. All the recent major urban cemetery excavations — Bath Gate, Cirencester; Poundbury, Dorchester; Lankhills and Victoria Road, Winchester — conform to a general picture of disuse in the early part of the fifth century. At Bath Gate[61] the latest dated burial was associated with a *siliqua* of Honorius. At Poundbury[62] the excavator suggests that the cemetery passed out of use by *c.* 420, the date also favoured for the abandonment of Lankhills.[63] The disuse of a town's cemeteries strongly suggests that there was no longer a parent population dying off. It could be argued that burial had been relocated to other sites, but quite apart from the question of why this should happen, no burial-ground of suitable date is known at any of these towns. The consistency of the evidence from a number of towns indicates that we are dealing with a generalised phenomenon of urban depopulation, which accords with our overall model.

The bulk of the evidence, therefore, from the buildings, from the cemeteries and from the rubble and 'dark earth' deposits points unequivocally to the abandonment of the 'large' towns of Roman Britain early in the fifth century, and to the fact that they had ceased to fulfil their functions as centres of population and of manufacture and distribution. Both this cessation and the date for it fit closely with the overall model for the causation and process of abandonment as consequent on the events of 411.

There are, of course, some sites where there is evidence for a more extended sequence, and these deserve to be studied both for their own sakes and because of the light they may throw on the generality of sites. But it must be borne in mind from the outset that the sites that we are about to consider are in a tiny minority. The most important sites are those at Canterbury, Exeter, Lincoln, Verulamium and Wroxeter. The Verulamium Insula XXVII sequence is one that has become a classic (fig. 35).[64] In about 380 an ample town house was constructed from scratch on a vacant site. Round three sides at least (any potential fourth side has been destroyed by a mediaeval hollow-way) of a courtyard or garden was laid out a building with twenty-two rooms on the ground floor, opening onto a corridor or colonnade around the court. Clearly the owner was confident of the future. After a period of use, two small extensions were added with mosaics laid in them. One of these mosaics was in use long enough to need patching before being cut through by the flues of what the excavator interpreted as a corn-drier, but which may in fact be a simple channelled hypocaust. The stoke-hole of this feature itself needed repair, before the whole structure was demolished. On the site was built a

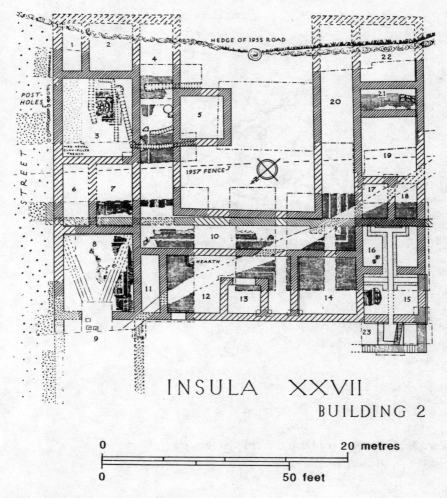

INSULA XXVII

BUILDING 2

Fig. 35 Verulamium Insula XXVII

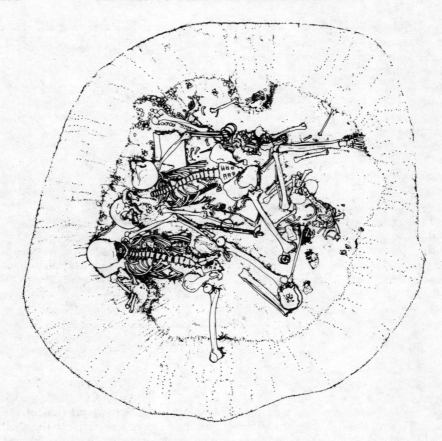

Fig. 36 Fifth-century burials from Canterbury

large, rectangular structure, interpreted as a barn, of which parts of two sides were recovered. After an unknown period in use this in turn was demolished, and a water pipeline laid across the site, consisting, in the Roman style, of hollowed-out trunks joined with iron collars. This site demonstrates neatly the sort of continuing stratigraphic sequence which must be encountered to posit use beyond the beginning of the fifth century. It also shows how different such a sequence is from what is generally encountered. It also points up the difficulties in dating. Only the earliest part of the sequence is likely to have been in place before the cessation of coin-supply, so everything thereafter — the later phases of the house, the barn and the pipeline — can only be said to be later than that. How much later is basically a matter of informed guesswork as to how long each element in the sequence would have remained in use. The excavator estimated that the sequence ran down to 475+. It should be noted that there are no new types of object in the middle and later part of the sequence, only the coins and pottery introduced by the end of the first decade of the fifth century which are residual in these later deposits. What does this sequence tell us about fifth-century Verulamium? The first thing is to remember that it is the only one of thirteen buildings to run this late; it is thus the exception and not the rule. After c. 420–30 there were no other inhabited buildings in its vicinity, and the urban economy and population of the town had departed. It is not, therefore, evidence for the continuation of a Roman-style urban way of life. It may have acted, as has been suggested,[65] as the centre of an agricultural estate. The survival of Roman hydraulic techniques to such a late date is wothy of note.

Canterbury has recently been the scene of a considerable number of important excavations, of which two concern us here. At the Marlowe IV site[66] in the south-eastern part of the walled area it was found that in the second half of the fourth century timber structures were inserted into the shell of an earlier building. Up to four phases of occupation had led to the accumulation of 1m. (3 feet) of deposit. This probably represents occupation on into the fifth century, but how far beyond the beginning of that century we cannot yet say. At 69a Stour Street[67] in the same area of the town a layer of earth formed over the latest Roman deposits, probably a form of the 'dark earth'. Into this was cut a pit (fig. 36); unfortunately we do not know from what level as its top had been removed by a later, mediaeval disturbance. The pit was found to contain the skeletons of one male and one female adult, two juveniles and two dogs. The female and the juveniles all had associated jewellery which has been tentatively dated to the first part of the fifth century. This group is significant, because Roman law forbade the burial of the dead within towns and this law had been scrupulously adhered to in the towns of Roman Britain, which is why all the great fourth-century cemeteries were extra-mural. Burial within the defences signified that Roman civic norms were no longer being adhered to at Canterbury. Again the majority of sites at Canterbury do not run this late, and the 'dark earth' and the Stour Street burial signify the abandonment both of the town and of its institutions and urban values.

Burials are the hallmark of the late evidence from Exeter and Lincoln, and at both these towns the burials came from the centre of civic power, the forum. At Exeter[68] the southern end of the forum-basilica was demolished in the early years of the fifth century and the site cleared. Where all that stone went and why is another problem. A quarry-pit, whose fill contained bronze-working débris, and a number of other, smaller pits were dug in the area before six inhumation graves were put in. These were on the alignment of the Roman buildings rather than that of the stratigraphically-later mid- to late-Saxon cemetery. Two burials yielded radiocarbon dates of 420±70 years and 490±80 years; a third centred in the eleventh century. Both by their stratigraphic position and two of the ^{14}C dates these seem to be late fifth or sixth century in date. How large the cemetery was overall we do not know; it may well have contained tens of burials. A case can be made that they are succeeded directly by the Saxon burials, which were associated with the minster church. If so then they may have been part of a Christian cemetery also. It may thus be possible to postulate more-or-less continuous activity on this site in the centre of Exeter, but the appearance of burials over the site of the forum equally suggests discontinuity of institutions and functions.

A similar situation seems to have obtained in the courtyard of the forum at Lincoln.[69] There in the seventh century was built the church later known as the church of St Paul-in-the-Bail. Earlier than this church and its associated burials there were other burials, and radiocarbon dates on some of these have yielded dates centring in the fifth century. It has even been postulated that there may have been a timber predecessor destroyed by the construction of the stone church. As at Exeter these burials show as much discontinuity in the way these sites were used as they show continuity of actual use.

The last site is Wroxeter (Pl. 10),[70] where Philip Barker's long, meticulous and brilliantly-conducted excavations have revealed a long sequence of late- to post-Roman use on the site of the baths-basilica. Sometime in the second half of the fourth century the roof, clerestorey and possibly the aisle colonnades were dismantled and, as at Exeter, cleared away. That the empty shell of the building continued to be used is shown by the patterns of wear on the floor and the construction of a small timber structure at the west end of the south aisle. This activity was associated with two coins of c. 375. Later the shell of the basilica was largely demolished to make way for a number of timber-framed buildings, some lesser timber structures and a street. The largest of these was to a Roman-derived plan. After an unknown period of use these buildings were dismantled and succeeded by two small structures. The final event on the site was the insertion of an inhumation burial into the now-abandoned area. A radiocarbon determination on this comes out at 610±60, which is a sort of *terminus ante quem* for the abandonment of the site. As with Verulamium Insula XXVII the problem is how long the various phases of occupation lasted. The latest dating evidence comes from the phase after the partial demolition of the basilica (two coins of the House of Valentinian); the final demolition of the basilica (two coins of c. 388–92); the construction of the timber buildings (a coin of 395–402). These of course can only give *termini post quos*; they could themselves be residual. But certainly the main timber building phase must be dated to the fifth century, though how far into that century the buildings remained in use is unknowable. There was then the one other, lesser, phase of timber structures. Also as at Verulamium, all the objects associated with this long sequence are of late Roman manufacture, and there is nothing identifiably of fifth-century post-Roman manufacture. The main phase of timber buildings is interpreted by the excavator as the residence and compound of a fifth-century notable.

These sites show, therefore, that on occasion occupation or use of sites within Roman towns continued into the mid- or later fifth-century. What is their general significance? The first thing to remember again is that they are a small minority, both of the sites dug within each town and in comparison with the total for all 'large' towns. They are therefore the exceptions and so should not be used to try to generate a rule of continuity into the fifth century at Romano-British towns. The evidence from the overwhelming majority of sites indicates abandonment early in the fifth century. This evidence is really reinforced by the exceptional sites, for what they consistently show is departure from the norms and practices of the fourth century. At Verulamium and Wroxeter the buildings can be argued to be the residences of fifth-century notables the basis of whose status was agriculture; at Wroxeter these private buildings had taken over the site of one of the public buildings of the Roman era. One even wonders whether they were farming the 'dark earth' of their towns (that this latter no longer survives in these cases can be attributed to mediaeval and modern ploughing). Other such sites will presumably be found at other towns, though the Wroxeter evidence is so finely-nuanced that at a town occupied in the mediaeval period it would have been largely destroyed by later activity, so these sites may be few and far between. The evidence from Canterbury, Exeter and Lincoln shows that though parts of the areas of Romano-British towns might have continued to be used, it was in ways utterly un-Roman. These late sites are often regarded as indicators of continuity from Roman Britain to Anglo-Saxon England (*cf.* p. 197), but they are in fact just as powerful symbols of a discontinuity.

It might be thought that the 'small' towns would have weathered the storm better, since they were essentially geared to the local economy and its needs, rather than being centres for the operations of the state or the landed classs in the way the 'large' towns were. The goods and services which they provided were those needed by the subsistence agricultural economy, and this was bound to continue, whatever the disruptions higher up the social and economic scale. In fact the evidence is that this was not the case and that the 'small' towns shared the fate of their 'large' cousins. The publications of a number of reports on modern excavations at Alcester,[71] Braintree,[72] Brampton,[73] Ilchester,[74] Kelvedon,[75] Neatham,[76] Scole[77] and Towcester[78] show that at these sites, walled and unwalled and with a wide geographical distribution, the tale was the same. The latest deposits, including abandonment deposits, were all associated with coins of the Houses of Valentinian or Theodosius, and after the introduction of the latest coin-types there was no significant addition to the stratigraphic sequence. Moreover, there has not yet been any long post-Theodosian sequence of the type we have just been considering for the 'large' towns found at any of the 'small' ones, though we shall consider the sequence from the temple courtyard at Bath below. The cemetery evidence for the 'small' towns is in general poor due to lack of excavation, but at Dorchester-on-Thames[79] the excavation of part of a large late Roman cemetery showed that its main phase of use ended in the early fifth century. At Ilchester[80] there is no evidence that burial in the extra-mural properties continued after the abandonment of the occupied areas. Nor is there any need for the latest burials at Kelvedon[81] to date far beyond the turn of the century. Again as at the 'large' towns there is no evidence for the manufacture or use of objects later than those of the end of the Roman sequence in the early fifth century, so even though the 'small' towns may have been more in tune with the needs of their hinterland, there is no evidence that they continued to serve that market. Nor is there anything detectable in the fifth-century rural archaeology that has a town-focused distribution. The evidence points to the 'small' towns going under as part of the same general collapse that overtook the 'large' towns.

At both 'large' and 'small' towns it was not just the structural and occupation sequence that came to an end in the first part of the fifth century, but also the artefactual. The artefact-type which is the most informative for this purpose, as for so many others, is pottery.[82] Earlier (p. 135) we saw that there were signs of stress in the Romano-British pottery industry of the late fourth century. The New Forest industry and that in the Nene Valley were apparently in decline, and the Oxfordshire industry had stagnated typologically and may have been having to make greater efforts to maintain or extend its market share. The fine-ware producers were very much geared to marketing through towns, as were many of the coarse-ware producers, though the latter also probably used other distribution networks independent of the towns. The demise of the towns should therefore sound the death-knell of the fine-ware producers, since the markets which made the economics of their large-scale production viable were gone. The smaller, coarse-ware industries might have been expected to cope better, since they were more localised and had few transport costs or problems. But the evidence for the small pottery industries as for the 'small' towns is that this was no help to them and that they too disappeared in the early fifth century. No production site has been found which can be dated after the end of the fourth century. Nor has late Roman pottery been found on sites used later in the fifth century in the quantities and fresh condition which suggest that it was still readily available. This is a crucial point, not only for the ending of the industry, but to confute the argument sometimes put forward that Roman pottery went on being made and used in the fifth century but that because of the problems of dating we consistently date its end too early. At sites such as Verulamium Insula XXVII and the Wroxeter baths-basilica the excavators are of the opinion that the pottery from the later levels was residual, as were the coins, so no new pottery was reaching the site. What is needed is quantification of the absolute amounts of pottery through these sequences, and of whether it was freshly-broken or abraded.

If it can be shown both that the amount of pottery declined and that increasingly it was long broken before getting into the ground that would be powerful evidence for it being residual. At none of the few identifiable fifth-century post-Roman sites discussed in the next chapter is there any argument that such Roman pottery as was present was other than residual. Crucially, the evidence from the Anglo-Saxon cemeteries and settlements of the mid- and later fifth-century is that Roman pottery was not available. There is little Roman material found at any of these, and it is as often as not earlier Roman rather than late,[83] suggesting that the Anglo-Saxons only had available that which happened to come to hand: that is to say, they did not have access to a still-functioning Romano-British pottery tradition. It might be argued that this lack of Roman material is a result of cultural aversion, and that therefore it tells us little or nothing about the state of the Roman industries. There are three vital pieces of evidence which tell against such an Anglo-Saxon attitude. The first is that provincial Roman artefacts are commonly found in Germanic graves of the fourth century within the empire, such as the *Waffengräber* of Gaul. Secondly, they are also commonly found (for instance the belt-suites) in graves in the Germanic homelands outside the lower Rhine. The third is that some Romano-British material is found on Anglo-Saxon settlement sites and in graves in Britain.[84] There was therefore no ethnic antipathy on the part of the Anglo-Saxons to goods of Roman manufacture. That these were so rare in Anglo-Saxon contexts, and were of a mixture of dates, can only suggest that the Anglo-Saxons were not in contact with a continuing Roman pottery industry, and that therefore that industry was already defunct by the time of the settlements. It is now generally agreed that the main episode of settlement started towards the middle of the fifth century, but even in the few cemeteries which can be dated earlier than that there was the same marked lack of Roman objects, so an end-date for the Roman industries early in the century seems likely.

Can we calibrate this any more precisely? Here the recent excavation and publication of the late Roman sequence in the precinct of the temple of Sulis Minerva at Bath is important (fig 37, Pl. 11).[85] Up to the mid-fourth century the paving of the precinct had been kept swept and garnished, but the paving was then covered by an accumulation of earth. Over this were six distinct levels of cobbling, each separated from the next by an accumulation of earth (the excavators' phases 5a–5f). Onto the top of this collapsed the masonry of the buildings around the precinct. This block of stratification was therefore sealed from below and above, minimising the problems of residual material from earlier phases, or disturbance of the deposits by later activity. This enhances the importance of an already interesting sequence. The pottery and a coin of Constans (347–8) agree in placing the earliest (5a) cobbling at about 350. The third level of cobbles (5c) sealed a coin of the House of Theodosius (388–402), and the pottery associated with it is of late-fourth century type. The coins of course only provide a *terminus post quem*, but the dating of the pottery is suggestive of their being lost not long after issue. There remain three phases of cobbles, each of them worn by the passage of feet. Again we have a sequence developing after the introduction of the latest coins. Because the significance of the deposits for late Roman problems was realised, a detailed study and quantification of the pottery was undertaken. Even after

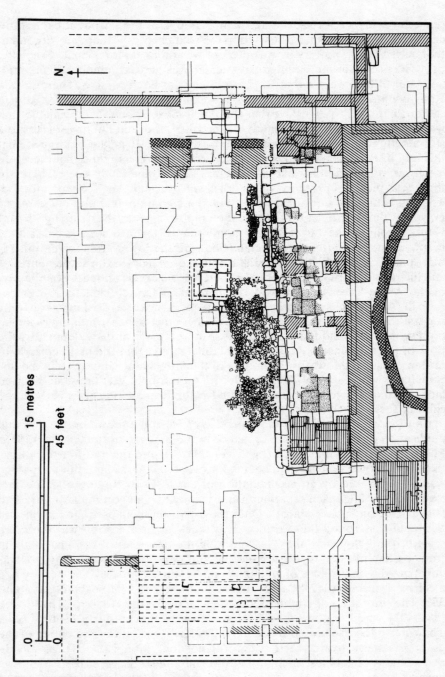

Fig. 37 The Bath temple precinct

phase 5c there was change in the proportions of pottery from the different sources, suggesting continued pottery supply. Phase 5e saw the appearance of types characteristic of a very late deposit at Dorchester (Dorset). Phase 5f, the final cobbling, was interesting because there was less pottery from it than from the earlier phases. This may mean that pottery was no longer readily available. The pottery experts opt for a compressed chronology, placing 5e at the end of the fourth century. The excavators opt for an open-ended, potentially very long, chronology, even down to as late as the sixth century, despite the violence this would do to the generally-accepted dating of late Roman pottery and its cessation. The pottery experts seem to be over-compressing the sequence, especially having regard to the coin of the House of Theodosius in 5c, which makes it very implausible that 5d and 5e could have been fitted in before the end of the fourth century. But if the late forms in 5e could be dated to the early fifth century, then it is possible to see the whole sequence ending comfortably within the first half, possibly the first third, of that century, with the pottery perhaps already being no longer supplied by the time of 5f. This would reinforce what we have suggested elsewhere as a terminal date for the recognisably Roman archaeological sequence in Britain, c. 430.

This discussion has focused on pottery because of its ubiquity and the amount of attention that it has been given over the years. But it is worth saying that there is no evidence from other classes of Romano-British material, such as metalwork, for their continuing any later than the pottery. Given that the technology of pottery manufacture of the type current in Roman Britain was not particularly complex, and given that pottery had been commonplace in the island through the Roman period, one might have expected that even if the fine-ware industries disappeared, more localised production of utilitarian pottery could well have continued. This is a not unreasonable hypothesis, and it is somewhat surprising, therefore, to find that the excavated evidence all points to a total cessation of pottery manufacture at all levels. This is a further vivid testament to the completeness of the breakdown of the Roman system in Britain. Indeed it suggests that that breakdown was more profound than one might have expected for the industries and their technologies did not revert, as might have been expected, to a pre-Roman level, but collapsed almost to nothing. The effects of this on those engaged in manufacture and trade and on the towns can only have been dire, adding to the other problems deriving from the ending of the Roman economic regime.

This consideration of the ending of Roman Britain has concentrated so far on the towns and town-related material. This is justifiable in the terms of this book because what we are seeking to define and explain is the passing of what was Roman about Roman Britain, and we have established that the town was the pivotal settlement in the dissemination of a romanised economy, society and culture. Thus the disappearance of towns was critical in the whole process. However, it is now time to pass in (fairly brief) review the evidence for what happened to the rural settlement types and patterns. Of course the same problems of dating apply in the country as in the towns. The most characteristically romanised rural settlement type was the villa. We saw earlier in the chapter (p. 134) that, as with the towns, there was evidence for a decline both quantitatively and qualitatively in the villas before the end of the fourth century. The evidence from the villas still parallels that for the towns in the early part of the fifth century. There is evidence from site after site of abandonment of the villa buildings in the early part of the fifth century, soon, in stratigraphic terms, after the introduction of the latest coins and pottery. In terms of the general process of decline and fall this need not surprise us. The villa was dependent on the town both as a place to dispose of its surplus and as a place in which the specialists necessary for the construction and main-tenance of the buildings, such as masons and mosaicists, were based. Thus when the towns failed, the economic and skill base for the continuance of the villa system was fatally compromised. At only a handful of villas such as Frocester (Gloucestershire)[86] or Thenford (Northamptonshire)[87] is there evidence for post-villa-building activity, and there is no evidence that that lasted long into the fifth century. But the disappearance of the villa buildings need not entail the disappearance of the villa estate. It is possible that the social and tenurial structures of the estate continued.

Overall, there is little evidence that the fifth century saw a significant decline in the global amount of land under cultivation in Britain. There would still have been a large population, descended from that of the late Roman period, and it would still have been reproducing itself and requiring to be fed, clothed and housed. The pollen evidence suggests that there was no great decline in the amount of cleared land overall during the fifth century. What probably changed were the uses to which that land was put. Some of the areas of more marginal land which were worked in the Roman period were allowed to revert, probably to grassland. The evidence from the detailed study of the upper Thames valley[88] is that immediately after the end of the Roman period settlement and land-use changed their pattern, with such settlement as can be detected reverting to the favoured land of the second-terrace gravels; the first-terrace gravels and the alluvium no longer being so intensively exploited and reverted to pasture. Thus the ending of the Roman system of things would seem to have had a two-fold effect. On the one hand there was a redefinition of the agricultural strategies in order to adjust to the (undoubtedly welcome) removal of the tax burden and in order to supply what was now needed. The second was the disappearance of the most obviously romanised features of the settlement pattern and hierarchy, principally the villas. The demise both of the vllas and of the towns must have meant that the residue of population from both classes of site must now have joined the general rural population.

But we have established that the majority of the rural population in Roman Britain never lived in villas anyway, but in the farmsteads. What can we say happened to them? The first thing is that we have precisely the same problems of dating as with all the other classes of site, indeed it is worse since Roman artefacts had never been common at such sites in the first place. If it was possible for a site such as the Wroxeter baths basilica to continue in occupation without any detectable new artefact types, then the same is most certainly true of a farmstead in the middle of nowhere. As yet we do not have a stratigraphic sequence from a farmstead comparable with that from a Wroxeter, but one may yet be excavated. There is some evidence from some farmsteads in the north[89] that occupation continued uninterrupted into the fifth century. Similarly, some sites in the south such as Bradley Hill (Somerset),[90] seem to have continued for a time after the introduction of the latest Roman artefacts. At Bradley Hill one component of the site was the cemetery. As we shall see in the next chapter, settlements founded in the fifth century are a great rarity, but there are some cemeteries which may derive from the late Roman period. If this was so and the locations of some cemeteries were not shifting, then the settlements also presumably remained in use.

Attention is increasingly being drawn to the persistence of features in the landscape, particularly fields, in such areas as East Anglia.[91] The field is a very basic unit of land-division and resource-definition, and it is at this level that continuity of land-use must be visible for us to be able to posit such continuity. The evidence that landscapes of Roman or pre-Roman origins were indeed perpetuated into the post-mediaeval period must mean that in the fifth century there were still people living there and tilling the ground and raising their herds within the physical framework of their ancestral landscape. The evidence is disparate and difficult, but we cannot doubt that the less romanised classes of rural society carried on through the ending of Roman Britain. In many ways the difficulties of locating and defining the fifth-century pattern of settlement in Britain is reminiscent of the problems with the rural settlement pattern in fourth-century Gaul. The people of Britain in the mid-fifth century will have gained from the removal of the Roman taxation system, and the demise of the industries producing pottery and other utensils may have seemed a fair price to pay. But as we saw in Chapter 3 (p. 114) the relationships between these people and the romanised élite was not purely utilitarian, and the removal of many romanised institutions will have affected their lives also.

If we step back from consideration of Britain in isolation, how does what we have been considering compare with the broader picture in Gaul and elsewhere? The first thing to say is that the ending of Roman Britain is entirely comprehensible within the framework of the ending of the western empire. The processes which led to it were processes operating within the late Roman state in the west and which affected other areas of the west. Britain seems to have suffered earlier and more completely the dissolution of the western empire than did her neighbours. Even within Gaul there was an observable gradient, with the northern parts suffering more profoundly, and the south and south-west suffering little by comparison. In part this was a measure of the empire's varying ability to control events in the different regions in Gaul. In part this was a measure of the ability of the Germanic successor-states to perpetuate or mimic the Roman system. The Franks in the north were not very able, the Visigoths in the south were better, as were the Vandals in north Africa. The acme was of course the Ostrogothic kingdom in Italy.

We may also see a similar division to that we saw at the end of the last chapter in our comparison of fourth-century Britain and Gaul (p. 128), between the fate of the structures of the state and that of more local formations. After the barbarian invasions of 407 and the suppression of Constantine III in 411 the north seems to have fallen out of Roman control in much the same way as did Britain. When the patrician Constantius summoned a council of the Gallic provinces at Arles in 418 the north was absent. It seems already to have been beyond effective Roman control. This may be one reason why the Frankish kingdom perpetuated Roman state institutions less than, for instance, the Visigoths; there was less there for it to perpetuate. In Britain the situation for the Anglo-Saxons was to be even worse (*cf.* p. 200).

On the other hand there is evidence for a continuation of Gallo-Roman families and Gallo-Roman ways into the period of Germanic rule. In the north this is more difficult to demonstrate, but there is for instance the Life of Remigius, bishop of Reims at the end of the fifth century, who owned and managed family estates in an entirely Gallo-Roman manner. Or there are the accounts of the various sacks of Trier during the fifth century. That it continued to be worth sacking suggests that there was still life and some wealth within the walls of the great city. On the material side there was a steep decline in the quantity and quality of artefacts, but not the stage of virtual extinction that we see in Britain. In both the state and local aspects Britain is comparable with the neighbouring areas of the Continent, but declined from Roman ways in both aspects early, sharply and totally.

By setting Britain in the context of the end of the western empire we may pick up and develop two of the themes outlined in Chapters 1 and 2 (pp. 8, 28). The first is the growing regionalisation of the economy in the fourth-century empire. Whilst overall political control and cultural and social unity were maintained by the empire this was no great matter. But when that unity could no longer be maintained, then the basic regionalisms of the west would assert themselves, and different areas would follow different trajectories according to their particular circumstances. The second theme is what caused the breakdown in that unity. We noted that in the fourth century the ability to pay tax, the ability to levy tax and the security provided by the army (on which the bulk of the tax was spent) were in rough equilibrium. But any disturbance would jeopardise the entire system. This was precisely what happened in the west from the first decade of the fifth century on. North of the Alps the events of 407 saw huge areas fall away from Roman control, which diminished the tax and manpower base of the state in those areas. At the same time the central authorities were preoccupied with the ravages of the Goths in Italy, and were temporarily unable to re-assert control in Gaul. By the time this became more possible under the patrician Constantius the damage was done. The north was effectively lost. In the centre and the south-west accommodations had to be reached with the Burgundiones and the Visigoths, who came to form politically and fiscally autonomous kingdoms, even if owing nominal allegiance to the western Augustus. Spain, Italy and north Africa were also dominated by Germanic peoples, all of whom deprived the Roman state of yet more resources. In 445 the western emperor

Valentinian III acknowledged that the tax-payers still within his power could no longer sustain ever-rising land taxes. Yet these taxes were needed to maintain the army both for external security and to levy the taxes ... It had become a self-fulfilling cycle of decline. The story of the passing of the west from Roman control is as much the story of Rome's increasing inability to reimpose her authority as it is of the seizure of control by the barbarians.

In conclusion, then, it has been argued in this chapter that the reasons for the disappearance of the Roman elements of Roman Britain lay within the general framework of the decline of the west; they had little or nothing to do with Anglo-Saxons. Specifically, in the aftermath of the suppression of Constantine III the central authorities could not or did not reimpose the structures of the state in Britain. In particular the disappearance of the taxation cycle came as a blow which an already-weakened economy could not withstand. The generality of the archaeological evidence points to a sudden and total collapse of the romanised way of life in the island in the generation or so after 411. In that time the towns, the villas, the industries and the other material evidence diagnostic of Roman Britain disappeared. There was no slow drawing-down of blinds: the end was nasty, brutish and short.

FIVE

Britons in the Fifth Century

The Roman government of and way of life in Britain were gone. Yet there remained a population descended from the inhabitants of Roman Britain and living in the lands of the erstwhile diocese. Even after the inception of the main phase of Anglo-Saxon migration in the middle of the fifth century they remained numerically the overwhelming majority and in control of most of the richest land of the island down into the sixth century. They therefore constituted a distinct entity and episode in the development of post-Roman Britain. They did not live according to the economic and social order of the defunct diocese, but neither did they live according to that of the Anglo-Saxons. It was with them rather than with late Roman Britain that the Anglo-Saxons interacted. Their history and archaeology are therefore of the greatest interest, both of their own sake and for what they mean for the study of the transition from Roman Britain to Anglo-Saxon England.

The archaeological evidence for these people is nugatory, both in absolute terms and relative to the historical sources. This has emphasised the importance of the documents at the expense of other sources, and has meant that the study of the fifth century has been one largely conducted by the minute examination of the texts. Out of this can be built a framework of events for the period from the suppression of Constantine III to the assumption of suzerainty over England by the Anglo-Saxons. It is this history that we must first recount and whose sources we must criticise, before returning to pick up the thread of the archaeological evidence.

In 429 worry about the spread of the Pelagian heresy in the heresiarch's homeland led the Church in Britain to appeal for help. At the instigation of Pope Celestine, the Church in Gaul sent Germanus, bishop of Auxerre, and Lupus, bishop of Troyes, to Britain to combat the heresy. After landing they met the Pelagian party who were *veste fulgentes* (showily dressed) and trounced them in theological debate. They then visited the shrine of Alban, presumably at Verulamium, where they healed the daughter of a *vir tribuniciae potestatis* (a man of the authority of tribune). Later, hearing that there was a threat from the Saxons they assembled a force of raw recruits, and having baptised them, won a victory over the Saxons by the simple expedient of shouting 'Alleluia' at them. They then returned to Gaul. This story apparently reveals the existence of a persisting wealthy class with the time to debate theological niceties. The visit to the shrine of Alban fell well within the timespan of the Verulamium Insula XXVII sequence, and there was a man whose titulature recalled that of the Roman period. This has been seen as evidence for the continuance of a Roman-style society, even if threatened by the Anglo-Saxons. Further ecclesiastical links across the Channel are suggested by the training in Gaul of Patrick for his mission to Ireland, and by the adoption by the Church in Britain of a change in the method of calculating the date of Easter promulgated by Pope Leo in 453. There is an account of a second visit to Britain by Germanus, in company with bishop Severus of Trier. This is conventionally dated to the 440s, but Germanus was probably already dead by then, so if it occurred it must have been earlier.[1]

In the 440s the Saxon storm broke. We are told that in 441 Britain which had been subjected to various disasters, fell under the control of the Saxons. In 446 the Britons appealed to the *magister militum* Aetius, the last effective Roman commander in Gaul: 'To Aetius, thrice consul, the groans of the Britons ... The barbarians drive us to the sea and the sea drives us back to the barbarians. Between these two types of death we are either slaughtered or drowned.' 449 is the year given by the Venerable Bede for the *adventus Saxonum*, the Coming of the Saxons. Though the process must have varied from area to area, the story of Vortigern, Hengest and Horsa is seen as probably representing a version of what happened. In this reading Vortigern was a sub-Roman potentate. To protect his realm from Anglo-Saxon incursions he invited in Hengest and Horsa and their warriors as a sort of *foederatus* force. Eventually they revolted against him and set up their own rule in Kent, defeating the Britons at the battles of *Aegelsthrep* (Aylesford) in 455 and *Crecganford* (Crayford) in 456, after which the Britons fell back on London. The account by the British author Gildas of a revolt of the federate Saxons added weight to this. 477 saw the arrival of Aelle who was to found the Saxon kingdom of Sussex. In 491 he defeated the Britons at *Andredesceaster* (*Anderida* – Pevensey Saxon Shore fort). Four years later Cerdic and Cynric, the founders of Wessex, landed.[2]

The Britons fought back, and their greatest successes came at the end of the fifth century under the leadership of Ambrosius Aurelianus, 'the last of the Romans'. This culminated in the battle of Mount Badon at which the Anglo-Saxons were comprehensively defeated and a generation of peace ensued. Other sources associate this battle with the figure of Arthur. King Arthur and the knights of the Round Table of course came to form the subject of the 'Matter of Britain', the cycle of heroic tales which flowered in England in the centuries of chivalry. But these earlier, unadorned references to Arthur led to the suggestion fifty years ago[3] that there was indeed a 'historical Arthur'. It was suggested that the tale of Arthur and his twelve battles (ending with Badon) and of the knights, were based on the remembrance of a sub-Roman war-leader who had fought the Saxons using heavy mailed cavalry in the late Roman style (*catafractarii*) against their infantry.

But around the middle of the sixth century the Anglo-Saxons were once more on the move, this time under the leadership of the new kingdom of Wessex under its warlike king, Ceawlin. In 552 the Britons were defeated at *Searoburh* (Old Sarum, Wiltshire), in 556 at *Beranburh* (Barbury hillfort, Wiltshire), in 571 at *Bedcanford* (in Bedfordshire), and in 577 at *Deorham* (Dyrham, near Bath) when the Anglo-Saxons reached the Bristol Channel, dividing the Britons of the south-western peninsula from those in Wales. At *Deorham* three princes of the Britons, Condidan (a derivative of Constantine), Coinmail and Farinmail were slain, and the towns of Bath, Gloucester and Cirencester fell to the Anglo-Saxons. Only twenty years later the harbinger of the new Roman conquest, St Augustine, landed in Thanet near the landing-place of Claudius' conquest of 43. But by then Anglo-Saxon England was rapidly crystallising out of the migration period, and in 610 the battle of Chester penned the Britons back into Wales and the north.

This, in bare outline, is the historical framework which can be constructed for the period which saw the change from Roman to English rule in eastern Britain. There are many other events and names which there was not room for here and which provide endless scope for discussion. Both in general terms and in particular details it provides a not implausible sequence of events. There is, of course, much scope for argument over particular events and their significance; nevertheless, taken as a whole it is a coherent narrative with all the comfort of names, dates, motives and circumstantial detail. This narrative has long held sway, partly because it was constructed before there was a discipline of archaeology, and partly because to scholars with a classical or historical training the written word took precedence. In this they were aided and abetted by practitioners of the emerging discipline of archaeology, who needed the historical dates to apply to the material they recovered. For instance if the area of Wiltshire was recorded as having fallen to Ceawlin in the 550s, then the Anglo-Saxon burials known from that county should not pre-date the mid sixth century. This gave a chronological horizon to the artefact-types from those graves. But this approach is now changing. Partly this is because the recovery of more archaeological data and their ordering according to archaeological principles is less and less concerned with histori-cal questions, which archaeology is usually not good at answering (*cf.* p. 45). But more especially it is because of the recent work of a number of historians who have been critically re-examining the nature of the evidence on which the narrative is founded.

The traditional narrative is a synthesis. It is a synthesis achieved by taking more-or-less at face value a number of statements from a variety of disparate sources. It takes them out of context — that is, out of the context of the work in which they are contained, and that work out of the context of the society in which, and the purpose for which, it was written. It then constructs a historical narrative, but many of the sources concerned were not attempting to write what we would regard as objective history. We must examine not only what was written but also who wrote it and why. What was the purpose of composing the work? At whom was it directed? How did the writer view his world? How did he view the past? How and why was he trying to relate the past to the present? What was the literary format of the work, and what constraints did that impose? It is now time to put the individual elements that make up the history of the fifth century back into context and see how this affects our view of their credibility.

We are dealing essentially with three groups of sources. The first is those authors working in a late-Antique style, historical or hagiographical, who were often near-contemporaries of what they describe, but were writing outside Britain. The second group comprises the two authors of British origin writing in the fifth and early sixth centuries. The third is those insular sources, both Celtic and Saxon, who write purporting to describe the events of the fifth century, but who themselves were of considerably later date.

Amongst the first group were Orosius and Zosimus, whom we have already discussed (p. 137), and whose work relates to the career of Constantine III. The statement that in 441 Britain fell under the control of the Saxons comes from the Gallic Chronicle of 452, which we have also already encountered (p. 138). This event took place only some eleven years before the Chronicle was set down, so presumably the reference is a reflection of some sort of reality. The question is whether a chronicler operating in Provence could have known enough about events in Britain for this statement to be taken at face value. The evidence for the actual presence of Anglo-Saxons in the island at the time suggests that it should not. The most substantial Continental source for the events in Britain after 411 is the narrative of the visits to Britain by St Germanus of Auxerre. The visits of Germanus have been received particularly kindly by scholars for the light they shed amid the encircling gloom of the early fifth century. The accounts occur in the *Vita* (Life) of the saint written by Constantius of Lyon.[4] Because of the desperate shortage of other evidence for Britain at the time, the accounts of the visits have been subject to particularly insular examination, divorced from the longer work of which they are a small part. The first point to make is that a *Vita*, following in the footsteps of Sulpicius Severus' *Vita* of Martin of Tours, was a work of hagiography as much as of biography. Its concern was to promote spiritual edification and moral improvement in the reader. It was therefore not necessarily overmuch concerned with details of birth, upbringing and adult life. Those taking the *Vita* as they would a modern biography are deluding themselves. The second point is that Constantius of Lyon was writing in central or southern Gaul, probably in the decade 480–90. Germanus probably died in 437, so Constantius cannot have got a first-hand account from the bishop himself. He could conceivably have met Germanus' collaborators, such as Severus of Trier, but by then they would have been extremely old men asked to recall the events of up to sixty years previously. In all likelihood, therefore, Constantius will have had to get his material from secondary oral and documentary sources. That he did so conscientiously is evident from the accuracy of the detail in much of the *Vita* where we can check it against other sources. But equally there are gaps, not because of the demands of hagiography but simply because he did not have the evidence. The principal gap is the account of Germanus' career, secular as well as ecclesiastical, before 429. Presumably Constantius could not find any information at the time he was writing.

The same lack of specificity prevails in his accounts of the saint's two visits to Britain, for the second even more than the first.[5] When Constantius is describing Germanus' later career on the continent, the range of geographical, chronological and personal detail is wide and accurate. The visits to Britain stand in stark contrast to this. There is not a single place-name given;

the best we have is the visit to the shrine of Alban, presumably at Verulamium. His great set-piece victories over the enemies of the true faith and of the Britons are not given locations. The chronology of the events of the visits is non-existent. In terms of what else we know about fifth-century Britain the mention of a *vir tribuniciae potestatis* may look like a model of clarity and informativeness. But for 'a man who can tell us that forty or fifty years ago Volusianus held the post of *cancellarius* to the Master of the Soldiers Sigisvult ... a man who did not shrink from laborious historical research' it is in fact the superficial precision that masks ignorance. Constantius simply did not know and could not find out about conditions in early fifth-century Britain, and cannot therefore be used as a reliable witness of what conditions were like in the island in the first half of the fifth century. He may have reflected the situation of Britain in his own day in his treatment of the Saxons, and of his own milieu in the appearance of a wealthy class. That the first visit at least did occur we cannot doubt; we have the independent testimony of Prosper of Aquitaine.[6] That the debate with the Pelagians and the visit to the shrine of Alban took place it would be captious to doubt. But much of the surrounding detail must lie under suspicion of being intended to add artistic verisimilitude to an otherwise bald and unconvincing narrative. The 'Alleluia' victory is clearly hagiographical rather than biographical, as are the healing miracles common to the accounts of both visits.[7] The *Vita* therefore is a source to be treated on its own terms, not as straight 'history', especially in the sections touching on Britain. To accept it as a historical source would be to be as credulous of its historical passages as the men of the Middle Ages were of its hagiographical ones.

Our two British sources of the fifth and sixth centuries differ widely in their relevance to the island at the time. After his capture by the Irish raiders Patrick never revisited his native land, and it scarcely figures in his writings except for mention of the Church in Britain. Our other source, Gildas, is very different both in the amount of information he gives us and the centrality of that information to the traditional historical framework. To him we own an apparently chronological narrative of events in Roman Britain and in the fifth century which includes the federate revolt, the appeal to Aetius, Ambrosius Aurelianus, Mount Badon and the peace that followed that battle, with other material besides. All these are to be found in the 'historical' section of Gildas' great work the *De Excidio et Conquestu Britanniae* — On the Ruin and Conquest of Britain. Gildas was a cleric, probably from northern Britain and probably writing in south Wales. The conventional date for the *De Excidio* is c. 540. Therefore the events of the sixth century and the second half of the fifth fell within the memories of Gildas himself, his father and grandfather and their contemporaries. That we should have a (near-) contemporary witness to the events of the fifth century is all that could be wished for: from Bede onwards historians of the period have turned to Gildas.

But was Gildas actually writing history? No: and this has long been recognised. So what was he writing, for whom and why? The *De Excidio* is a tract for the times. It is a work of polemic excoriating the kings and ecclesiastics of Gildas' day for their manifold sins and imperfections and threatening them with the imminence of divine retribution should they not mend their ways. This purpose and message condition the overall structure of the work and the choice of what was included and what was excluded. Most of the *De Excidio* consists of two long passages (§27–65, §66–110) inveighing angrily against the wickedness of the kings and ecclesiastics respectively of Gildas' own time, with a wealth of biblical example and patristic authority. So how does the long 'historical' prologue (§2–26) fit into the literary and minatory structure of the work? The answer is simply that it is there as an awful warning. It shows how Britain had been brought to the plight it was in as the direct consequence of past sinfulness. For this divine retribution had been visited on the Britons, particularly through the agency of the Saxons. If the rulers of Church and state of Gildas' day did not repent of their evil ways, further divine justice would be meted out to them at the hands of the 'impious easterners'. Gildas' concern, therefore, was not to write an accurate chronological narrative of the past, but to use a series of events in the past to point up the moral for the present.

Another problem about Gildas' 'historical' section which has long been recognised is that where it can be checked against other sources it can be shown to contain errors. The classic case of this is where he ascribes Hadrian's Wall and the Antonine Wall, early and mid-second-century respectively, to the late fourth century, making the Antonine Wall the earlier of the two. There are also accounts of military expeditions from Rome in the late fourth or early fifth century which only considerable ingenuity can reconcile with the known late military history of the diocese. And not only is there the problem of error in that which is included, there is also the problem of exclusion. The usurpation by Magnus Maximus figures, but that by Constantine III is totally ignored. Yet Gildas' late-Antique sources such as Orosius will have told him about Constantine III. Clearly Gildas did not see him as useful in furthering the argument of the *De Excidio*, so he was ignored. How much else was similarly ignored?

Allied to these problems are those of the sources Gildas had with which to work. He clearly had access to a number of late Antique writers down to the early fifth century (for instance, Orosius). But for events of the mid- and later fifth century he seems to have run out of written sources. For example, he makes no mention of Germanus of Auxerre, though such a tale of Orthodox virtue triumphing over Pelagian and Saxon impiousness would, one feels, have been grist to his mill. Only in the appeal to Aetius (the Groans of the Britons) do we appear to have a direct quote from a written source. But that passage stands in sharp stylistic contrast to the rest of the narrative. For most of the events of c. 440–500 it is now thought that Gildas was relying on oral tradition which, unfortunately, is not necessarily a trustworthy source. Add to this the chronological vagueness — the only reconstructable dates are 388 for the death of Magnus Maximus, 446 or later for Aetius in his third consulship and c. 540 for the composition of the *De Excidio* if the Maglocunus addressed in it is to be identified with Maelgwn of Gwynedd[8] — and the difficulties compound themselves.

The conclusion must surely be that Gildas is not a reliable source for the events of the fifth century. His concern was to sketch agencies — Picts, Saxons, plague, sin — which had brought about the ruin of Britain; it was not to write what we would call history. As with Constantius of Lyon, some of what he relates must have happened, in particular important events near his own day such as Badon. But the rest lacks independent verification. And it needs that verification because the nature and purpose of the *De Excidio* are not concerned with historical accuracy. Episodes in the work may be used to complement or illustrate a narrative of the fifth century derived from other sources, but the *De Excidio* should not be used to devise a set structure for the fifth century into which the other evidence must fit.

To turn to the later insular sources, Celtic and Saxon. The principal later Celtic source is the work usually known as the *Historia Brittonum* and attributed to one Nennius writing somewhere around 800. Much of the work consists of passages which, save that they lack the introduction 'once upon a time', have all the historical reliability of fairy-stories. There are also some short passages derived from reputable earlier authors. A good example of both is in Nennius' treatment of St Germanus. When the narrative opens it is based on Constantius of Lyon, but it soon turns into a tale which the brothers Grimm would have thought fantastical. The problem lies in the facts and events which lie between these two poles. In his Preface to the *Historia* Nennius states '*coacervavi omne quod inveni*' — 'I have made a heap of everything I have found'. Most historians have taken this to be an accurate description of Nennius' historical method, and have thus argued that Nennius must preserve some gobbets of information on the fifth and sixth centuries. The problem is that an objective method of sorting the wheat from the chaff has never been forthcoming; you pays your money and you takes your choice of what commends itself to you at the time. Recent research[9] has shown that in fact Nennius was trying to write to a well-known, early mediaeval literary format; a synchronising history. This is a history which tries to reconcile a number of sources to produce, as it were, parallel chronological columns. The result in Nennius' case happen to be bizarre, but the intention was there. But the exposition of the sources Nennius used led to the conclusion 'I trust that the mere recital of these sources will suggest their utter flimsiness as records of this obscure century of our history'.[10] With Nennius fall amongst other things, Arthur, his twelve battles and his presence at Badon. Arthur, in fact, seems to be essentially a creation of later (eighth/ninth century on) Celtic literature and lore. He does not appear in Gildas. The earliest mention of him is in the *Gododdin*, a poem which describes events of the late sixth century, though probably not written down until much later. In it the warrior Gwawrddur is commended for his prowess 'though he was not Arthur'. This seems a curiously sideways means of first meeting such a notable figure. In fact the *Gododdin* as it stands is much later than the events it describes and it is perfectly possible that the comparison with Arthur was interpolated at a time when the Arthur myth was already influential. The same applies to other Welsh sources which mention Arthur; they are all much later than the late fifth century and date from a time at which Arthur was already an important figure in Welsh lore and genealogy. They must therefore all stand under suspicion of reflecting the situation of the time at which they were written and not of the fifth century. Though we can never disprove the existence of a historical Arthur, we have no evidence for him.

Included in the same manuscript (BL Harleian 3859) as the *Historia Brittonum* are the *Annales Cambriae* and a set of Welsh genealogies. The *Annales* are a set of tables for determining the date of Easter over long periods. They take the form of columns, and in due course historical memorabilia were added in the generous margins. These records include the dates of battles, those of the births and deaths of rulers and saints, and other items of interest to the compilers. The latest entry is the record of the death of Rhodri ap Hywel Dda in the 950s, but the basic compilation seems to have occured at St David's from the late eighth century on.[11] Like Nennius, therefore, the *Annales* are long distant in time from the fifth century, for which there are nonetheless entries. They include two for Arthur; his presence at Badon (518) and his and Medraut's death at the battle of Camlann (539). Whence were these data derived? We do not know, and though the records for the later centuries seem reliable it is still not possible to accept the fifth-century and Arthurian entries uncritically, especially the latter given what we know of the special place of Arthur in the society in which the *Annales* were written down. Nor are the Arthurian entries the only ones for the fifth century in the *Annales* which are suspect.

Genealogies and king-lists have been much used by those lacking more precise historical records, particularly as a means of dating. The list usually begins or ends with the ruler alive at the time of compilation, and he can often be independently dated. By allotting a nominal span of years to the previous rulers one can have a retrospective chronology, at least for as far as the rulers were human rather than mythical or semi-divine. Thus the reigns of earlier rulers and any events associated with them may be (roughly) dated. The basic assumption, of course, is that the genealogy or king-list is an accurate document compiled with bardic precision: this is naive. First of all there are the problems inherent in compilation; back beyond the stage of about great-grandfather one is passing out of reliable human memory of actual persons and is thus dependent on pre-existing lists which may or may not be accurate. Second, and far more important, is the question of the functions such genealogies served and how these affected their compilation. Lists of descent are a widespread human phenomenon, and study of them in better-documented societies allows us to assess their place in Celtic and Anglo-Saxon society.[12] They are essentially a means of validating claims either to status or to possessions (generally territory). That claim is being made by the ruler alive at the time of compilation and thus the genealogy will be structured so as to show that claim in the best light. In terms of status this means linking the ruler through to the founder of the line or dynasty and any other important figures in the descent from whom the authority derives. This may not always be scrupulously truthful and may demonstrate a need to link back to an acceptable progenitor. For instance the Anglo-Saxon dynasties are headed by the Gods Woden and Saexneat, and some of the Welsh pedigrees are headed by the unlikely figure of Magnus Maximus.[13] This tells us about the concerns of the compilers, not about the actual ancestry of the English and Welsh rulers. Political power went hand-in-hand with territorial; thus one may find 'ancestors' who give substance to a territorial claim. For instance, the dynasty of Wessex was founded by two men, Cerdic and Cynric, with British not English names. Is this an attempt by an Anglo-Saxon dynasty to legitimise its rule over formerly British lands? Given the ulterior motives behind the compilation of these genealogies it is not at all surprising to learn that they can be heavily manipulated, for instance by the omission of 'bad' or inconvenient rulers, by the suppression of periods of external domination, by the inclusion of prestigious names or simply by lengthening to fill out the list back to the founder. Genealogies are thus fascinating sources for the politics of the kingdoms and times that produced them, but not for the accurate history of the fifth and earlier sixth centuries in Britain.

The Anglo-Saxon sources are similarly problematical. The earliest is the Venerable Bede, writing his *Historia Ecclesiastica Gentis Anglorum* (Ecclesiastical History of the English People) in the years up to 731. Despite the title, Bede was too good an historian to deal with ecclesiastical history divorced from the society within which it took place. He was also, to the best of his ability, an objective historian with a marked concern for chronology. In his Preface he tells us that for the period from the Conversion of the English he consulted learned clerks all over England. But for the period before 597 'I have obtained my material from here and there, chiefly from the writings of earlier writers' (§5). When we look at Bede's account of the fifth century we see that it is almost entirely taken from Constantius of Lyon and Gildas, the latter a peculiarly jaundiced source for the early history of the Anglo-Saxon settlement. To what he culled from these two writers he added the accession-date of Ida of Northumbria (547) and a list of seven kings of Sussex. He also gives the famous passage retailing the continental origins of the Angles, the Saxons and the Jutes, and the date of 449 for the *adventus Saxonum*. But remove the contributions of Constantius of Lyon and Gildas, whom we have already considered, and Bede ceases to be an important source for the history of the fifth century. It is interesting that, bar Constantius and Gildas, so diligent a worker could not lay his hands on any Anglo-Saxon or other source for the period.

The last major source is the *Anglo-Saxon Chronicle*, a document first set down in the reign of Alfred of Wessex at the end of the ninth century, though incorporating material from late-Antique sources, from ecclesiastical records, from Bede and from existing middle- and later- Saxon annals of which the earliest appears to be mid-seventh-century in date.[14] The *Chronicle* is the source for most of the history of the origins and expansion of the Anglo-Saxon kingdoms of southern Britain, yet all these occur in the years for which we do not know what the *Chronicle's* sources were. We have seen that Bede could find no Anglo-Saxon source for the period. This is perhaps not surprising since until the setting-up of the Christian Church in their land the Anglo-Saxons were to all intents and purposes illiterate. Some of their artefacts may bear runic inscriptions, but there is no evidence that they had the desire or the ability to keep any sort of records. This must mean that for the fifth- and early sixth-century entries the compilers of the *Chronicle* depended on oral tradition and the accumulated legends purveyed by the praise-tellers of the royal houses. As we shall see there is good evidence that myth and legend formed an important part, and that is not good evidence for history. It has long been recognised that the *Chronicle* is geographically heavily biased. Apart from the Bedan date of 547 for Ida of Northumbria, it is solely concerned with the kingdoms of Kent, Sussex and Wessex. This is none too surprising considering that it is a product of late ninth-century Wessex, but it does severely limit its usefulness. For the fifth century there are grounds for the gravest reservations over both events and persons. For instance, the foundation of the three kingdoms is portrayed in remarkably similar terms — Kent, *sub anno* 449 'the Angles came hither to Britain in three ships'; Sussex, *s.a.* 477 'Aelle came to Britain and his three sons Cymen, Wlencing and Cissa with three ships'; Wessex *s.a.* 495 'Cerdic and Cynric his son came to Britain with five ships'; *s.a.* 501 'Port and his two sons Bieda and Maegla came with two ships'; *s.a.* 514 'Stuf and Wihtgar came to Britain with three ships'. Clearly we are dealing here not with historical fact but with an origin-myth. Some of the names are also clearly suspect. Some are invented to explain the ninth-century place-name of particular locations. For instance, Port is there to explain the place-name *Portesmutha* (Portsmouth), which in fact means exactly what it says. Wihtgar is there to explain *Wihtgaresburh* (Carisbrooke, Isle of Wight). This makes the name mean the *burh* (fortification) of Wihtgar. In fact the name is formed in the same way as *Cantwaraburh* (Canterbury — the *burh* of the *wara* (people) of Kent); the *burh* of the *wara* of *Wiht* (The Isle of Wight). This conscious attempt to improve the record can also be seen in the names of the early battles of Kent mentioned above (p. 163), *Aegelsthrep* and *Crecganford*, neither of which is the correct linguistic form to yield Ayelsford and Crayford; they are conscious and inaccurate archaisms by the compilers of the *Chronicle*. The politics of ninth-century Wessex must also be watched for. For example, the battle of Deorham in 577 resulted in the fall of Bath, Gloucester and Cirencester to Wessex. But at the time of the compilation of the *Chronicle* this area formed part of the kingdom of Mercia. Is the record of Deorham a record of a real battle, and/or an attempt to stake a title to Mercian territory? Such problems, and they can be multiplied, make the *Chronicle* narration of events in the fifth and first half of the sixth century very suspect. Some of the events listed concerning the early history of the Anglo-Saxons in Britain may have happened, but we can be fairly certain that the majority did not. Moreover we have no independent source with which to discriminate between the true and the false.

It should by now be clear that the exercise of putting the various snippets of 'history' for the fifth and early sixth centuries back into the contexts of the works from which they have been culled has far-reaching consequences. To return to some of the considerations which we outlined at the start of this discussion: most of the writers with whom we have been concerned were writing for purposes concerned with the politics and personalities of their own times. They saw the past through the preoccupations of those times, and they used the past for purposes bound up with what they wanted to say to their own generation. They were not attempting to write what we call history. All of them suffered from very weak sources, mainly due to having no written narratives on which to draw, but rather the vagaries of oral tradition. A critical examination of what they say and why they said it can only lead to the conclusion that the bulk of it must be rejected as evidence for the events of the fifth century. Some few events will remain, but so few that they cannot yield a connected narrative for that century. This is not by any means a recommendation that we should cease to study these sources. Far from it; for a start it is only the recent study of them that has shown how badly we have misled ourselves by our previous acceptance of them. This recent work has been of the highest quality and interest. What it is a recommendation for is that we (especially archaeologists and other non-historians) should cease to read these sources as history for the fifth century. They have a great deal of the first importance to tell us about the societies in which they were written, but next to nothing about what actually went on in the fifth century. The literary evidence cannot any longer be used to build a framework within which all other types of evidence will be comprehended. It is to the other types of evidence that we shall increasingly have to turn, and start again to build our picture of the dark fifth century.

As was said at the beginning of the chapter the archaeological evidence for the inhabitants of Britain in the fifth century (other than the Anglo-Saxons) is nugatory. This is of course why so much emphasis was laid on the written sources. This poverty of evidence is going to make our task both now and for many years to come a hard one. But before going on to examine what little evidence there is and what it may tell us, we must first examine the implications of the change in the quantity and quality of the archaeological record.

Fourth-century Roman Britain had a complex political, economic and social hierarchy which was expressed tangibly in a great range of settlement types and a multitude of objects. In the first third of the fifth century all this came to an end. Given that the reasons behind much of the wealth of archaeology for late Roman Britain were bound up with being a part of the Roman empire, then a decline consequent upon ceasing to be a part of that empire was entirely to be expected. It might also be expected that this decline would return the material culture of Britain to a level roughly comparable with that prevailing before the expansion of Roman influence and ultimately the conquest of the island. But this did not happen. Instead of the graph of the observable material culture dropping back to such a level and steadying, there was instead a vertiginous drop practically to zero. In addition there seems to have been technological recession with, for instance, the loss of the potter's fast wheel. This is far greater than could be expected and signals a massive dislocation. It also tends to confirm that the Roman socio-economic system was in fact deeply embedded in all levels of society and that its removal affected them all.

Material culture is not simply a function and expression of economic and technological capacity. Material objects also have social significance and uses. A particularly important one is the identification of the social context of an individual or group either horizontally to other individuals and groups of similar social and economic status, or vertically up and down a social and economic hierarchy. Much archaeological and anthropological ink has been shed over how material culture and socio-economic status and groupings may correlate,[15] but that such a correlation exists is axiomatic. Thus the plunging decline and disappearance of Romano-British material culture and the virtual absence of any detectable material culture to succeed it must be expressions of a social crisis as profound as the economic and material ones.

In late Roman Britain the hierarchy of settlement types, building types and the materials and workmanship of material goods were clear expressions of social status: 'large' as opposed to 'small' towns; town house as opposed to strip building; villa as opposed to farmstead; military as opposed to civilian; official as opposed to private; silver as opposed to pewter. Sometimes they also afford us a glimpse of cultural oppositions; for instance Christian as opposed to pagan. So buildings and objects were not simply functional; they also proclaimed the acquired or inherited group-membership and status of an individual, a family or a larger body of people. These distinctions and the means of expressing them had evolved over some considerable time. Though an individual or group might prosper or decline or, for instance, change religious allegiance, this took place within a relatively unchanging set of horizontal and vertical structures. The means of expressing identity also changed only gradually, and were almost always clearly linked with the preceding means of expressing membership. The fifth century saw a sudden and brutal rupture, and materially a massive discontinuity with what had gone before. This must have been both the product and cause of massive social turmoil as the accepted markers of identity and status were swept away. Such turmoil must have contributed to the steepness and depth of the decline of the graph of material culture. Whether what we are witnessing was revolution or traumatic evolution we cannot now say, but it does suggest that the old order inherited from Roman Britain may well have been brought to nothing. Such a process would complement the ending of the Romano-British socio-economic system and clear the ground for the evolution of a new order.

The group which would have suffered most severely from this dislocation was the landowners, since they were dependent on the labours of others for the sustenance both of their bodies and their styles of life. What is odd is that we have no literary or archaeological evidence that they tried to maintain the style to which they were accustomed in the way that the Gallic aristocracy did. As we have seen, even in late fifth-century northern Gaul there were men such as Remigius who were very conscious of coming of Roman stock and who maintained forms and institutions along fourth-century lines, even if the material culture in which these were expressed had declined greatly since the fourth century. In Gaul there remained a consciousness of the Roman way of doing things and a desire to try to preserve the manners of the late empire. In Britain we have virtually no evidence for perpetuation of either such an attitude or of the material culture. To Gildas the inhabitants of Roman Britain were as alien to his experience as were the Romans who had once ruled them. Gildas did not think of himself as a continuer of Roman culture in the way that a Sidonius Apollinaris or even a Gregory of Tours did in Gaul. It seems that not only had the Roman politico-economic system collapsed in the early fifth century, but so also had the socio-cultural system. Why this should be we cannot as yet say; it is the more puzzling given the apparently very romanised values of the Romano-British aristocracy noted in Chapter 3. It may be that the contrast with Gaul lies in the differing experiences of the third-century crisis and the responses to it. Central and northern Gaul had suffered barbarian invasion and an apparent collapse of the romanised material culture inherited from the early Empire. The fourth-century synthesis was therefore a response from a society which had suffered a profound shock; when the events of the fifth century supervened, it was perhaps more resilient. Britain, on the other hand, had had a far less traumatic time until the onset of the fifth-century crisis, and her social and cultural institutions may have been less able to cope, so collapsed to a level comparable with that of the material culture.

We may in passing note two Britons who escaped the wreck of their native diocese and went to Gaul under very different circumstances. One was Faustus, a Briton who became bishop of Riez in Provence and a correspondent of Sidonius Apollinaris. Sidonius also had cause to write to one Riothamus, a Briton who had established himself as a war-lord, probably in the lower valley of the river Loire.

What we must now examine is the archaeological evidence for the period ensuing on the collapse of Roman Britain. Our period therefore begins c. 430 and lasts until the end of the fifth century, by which time we may see new structures of society and culture emerging; in the west the 'Celtic' and in the east the 'Anglo-Saxon'. Though the amount of archaeological evidence for the people of the fifth century is paltry, there can be no doubt that there was still a significant level of population descended from the peak in late Roman Britain. This is shown most clearly in the pollen record.[16] There is no evidence for significant regeneration of woodland at the expense of agricultural land until the sixth century. Indeed in the north-east the evidence shows that the Roman phase of deforestation continued through into the early post-Roman period. Therefore, though the high, perhaps over-high, level of agricultural exploitation reached in the late Roman period was not maintained the countryside was still being farmed and kept open. The level of population in the post-Roman centuries in Britain has long been a matter for discussion. From the evidence of Domesday Book it is reckoned that the population of England in the late eleventh century was of the order of two million and on an upward curve. The population of late Roman Britain is almost impossible to estimate, but the best-informed guesses[17] place the figure at at least two million, quite possibly three. Thus for the Domesday population level to have been moving up there must have been a drop between, say, 400 and 1000. One mechanism that has been invoked for this is plague. A throwaway line of Gildas (§2) mentions *famosa pestis*, a renowned plague. In §22 he also mentions *pestifera lues*, a deadly plague. This has led some to suggest that one of the plagues attested in the fifth-century Mediterranean reached Britain. There is, in fact, no evidence that any of these plagues spread anywhere nearer to Britain than the eastern Mediterranean.[18] Even if one did reach Britain it cannot be claimed, as has sometimes been tried, that it was a cause of the British succumbing to the Anglo-Saxons, since the disease would have struck both peoples equally.

Since we have so little archaeological evidence, before we consider it it may be helpful to outline a general model of the sort of economy and society we might expect. With the disappearance of the Roman system the population of Britain would have reverted totally to a subsistence agriculture mode. We may thus expect for the area that is now England to find a settlement pattern made up of farmsteads for nucleated or extended families practising agricultural strategies designed to yield little in the way of surplus above that necessary to perpetuate the crops and herds. Settlements within the same area can be expected to have maintained social relations, not only for purposes such as marriage, but also for co-operation at times of the agricultural year requiring more than usual labour, for instance harvest. Such a system could have been organised along essentially co-operative lines. It is also possible that it was organised more hierarchically, with a central authority determining the workings of the population of a given area. Such an authority might well have become established as a response to external threat, either from the Saxons or from other British groupings. If that were the case, then we might expect to see differentiation in settlement type and perhaps burial, and perhaps also prestige displayed in objects. In fact this is very seldom the case. We are forced to suggest that social relations were mediated in ways which leave little archaeological trace. One way in which rulers and the élite may have validated their status and disposed of their surplus was in feasting. This was noted by Classical commentators such as Poseidonios and Caesar as being a Celtic pastime, and it is also well attested from early mediaeval Wales. Another possibility is that status was defined through gift-exchange, the gifts involved being high-value and thus unlikely to have been casually lost or disposed of. If the society was becoming Christianised then it is not surprising that these objects do not survive as grave-goods.

This period was also crucial for the development of the Church in Britain. In the early fifth century Christianity was still probably a minority religion, if a very influential one. In the early sixth century Gildas wrote in a totally Christian milieu. Paganism was something which did not touch upon his contemporary experience, and the *De Excidio* castigated a range of Christian rulers and prelates. Whatever his shortcomings as a historian of the fifth century, Gildas could not have falsified so totally the state of affairs of his own time and still have expected his admonitions to be received seriously. The Church at the beginning of the fifth century was rooted in the romanised sections of society of the diocese of the Britains. In the sixth century it was a rural-based religion with very little in its structure resembling anything inherited from Roman Britain. So during the fifth century it must have changed almost completely its organisation and locations. Indeed, the mutations of this Roman institution into its Celtic version could almost be taken as a paradigm for discussion on the fate of the romanised, landowning classes of the island.

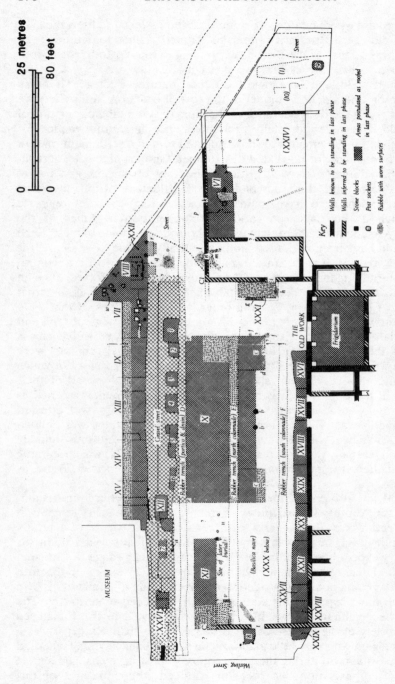

Fig. 38 Wroxeter baths basilica

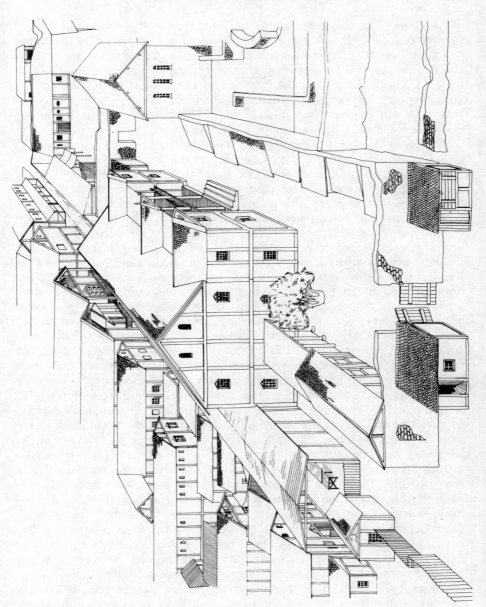

Fig. 39 Wroxeter baths basilica reconstruction

So what archaeological evidence do we have for this continuing British population? On general grounds we might expect it under the following heads: settlements; cemeteries; artefacts. So far settlements are a rarity. This must be the result of their having consisted of timber buildings of types which have left insubstantial archaeological traces. The same is broadly true of the contemporary Anglo-Saxon settlements, and it is only in the last twenty years that many of these have been located and we have begun to learn something about their nature. The same process seems just to be starting for the British settlements. The lack of cemeteries is more difficult to explain since human bone is far more readily recognisable, even as a casual find in building or ditch-digging, than the remains of a timber structure. British cemeteries of the fifth century are now coming to light, and as we shall see there may have been others that have been mis-identified in the past. There is an almost total lack of archaeologically-detectable artefacts. It may be that people used organic materials such as wood and leather which have perished from the archaeological record. If so, then that is in itself interesting as a contrast with the late Roman artefact suites. At present the main concentration of sites which can be shown to be of this date comes from the counties of Dorset and Somerset and up into Gloucestershire. These are areas well to the west of the areas of early Anglo-Saxon settlement and therefore the building-, burial- and artefact-types are not confused by the presence of Anglo-Saxon material.

In Chapter 4 we saw that two urban sites of Romano-British origin continued in use well into the fifth century: Verulamium Insula XXVII and the Wroxeter baths basilica. At Verulamium a large, late fourth-century town house was replaced by a rectangular structure interpreted as a barn, which was itself replaced by a wooden, gravity-fed water-pipe of Roman type. To want a piped water supply and to be able to command the technical expertise to have one laid argues that there was a person or body of authority in the area. It would be interesting to know the destination of the water-pipe. At Wroxeter the area of the former baths basilica (fig. 38) was taken over in the fifth century and turned into what seems to have been the compound of a local notable. There was a large, timber-framed residence whose plan was derived from that of the Romano-British 'winged corridor' villa, and around it were various lesser structures (fig. 39). Late in the fifth century a tombstone to an Irishman called Cunorix was set up outside the Roman defences. The deceased's name and filiation had been carved on part of a Roman tombstone in a debased Latin script.[19] So at the end of the fifth century Wroxeter contained at least one high-status site and someone literate in Latin.

What may have been a more 'ordinary' agricultural settlement developed in the fifth century over the site of the great fourth-century Christian cemetery at Poundbury, Dorchester (fig. 40).[20] This marked a complete break in the use of the site. The settlement consisted of a group of simple, rectangular, post-built structures of a type not found on Anglo-Saxon sites, but reminiscent of some of the simplest of Roman-period timber structures.[21] In addition there were six grain-driers and a threshing-floor. The grain-driers were unlike the classic Romano-British H-shaped driers, but did resemble some of the simplest driers of that period. This was a type of feature again not to be found at early Anglo-Saxon settlements. The artefactual assemblage from this phase of the site was small and not particularly distinctive — some knives, a few sherds of coarse pottery, parts of some bone combs, evidence for weaving and metal-working. It was clearly a subsistence agriculture that was being practised here. In its level of material culture it was not too dissimilar to contemporaneous Anglo-Saxon sites, but the range of building- and artefact-types was distinct from those of Anglo-Saxon settlements. This is the best example of such a site to have been excavated and published in recent years; its structural and artefactual poverty both show the change from the late Roman period, and also demonstrate that whilst such sites exist, they will remain very hard to detect.

Another, better-known, class of fifth-century site is re-used Iron Age hillforts; the most famous of these being South Cadbury (fig. 41).[22] There in the post-Roman period the inner defences of a 7–ha. (18-acre) hillfort were refurbished. The 1.2 km (3/4 mile) rampart was rebuilt, and there was at least one gateway. Within the defences lay a large, post-built structure, its building technique not unlike that of the Poundbury buildings. It has been interpreted as a hall where a lord would feast and live with his retainers. This phase of use of the hillfort was associated with imported pottery, including Mediterranean amphorae and ARSW, datable to the turn of the fifth and sixth centuries. The labour required to rebuild so long a rampart enclosing such a large area was of an entirely different order from that taken to construct, for instance, the Poundbury settlement. This combined with the large 'hall' indicate that the settlement was a high-status one with more than local significance and resources. A number of other hillforts in the Somerset area and in the Welsh Marches[23] have yielded late Roman pottery[24] and some also have traces of refurbishing of the defences. If there was solely late Roman pottery, then it may be that we are dealing with a phenomenon analogous to the (re-)fortification of hilltop sites in eastern Gaul during the fourth century (cf. p. 32). There are, however, a few hillforts such as Cadbury Congresbury[25] in Somerset and Coygan Camp[26] and Dinas Powys[27] across the Bristol Channel in south Wales which have defences and occupation also associated with these late fifth- or early sixth-century imports. These also, therefore, were presumably the residences of local rulers. At Dinas Powys the artefactual assemblage included ARSW and glass from the Rhineland, which indicates extensive contacts. The site itself was defended and therefore could presumably call upon the labour and resources of a large area round about. Yet the buildings were small and simple. Status must have been proclaimed largely by means which leave us little or no trace.

Another class of site which has been shown to have, in some instances, a post-Roman phase is Romano-Celtic temples, particularly again in the Somerset area. At Brean Down,[28] Lamyatt Beacon (fig. 42)[29] and Uley[30] the Romano Celtic temple was demolished at the turn of the fourth and fifth centuries. At Brean Down and Uley the temple was succeeded by a small, rectangular, stone-built structure. A similar structure existed at Lamyatt Beacon but the only dating was a terminus post quem of the late third century. It was, nonetheless, so similar to the other two that a fifth-century date is

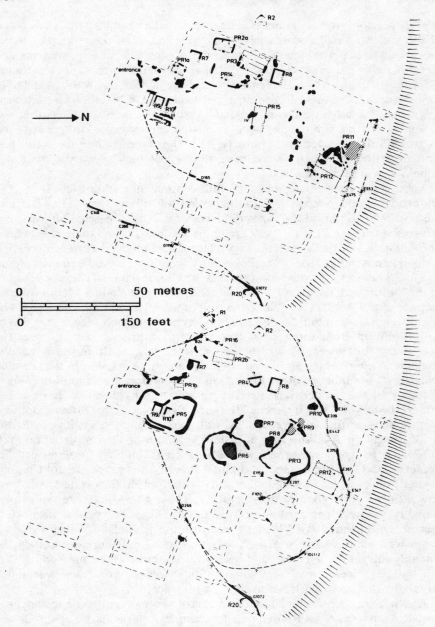

Fig. 40 Plan of Poundbury settlement

Fig. 41 Reconstruction of South Cadbury gateway

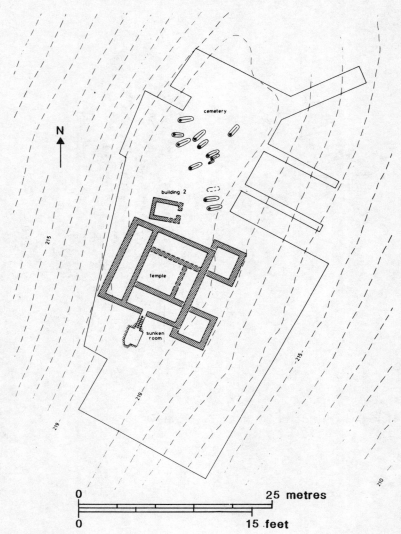

Fig. 42 Plan of Lamyatt Beacon

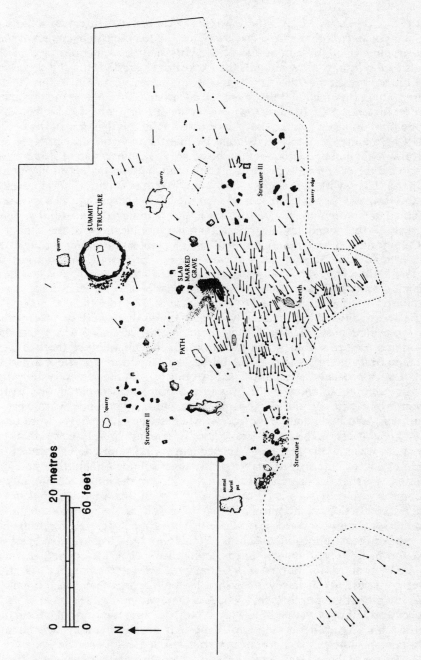

Fig. 43 Plan of Cannington

entirely acceptable. At Uley there was also a timber structure over the site of the temple and another a little way away. As the temple had been demolished and fragments of the cult statue of Mercury had been incorporated in the walls of the little stone structure, the excavator suggested that this represented the suppression of the pagan cult by and in favour of Christians. If this were so then the small building might be a Christian shrine, and the argument can be extended to Brean Down and Lamyatt Beacon. This is possible, though it does again assume that the principal religious dynamic of the period was Christianity; an alternative could be that the technological collapse and cultural realignment consequent on the end of the Roman rule of Britain gave rise to a different physical expression of the cult. This had, after all, happened earlier at Uley, with the religious site of late Iron Age origin being superseded by the Romano-Celtic temple. If so then the latest phase could as easily have signified a continuing pagan use, with the coming of Christianity being marked by the abandonment, rather than the modification, of the site.

Cemeteries of this date are gradually being recognised, either through new excavations or the reassessment of earlier ones. Perhaps the most important, so far, is the cemetery at Cannington (fig. 43).[31] Most of the site had been quarried away and only some 500 burials remained to be excavated. It was estimated that the original total of burials was of the order of 2000–5000. The burials were aligned approximately east-west, and there were two foci within the excavated area. At the highest point of the cemetery was a circular, wooden structure within which was a burial, though whether the two were contemporary is impossible to establish. The other was a grave marked by slabs and approached by a path. The few objects from the cemetery and some ^{14}C determinations show that it was in use from the second century to the seventh or eighth. In the earliest phase the burials lay more north-west — south-east and had some grave-goods, whereas the later phases were more nearly east-west and lacked grave-goods. It may therefore be that the cemetery was initially pagan and subsequently Christianised. The size of the cemetery is of interest. It lay close to the Cannington hillfort, and one possibility is that it represented the burial-ground of the hillfort community — though it would be surprising to find a hillfort in this area occupied in the second century. An alternative is that it served as the communal burial-ground for a number of local settlements. We have suggested that this may have been the case for fourth-century Poundbury, and it must have been the case for the large, early Anglo-Saxon cemeteries such as Loveden, Sancton or Spong Hill (all contemporary with Cannington) where the number of burials ran into thousands. If this were so then it would again mean social organisation at a more than purely local level. A cemetery that may also have served a reoccupied hillfort was that at Henley Wood, dug into the ruins of a Romano-Celtic temple. Another cemetery of some sixty burials that may have been of fifth-century date has recently been excavated at Ulwell near Swanage.[32]

Apart from these larger cemeteries it is now clear that there are many, perhaps a hundred or more, small cemeteries of post-Roman date in Britain, which are not usually recognised as constituting a distinct class. Many of them have been found by archaeologists excavating Romano-British sites, dug into the abandoned Roman buildings.[33] Others which consisted of small groups of inhumations without grave goods have been argued to be Christian, but often therefore assigned to a Christian, Anglo-Saxon context in preference to any other.[34] It may be that many in fact were cemeteries of settlements of the post-Roman population. Their frequent occurrence in or over the ruins of Romano-British buildings is noteworthy. Some of them, as at Henley Wood, overlay temples. The same may be seen at Lamyatt Beacon,[35] but there the cemetery was a century and a half or more later than the end of the temple. It is debateable whether such cemeteries from former temple sites should be treated as a group distinct from those overlying other types of Romano-British sites. It is also debateable whether there was any particular link between the Romano-British settlement site and the post-Roman British cemetery. We need to locate and excavate a lot more cemeteries both on and off such sites to see whether the ones over buildings were a definite sub-group. Nevertheless it does seem the case that we can now identify a cemetery type: small in numbers, with male and female, adult and juvenile burials, often without grave-goods, often east-west oriented, which may be the cemeteries of the post-Roman, British population (cf. also p. 201).

In the preceding discussion of early post-Roman sites we have seen that despite the overall material poverty there were nonetheless some artefacts proper to this chronological and cultural horizon. The most notable were the imported Mediterranean amphorae and red-slipped wares. With the end of Romano-British material culture in the first part of the fifth century there seems to have been a cessation in contact between Britain and the Roman world, at least so far as is recognisable through objects. The Church may have remained a channel of communication, for instance with the acceptance of the change in the way of calculating Easter promulgated by Pope Leo in 453. But in the late fifth century Mediterranean pottery again reached Britain, exclusively in the west rather than the Anglo-Saxon east.[36] At present we do not know what the mechanisms of trade were. The amphorae were clearly being traded for the wine in them, but it could be that there were other items of trade on which the pottery was parasitic. Nor is it clear what Britain had to offer in return, though tin is a possibility for the south-west. Once contact had been re-established it seems to have been maintained through the sixth century. Unfortunately it is often not possible to date the imported pottery very closely, so it may be that many of the small settlement sites in the south-western peninsula at which this pottery was present in small quantities were of sixth- rather than fifth-century date. The site with the largest amount was Tintagel. This site has occasioned much debate: 'Arthurian' or not; Celtic monastery or secular site; early or late?[37] Despite the dating problems, some of the Tintagel pottery did date to the turn of the fifth and sixth centuries. Overall the site had far more than other sites — perhaps some seventy or eighty vessels all told whereas other sites with more than one were in a minority.[38] The site was a defensible headland accessible from the sea. To an archaeologist it is reminiscent of an emporium or port-of-trade site.[39] Such a site was one on the edge of a political or economic unit where imported goods and foreign merchants were received. This made control of the merchandise by the native authority very much easier whilst affording the merchants a degree of protection at a controlled site. It is a characteristic of such sites, for instance Hengistbury Head in the Late Iron Age or *Hamwic* in the middle Saxon period, that the exotic goods which were so common at them rarely penetrated to sites in their hinterland. If Tintagel was a site of this type then that again would argue for a degree of political cohesion and organisation in south-western Britain from the end of the fifth century.

The only other distinctive artefact type linked with this chronological horizon is a type of penannular brooch; Fowler's Type G.[40] This was a small, bronze, almost circular brooch with facetted terminals either side of the break in the circle. Its distribution centred in the Severn basin, and the dating, evidence, suggest that it was first made in the late Roman period and continued in use into the fifth century, coming from sites such as Cadbury Congresbury and Cannington. Otherwise the artefacts from these sites are simple and undistinguished as we saw for the material from Poundbury, the local pottery being hand-made and often marked where grass or chaff incorporated into the clay had burnt out during firing. One is forced to the conclusion that the vast majority of vessels for cooking, eating and drinking must have been of perishable materials such as wood, leather or horn, and it may have been there that the technological skills so sadly lacking in the surviving material were exercised. This does mean, though, that it is very difficult to use the normal, artefact- and settlement-based techniques of archaeological analysis to examine the hierarchy and structure of this society, since the data are so sparse.

But material poverty need not entail poverty of social or cultural structure. All so-called 'primitive' peoples in the modern world have turned out on examination to be primitive only in their technology, not in their social formations or cultural expressions. There are, though, some indicators that post-Roman British society did have a complex cultural side to it that leaves no archaeological trace. To examine this we shall have to return to a further consideration of the literary sources, in particular certain aspects of Gildas, and the Llandaff charters. For all his manifold sins and imperfections as a historian of the fifth century, Gildas has something interesting and important to tell us in the style of the *De Excidio*.[41] For a start it is in Latin. It displays a knowledge of history (however imperfect) and a familiarity with some of the historical sources which have also come down to us. It is therefore the product of a man who had received a formal education in Latin and had access to a library. Moreover, there is the evidence from an analysis of the structure of the *De Excidio*. Gildas was a cleric writing a work of theological import. He might therefore be expected to write in an ecclesiastical style; the more so as the Church is an obvious channel for the transmission of education and knowledge. Yet the work is not written in the style of contemporary ecclesiastical works. Its structure and methods of argument are derived from the Roman forensic tradition. The *De Excidio* is a distant cousin of the speeches of Cicero. That there should have been education available in early sixth-century western Britain is interesting enough; that it should have preserved the forms of late Roman secular education is totally unexpected.

And this was happening alongside the material poverty which we have just been considering.

The Llandaff charters[42] are documents of the late sixth to eleventh centuries, which record the transmission of land-holdings in south-eastern Wales. The earlier ones among them have several features of interest. For a start they are again in Latin rather than the vernacular, unlike the early Anglo-Saxon laws. Moreover, both the general legal concepts and forms and the specific legal terminology are derived from the late Roman. Though they reflect Celtic practices, they do so in a way which has been adapted to Roman usage. The estates mentioned in these early charters were large, hundreds or thousands of acres in extent. The questions are; from how long before the date of the charters did the formation of the estates date? Can they be linked back to the Roman period? An analysis of the known locations of the estates as compared with that of Romano-British forts and villas is inconclusive. The geographical correspondence is not good, but that can be got round by saying that what had been perpetuated was the estate, not the location of the estate-centre. It could equally well be that the estates represent the re-division of the landscape following on the collapse at the end of the Roman period. But this is a secondary point; the important one is the existence and form of the charters themselves. The charters are also important in that they afford us a glimpse of the archaeologically-undetectable means whereby the élite organised its affairs and maintained its land-holdings.

Clearly then, for all the paucity and poverty of the archaeological record there was a distinct phase of settlement and society that was neither Romano-British nor Anglo-Saxon. As yet we can but see it through a glass darkly. On the one hand there is the archaeological evidence. At present this may be divided into three overlapping horizons. The first is those sites, such as Cannington or Wroxeter, whose origins lie in the late-Romano-British period but continue thereafter. The second is those sites, such as Poundbury, which originated in the mid-fifth century, and may have continued for some time thereafter. They are not numerous. More numerous are sites of the third band, those, such as South Cadbury, that originated in the late fifth century and ran on into the sixth and seventh. In many ways these seem to be a prelude to the Celtic culture of the sixth century on. This can now be argued to emerge as a distinct entity at some time around 500, from and after the dislocations of the preceding half century. On the other hand we have the literary sources, and such odd pieces of information as the Cunorix stone. These show that despite the material poverty there was a rich social and cultural formation. This again foreshadows the world of the Celtic west, where saints, scribes and scholars worked and taught in small, simple settlements, and where craftsmen produced some of the loveliest and most complex objects ever made in these islands. More attention will have to be paid to the mid- and later-fifth century both in its own right and as a time of transition from Roman Britain, to the Celtic culture of the lands around the Irish Sea in the west, and to early Anglo-Saxon England in the east. The problem lies in locating and identifying the sites of this period; judging by our experience to date one can do little more than recommend a strategy of rigorous serendipity.

SIX

Postscript: Continuity and Change

Roman Britain was in due course to be succeeded by Anglo-Saxon England. What influence did the former have on the formation of the latter? For many years this was an irrelevant question as it was thought that the Anglo-Saxons shunned the decaying works of the Romans. But since the Second World War the subject of continuity between the two has been a major topic of debate and research. This change in attitude came about for two main reasons. The first was the realisation that if there was a complete break between Roman Britain and Anglo-Saxon England, then that was utterly unlike the situation on the Continent. Surely, therefore, threads of continuity on the Continental model should be sought? The second reason was the growing realisation amongst archaeologists and historians that even when there was a known invasion, the changes that this wrought overlay a huge continuum from the pre-existing society. For instance, the Norman Conquest changed many things, but even more remained as they had been in late Saxon England. Should not, therefore, the change from Roman Britain to Anglo-Saxon England have also entailed a measure of continuity between the two?

To date, this continuity and the agencies for it have been sought in two different ways. One has been the attempt to identify Anglo-Saxons in or alongside still-functioning Romano-British settlements. The other has been the notion of the continuity of institutions of secular or ecclesiastical authority. Both of these latter are phenomena well-attested on the Continent. The word 'continuity' was also discussed. At one end of the spectrum of its possible meanings in this context was a perpetuation of late Roman practices little changed. That was clearly not the case in Britain, so discussion in those terms was futile. At the other end was spatial juxtaposition of settlements of the two cultures; for instance, an Anglo-Saxon village beside a Romano-British villa. This latter entailed no functional or causative link between the two, just physical coincidence, and so was never a serious contender as an expression of continuity. The generally-accepted area of study lies in the middle and may be formulated as the taking-over by the Anglo-Saxons of a Romano-British site or social feature and its adaptation the better to respond to Anglo-Saxon priorities. The end product may not be particularly recognisable as Romano-British, but neither is it explicable without reference to its Romano-British origins. So far the discussion has usually been concerned with links between Romano-British and Anglo-Saxon. We shall therefore examine the question of the relationship between the earliest Anglo-Saxon settlement and late Roman Britain. Then we shall examine some of the other mechanisms which have been proposed for permitting continuity, for instance 'institutional' continuity. Finally we shall examine the concept and processes of continuity in the light of what has been said in Chapters 4 and 5. Though this chapter will inevitably involve the discussion of certain, individual Anglo-Saxon sites, its purpose is not to afford a consideration of the early Anglo-Saxon migrations into and settlement in Britain. It is concerned, rather, with exploring possible modes of contact between late Roman and/or post-Roman Britain and early Anglo-Saxon England. Such Anglo-Saxon sites as are discussed are mentioned, therefore, because they contribute to these more thematic discussions.

Several attempts have been made to try to identify an Anglo-Saxon presence in fourth-century Roman Britain. One obvious method is to be able to identify objects of Anglo-Saxon as opposed to provincial Roman manufacture in Britain in that century. The best-known example of this was the early date ascribed to some of the cremation urns in the Anglo-Saxon cemetery at Caistor-by-Norwich (fig. 44),[1] outside the eastern walls of the Romano-British *civitas*-capital, which was certainly still occupied through the fourth century. These vessels were given dates as early as the late third century on the basis of comparisons with those from the Danish island of Fyn. The dating of the Danish material is not secure, resting on a chain of associations with datable Roman objects. Scholars of the Anglo-Saxon period would not now care to put so early a date on the Caistor-by-Norwich urns. Moreover, had it been the case that the cemetery was in use through the fourth century, then the lack of Romano-British artefacts from it would be inexplicable, for, as we have seen (p. 33), Germanic peoples, including the Anglo-Saxons, had no aversion to Roman material. It is now generally accepted that even the earliest Anglo-Saxon objects from this country should not be dated earlier than 400, and there are very few of those.

Failing identification of Anglo-Saxon objects in fourth-century Roman Britain, the alternative was to try to identify classes of object which were of Roman manufacture but betrayed a Germanic presence in the fourth century. The first category of artefact proposed as falling within this definition was two classes of pottery.[2] The first was vessels made by hand and in typical Anglo-Saxon fabrics, but imitating Romano-British pottery. That the Anglo-Saxons should on occasion have aped the Roman pottery they saw is understandable enough; but at present none of these vessels need be earlier than the general run of Anglo-Saxon pottery, that is fifth-century. The second class was held to be much more significant. This was pottery made in the Romano-British tradition, of well-prepared clay and on a fast wheel, but decorated with motifs and in a style felt to be reminiscent of that on Anglo-Saxon pottery of the fifth and sixth centuries. Its distribution was on impeccably Roman sites of the fourth century, with a concentration in East Anglia which was also where the early Anglo-Saxon cemeteries clustered. It was thus thought to be of Romano-British manufacture, but designed to appeal to Anglo-Saxon tastes, thus implying that these people were present in eastern Britain during the fourth century. The name for it, 'Romano-Saxon' ware, reflected this ethnic ascription.

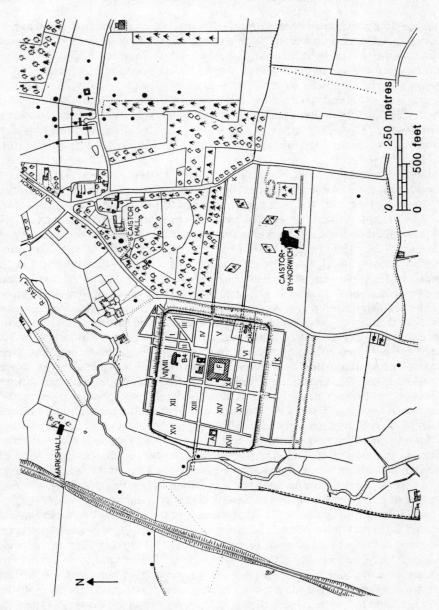

Fig. 44 Location of Caistor-by-Norwich cemetery

Re-assessment of this pottery suggests that it is in fact standard late Roman provincial with no ethnic overtones.[3] It has been pointed out that the decorative styles on Anglo-Saxon pottery which were held to be imitated on Romano-Saxon ware were in fact of the later fifth century onwards, rather too late to have influenced a fourth-century pottery type. Moreover, the bulk of fourth-century pottery from the Anglo-Saxon homelands was plain or had little decoration. The decorative motifs on Romano-Saxon ware, such as dimples and triangular panels of decoration, can be paralleled on other pottery and on glassware and metalwork of Roman manufacture and fourth-century date. The sites of the kilns at which this pottery was made are now known, and the East Anglian distribution can be explained by the fact that they were located in Hertfordshire and Cambridgeshire. All in all this pottery is far more easily and far better explained as standard Romano-British than linked with the Anglo-Saxons. The ethnic designation 'Romano-Saxon' should be abandoned, and the ware named after its kiln-site or area, like New Forest ware.

The other category of artefact linked with the Anglo-Saxons in fourth-century Britain was metalwork, principally that associated with the elaborate belts of late Roman manufacture. Again because it was found in Germanic graves on the continent (for instance, the *Waffengräber*) and in fifth-century Anglo-Saxon graves in Britain, and because of the relationship of the art-style on this metalwork to that of the Germanic peoples, it was seen as a class of material of Roman manufacture to barbarian taste, and issued to Germanic troops such as *foederati*. This also may now be discounted. Again there was a chronological inversion in the direction of transmission of the art-style; it was the fourth-century Roman that influenced the fifth-century Germanic, not *vice versa*. As we have seen in Chapter 2 (p. 34) these belts were the standard insignia of office of late Roman civil as well as military officials, no matter what their ethnic origins. Some of the people who wore these belts will have been Germanic, many more will not. It is no longer permissible to refer to this fourth-century metalwork as specifically linked with Germanic peoples.

The assumption underlying these discussions was that if Anglo-Saxon personnel could be identified serving in late Roman Britain as *foederati* then these people would be in a good position to take power at the time of the collapse of the Roman system. We saw in Chapter 1 (p. 7) that occasions of treachery by barbarian troops in the fourth century were rare. Moreover, the Germanic peoples who seized power on the Continent in the fifth century were precisely not those who were already present within the Roman empire as *foederati*, but were those coming in from outside the empire. It was not the sites associated with the *Waffengräber* which developed into the centres of Frankish or Visigothic power, but other sites altogether. Germanic troops had been used in Britain from the time of the conquest on. In the late period we know, for instance, of the *numerus Hnaudifridi* (Nottfried's Unit) at Housesteads, which even used a distinctive type of Germanic pottery,[4] but there is no question of it being a means of transfer of power from Roman military to Germanic.

Attempts to juxtapose Romano-British and Anglo-Saxon by trying to pull

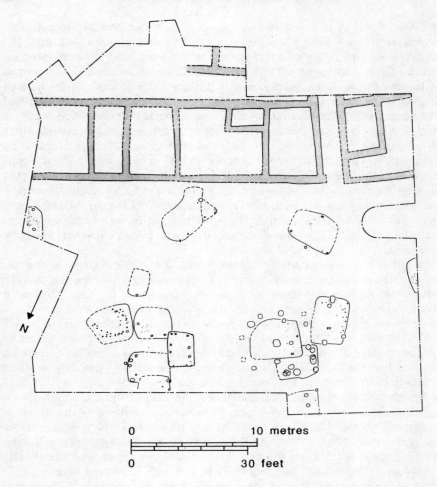

0   10 metres

0   30 feet

Fig. 45 *Grubenhäuser* at Canterbury

the latter back into the fourth century have come to naught. In fact that ought not to surprise us since the evidence for the better-documented transitions in Gaul is against such a scheme. What of the alternative of pulling the Romano-British into the fifth century so that they could then have been in contact with the Anglo-Saxons? There are a number of late Romano-British sites which have yielded early Anglo-Saxon material; was the latter there in the last days of the former? At four 'large' towns, a couple of 'small' towns, a Saxon Shore fort and some rural sites there was Anglo-Saxon material. The 'large' towns were Canterbury,[5] Colchester,[6] London[7] and Winchester.[8] The most substantial case for contact can be made for Canterbury. There, as we have seen (p. 151), there was occupation on some Roman sites into the fifth century. Dug into the 'dark earth' while it was still forming were the earliest of a number of *Grubenhäuser* now known from the town, containing Anglo-Saxon pottery of the late fifth century. Nonetheless, none of the Anglo-Saxon pottery has been recovered from the latest Roman levels, and the *Grubenhäuser* were dug into the 'dark earth', which as we have seen (p. 147) betokens the abandonment of the underlying town. The current estimate is that there was a gap of at least a generation between the latest Roman and the earliest Anglo-Saxon occupation.

At Colchester, likewise, two *Grubenhäuser* have been found dug into the latest Roman levels. But the material from them is of later fifth-century date, and Colchester appears to have been a town where the late-fourth-century decline was steeper than at most towns. There is thus no convincing case for contact between the two cultures. At London an Anglo-Saxon disc brooch was found in the excavation of the bath-house at Huggin Hill, but it was in the rubble of the building, which must therefore have been deserted at the time. At Winchester there are a number of sherds of early fifth-century Anglo-Saxon pottery and a triangular bone comb of Germanic type from the town. Unfortunately most of the pottery was residual in later, mediaeval deposits. The bone comb, though, was in a small pit cut into the latest metalling of the street along the southern side of the forum insula. In all these cases, therefore, the evidence for a direct relationship between the two cultures is thin. Moreover, whatever the nature and level of the contact between late Roman and early Anglo-Saxon settlement was in the early fifth century at Colchester, London and Winchester, there is no evidence for the Anglo-Saxon activity continuing. At all of them the archaeological evidence is that the sites of the towns were deserted from the early- to mid-fifth century until the seventh century at least. So if they were centres for the transmission of Roman culture, that process has left no trace, and arguments from silence are not always easy to accept. So at all four 'large' towns there is evidence for a break in occupation before the start of urban regeneration in the middle or later Saxon period.

At the 'small' town of Dorchester-on-Thames (fig. 46),[9] there were three types of evidence. The first was the burial with the late fourth- to early fifth-century belt suite discussed in Chapter 3 (p. 55), and possibly two other burials with Anglo-Saxon brooches, one from near the first burial and the other to the north of the town. The second was that Romano-British

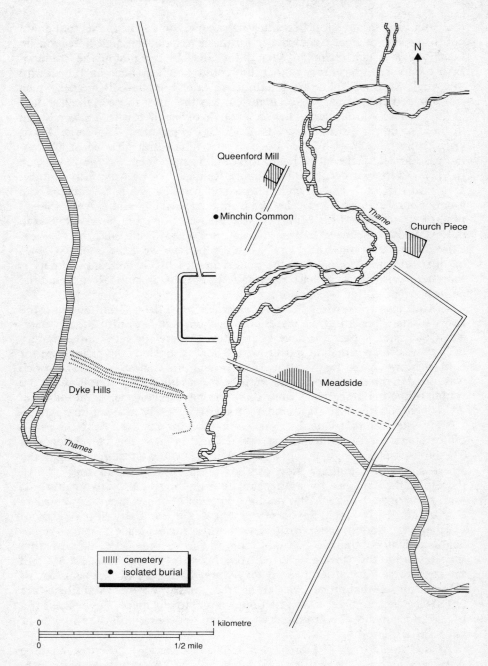

Fig. 46 Dorchester-on-Thames

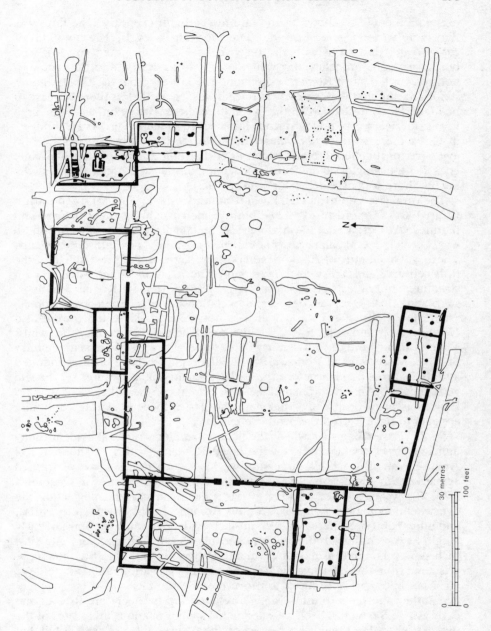

Fig. 47 Plan of Orton Hall Farm

occupation could be shown to run into the early fifth century. The third was that there were *Grubenhäuser* dug into the Roman levels. The problems of categorising the burial with the belt we have already noted (p. 56). The burials with the brooches may well be early fifth-century, and thus contemporary with the latest Roman occupation. The pottery from the *Grubenhäuser* is not now thought to be as early as once it was. Nevertheless there is a case to be made for contact between the two cultures here. But again, as at the large towns, there is a gap in the evidence for occupation thereafter. At Heybridge[10] in Essex there were *Grubenhäuser* dug into the late Roman levels, but no evidence for functional relationship rather than coincidence of site. The same goes for the Anglo-Saxon features cut into the latest Roman levels at the Saxon Shore fort of Portchester[11] (cf. p. 143).

The rural sites at Orton Hall Farm (Cambridgeshire) (fig. 47)[12] and Barton Court Farm (Oxfordshire)[13] have both yielded Anglo-Saxon structures and features. At Orton Hall Farm alongside the late Roman estate centre there was a small, rectangular, post-built structure, and a possible *Grubenhaus*. There was a quantity of Anglo-Saxon pottery, some of it of the first half of the fifth century, and a Frisian bone comb. The location of the Anglo-Saxon structures and objects clearly respected certain of the late Roman buildings, suggesting that there was contact and a relationship between the two peoples. At Barton Court Farm the evidence is not so good. Here there were also *Grubenhäuser* and other features containing Anglo-Saxon pottery, but whilst some of them were of fifth-century date, some of the rest were sixth-century or later. Moreover the Romano-British villa seems to have been abandoned and its features derelict before the earliest Anglo-Saxon features on the site were created. An Anglo-Saxon take-over of parts of the villa at Rivenhall in Essex has been proposed,[14] but here the desire to demonstrate continuity appears to have outrun the available evidence.[15]

So there are some sites where the material and/or structural evidence may indicate direct contact between the latest Romano-British and the earliest Anglo-Saxon. But in this discussion we have been doing what we warned against in our discussion of very late Romano-British features in Chapter 4 (p. 148); we have been looking at particular instances and neglecting the overwhelming majority of sites. At most Romano-British towns, forts, villas, and other rural sites there has been no such evidence for the presence of early Anglo-Saxon settlers. Indeed it is noticeably absent from the very late sites such as Verulamium Insula XXVII and the Wroxeter baths basilica, and there was none from the extensive nineteenth-century excavations at Silchester. We must not allow the exceptions to prove the rule too far.

Another approach to establishing a relationship between late Roman and early Anglo-Saxon has been to examine the spatial relationship of sites of the two periods rather than direct contact on the same site. It has been noted that a number of the earliest Anglo-Saxon settlements lie on agriculturally unfavourable land in close proximity to areas of much better land. An example of this is the Anglo-Saxon 'village' of West Stow[16] in Suffolk which lies on the edge of the sandy soils of the Breckland, but near the fertile gravels and alluvium of the valley of the little river Lark. It has been proposed that the post-Roman population controlled the better land, and that the incoming Anglo-Saxons were forced onto the peripheral location. A similar situation may have obtained at the early Anglo-Saxon settlement at Mucking[17] on a particularly barren part of the northern shore of the Thames estuary. The settlement at Catholme (Staffordshire)[18] lay in a gap in a pattern of Romano-British farmsteads known from field surveys. In all these cases there is a case for a spatial relationship with an existing population. The nature of the Romano-British sites in these areas and the precise chronology both need further clarification. At Catholme and Mucking the Romano-British evidence suggests that we may well be dealing with Romano-British sites of the farmstead rather than the villa level. At all three the Anglo-Saxon settlements are of the first half of the fifth century at the earliest, and it may be that therefore it is the post-Romano-British settlement pattern we should be considering, not the Romano-British. These spatial relationships of the Anglo-Saxon settlements may be an oblique clue to the whereabouts of those elusive folk, the post-Roman Britons.

So far the amount of evidence for sites where there was contact between early Anglo-Saxon and late Roman is pretty small, especially in the face of the hundreds where there is no such evidence. Given this, more general models have been advanced. The most favoured have been 'institutional' continuity and ecclesiastical continuity. Institutional continuity is concerned not with population but with power. It is therefore less concerned with direct evidence, though in the fullness of time it is to be hoped that archaeological evidence for the people who perpetuated the power will emerge. The scenario is that there were early Anglo-Saxon personnel in positions of influence in latest Roman Britain, or possibly early post-Roman. The favoured theory is that they were there as mercenaries, quasi-*foederati*. With the breakdown of the Romano-British power structures they were in a favourable position to assume the reins of power from the Romano-Britons. It is suggested that this may have lain behind Gildas' tale of the revolt of the federates. Sites which were felt to be important in this scheme were those where an important Anglo-Saxon site lay on or near one from which power may have been exercised in the late Roman period. For instance, at Winchester the site of the Anglo-Saxon royal palace overlay part of the Romano-British forum, and at London the palace of the Mercian kings probably lay within the Cripplegate Roman fort. Another class of buildings thought to be important are Saxon churches over important Roman sites, such as the Minster or the church of St Paul-in-the-Bail over the fora of Exeter and Lincoln respectively (cf. p. 152), or the chuch of St Peter, Cornhill over the western part of the London forum basilica. At York the Saxon cathedral overlay part of the site of the Roman *principia* (headquarters building) of which the basilica had apparently remained standing into the ninth century. In these cases the transfer of power was from secular to ecclesiastical bodies.

The arguments for this model rely very much on physical coincidence and have not been rigorously developed. One particular weakness is that the nature of the authorities concerned and the degree of complexity of social structure are not analysed in any detail. For the late Roman period, is it state authority or local authority? How was such authority expressed on late Romano-British sites? Were fora necessarily any longer the centre of government? We have seen (p. 71) that some cannot have been. On the Anglo-Saxon side, what was the nature of early Anglo-Saxon social structures and how was power expressed in them? The archaeological evidence from cemeteries and settlements is that the social hierarchy of the Anglo-Saxons in the fifth century was relatively flat and undeveloped. It was only in the late sixth century that we see the kingdoms developing out of simpler, more localised, earlier structures. This must lead us to ask whether there was in the first half of the fifth century any Anglo-Saxon power structure which could have meshed with something of the order of the late Roman state or municipalities? The underdeveloped nature of the early Anglo-Saxon social hierarchy and power structures strongly suggests not. Indeed, this lack of development may be used further. On the continent the Franks[19] seem originally to have had a similarly flat social structure, but when they came in contact with the Gallo-Roman hierarchies they soon developed a more differentiated hierarchy. The fact that the Anglo-Saxon did not do so in the mid-fifth century strongly suggests that they were not interacting with relict, Roman-derived, hierarchies of authority and society.

Another approach which has been tried is the examination of the parish or other early boundaries around selected Romano-British towns. In the case of Silchester[20] the parishes of Silchester and Mortimer West End form a rough circle of 4.5 km (2.7 miles) diameter around the town. This is an anomaly in the pattern of parish boundaries in the area. Clearly it is influenced by the presence of the Romano-British town, but when? It could be that there was a post-Roman-British power centre there; there are some fifth- to sixth-century British objects from the nineteenth-century excavations.[21] Alternatively it could have influenced the Anglo-Saxons in their demarcation of the landscape. In neither of the latter cases could one argue for a direct link between Romano-British and Anglo-Saxon. A similar argument has been advanced for the origins of the Manor of Chilcomb around Winchester,[22] though the area contained within these boundaries is much less regularly-shaped. There have also been suggestions for places such as the 'small' town of Great Chesterford. There and at Silchester there are anomalous parish boundaries, but no good case can be made for these representing a late Roman rather than a post-Roman land-unit. There is no known late Roman unit of administration to which such a unit would have corresponded — a *territorium* was allotted to *coloniae* only, and that in the early empire. Moreover, had there been such a unit one would have expected the occurrence of these anomalous parish and other boundaries to be a more widespread and uniform feature. It is possible that the ruins of the Romano-British town acted as a focus in the creation of post-Roman or Anglo-Saxon landholdings and their boundaries. If the former then the continuity is again from post-Roman, not Roman Britain. The evidence from the Continent is that analogous zones around Gallo-Roman towns (the *bannum leugae* or *bannlieue*) is again a post-Roman — Merovingian — feature.[23]

Ecclesiastical continuity has been suggested in two main forms. One is continuation of a late Roman church in use into the later Anglo-Saxon period. The other, which we have already briefly encountered, is that the siting of certain churches was in a significant relationship with centres of Roman civil or military authority. The first of these derives from the observed situation on the Continent, where some churches, particularly cemetery churches, of late Roman date continued in use and formed the nucleus of the early mediaeval settlement. This model caused a spate of proposed identifications of such sites in Britain during the 1970s, generally marshalling more enthusiasm than evidence. As we saw in Chapter 2 (p. 38) such cemetery churches were a phenomenon of the fifth rather than the fourth century in northern Gaul and the Rhineland. It is therefore *a priori* doubtful whether they are to be expected in Britain in any number. In Chapter 3 (p. 127) we saw that the only decent candidate in Britain for a cemetery church mediating continuity on the Continental model was St Albans, but even there we are dealing with likelihood rather than proof. Otherwise there are no sites which can demonstrate both a proven late Roman cemetery church and a continuous sequence from that to the late Saxon period.

Rather different are the ecclesiastical sites overlying places felt to be of secular significance such as forts and fora. For here we have the conversion of one form of authority to the other. On the Continent it is true that during the fifth century bishops became the leaders of urban communities as the Roman secular arm withered. But they did this through their ecclesiastical position and they exercised that power through ecclesiastical forms and on ecclesiastical sites.[24] We do not find bishops in fifth-century Gaul passing judgement from the *tribunal* of secular basilicas. In addition, the evidence from the Continent is that secular basilicas were not converted into Christian churches before the sixth century,[25] so we should treat with caution suggestions that this may have happened to secular Roman basilicas before Augustine's mission of 597. The occurrence of Anglo-Saxon churches on Roman forts has as yet only been partially treated. So far those sites where there is such a coincidence have been treated in isolation. More work is needed to set them against the background of Roman forts which do not have an Anglo-Saxon church on top of them and of Anglo-Saxon churches with no relationship to Romano-British sites. For the moment it would perhaps be preferable to seek Anglo-Saxon reasons for the siting of Anglo-Saxon churches on these sites of former Roman secular authority. Indeed the change from secular to ecclesiastical authority has not been considered in any detail either. As with simple 'institutional' continuity, the mechanisms of transition have not been thought through.

The premise on which all the preceding hypotheses were based and the result which they wished to demonstrate were that there was some sort of contact and continuity between the incoming Anglo-Saxons and the late Romano-British system. It is now time to examine the effect of the arguments in the two preceding chapters on this overall model. The argument of Chapter 4 was that the Romano-British system was a product of and response to the conditions consequent upon inclusion within the late Roman empire. When Britain ceased to be a part of the empire that system collapsed virtually completely and in the space of about a generation; say by c.430–40. On the other hand work on the chronology of Anglo-Saxon settlements, cemeteries and artefacts now suggests that the main phase of immigration started in the middle of the fifth century, and that is was in eastern Britain. In the centre and west of what is now England the time-lag was even longer. There was thus a perceptible gap between the end of the Romano-British system and the main phase of Anglo-Saxon settlement. Nor is it by any means certain that fifth-century Saxon society would have had the necessary sophistication to be able to comprehend and perpetuate Romano-British institutions had they come across them.

It has long been recognised that compared with the Germanic successor-states in the rest of the western empire. Anglo-Saxon England in its political and social institutions, its language and law, to say nothing of its material culture, owed little or nothing to Roman Britain. Whereas the Vandals, the Visigoths and the Franks tried with differing degrees of lack of success to perpetuate or imitate late Roman institutions, the Anglo-Saxons could not or did not.[25] The states on the continent and in north Africa tried, eventually unsuccessfully, to maintain the late Roman land tax, they minted coin, they had a centralised administration, and they sustained some form of town life. In all this they were greatly aided by the presence and active co-operation of a late Roman aristocratic and administrative cadre, which provided the specialists competent (if anybody was) to try to maintain the late Roman forms. The Anglo-Saxons did none of these things. It is often stated that this was because, of all the incoming Germanic peoples, the Anglo-Saxons had had the least contact with the Roman empire and thus had little appreciation of or desire for Roman forms. We may suggest a less condescending alternative. First, when the main phase of Anglo-Saxon immigration began, it was happening in a country which no longer had functioning Roman institutions in the way Gaul, Spain and Africa had for the Franks, the Visigoths and the Vandals. Second, there was no-one left in Britain who could have operated such institutions on the Anglo-Saxons' behalf, for the post-Roman Britons too had little or no experience of them. The option of maintaining a modified Roman-style set-up was simply not open to the Anglo-Saxons. This accords with what we noted about the way in which the social development of the Anglo-Saxons differed from the Germanic peoples on the Continent, suggesting the absence of a Roman-style model.

In this case, continuity into Anglo-Saxon England must be sought not from Roman Britain, but from post-Roman Britain; the shadowy society and economy we considered in Chapter 5. From this consideration we may see that post-Romano-British society and early Anglo-Saxon society probably had many basic features in common. Both comprised subsistence agricultural economies. Both had social organisations based on the family and the kin. Both had relatively undeveloped social hierarchies, consisting probably of local rulers and the occasional paramount war-leader. Their settlement and cemetery archaeology show comparable levels of technological attainment, despite obvious cultural differences. Thus, though the two peoples came into conflict often — that after all was a standard way for a ruler to attain or maintain his status — there were also the preconditions for acculturation and assimilation. The written sources concentrate on the conflict because that was what the heroic ethos of society required. Peaceful interchange was not appropriate material for relating. So it is at this much lower level of sophistication that we should search for such continuity as there is. We may continue to examine categories of evidence such as we have already reviewed in this chapter, particularly that from cemeteries and settlements.

It is becoming clear that there are a number of features of cemetery archaeology which suggest contact and influence from Briton to Saxon and *vice versa*. One such feature is those cemeteries which have evidence for both British and Anglo-Saxon practices. A good example is the one recently excavated at Wasperton (Warwickshire) (fig. 48).[26] There a cemetery comprising both cremations and inhumations has been almost completely excavated. The dating evidence suggests that the burial-ground was first used in the late Roman period, and there are features of the burial rite, such as the presence of footwear in the inhumation graves, which support this. Stratigraphically-later cremations and inhumations were accompanied by Anglo-Saxon grave-goods, including weaponry and disc- and great-square-headed brooches. An earlier generation of workers would have classified this as an Anglo-Saxon cemetery on the basis of the presence of Anglo-Saxon artefacts. But we can see that it is in fact far more likely to have been the burial-ground of a family farmstead, starting in the fourth century and continuing into the seventh. During that period the nature of the material culture available changed from 'Romano-British' to 'Anglo-Saxon'. The appearance of Anglo-Saxon objects may be put down to one of two mechanisms. The first is that there was an influx of Anglo-Saxon settlers who continued to use the burial-ground of the people they had supplanted. The second is that it was the same group of people there all the time, but that in the fifth century they took to using and burying Anglo-Saxon objects; if only because they seem to have had no equivalent British ones. This raises the simple but important question of what grave-goods can tell us about the ethnicity of the people with which they were buried. To put it in contemporary terms; if I own something 'Made in Japan', does that make me ethnically Japanese? The answer of course is no. Obviously the range of objects to be found in settlements and cemeteries conventionally labelled Anglo-Saxon were of Anglo-Saxon origin. Their antecedents and parallels may be traced in the Continental homelands, and they were utterly unlike anything Romano-British or what we know of post-Roman material. But that does not mean that everybody who used or took to the grave with them such objects was in turn ethnically or linguistically Anglo-Saxon.

The evidence is that Anglo-Saxon objects were acceptable to the British population. They occur at such undoubtedly British sites as Cannington and South Cadbury. There are other cemeteries similar to Wasperton, for instance not far away at Stretton-on-Fosse, or much further to the east at Saffron Walden.[27] This being so, one may wonder how many of the small cemeteries usually classed as Anglo-Saxon[28] on the presence at them of a few Anglo-Saxon objects merely represent the adoption of Anglo-Saxon objects,

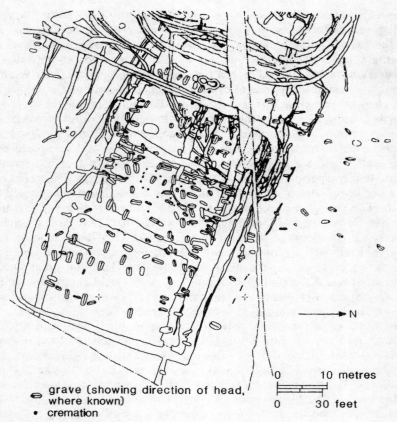

grave (showing direction of head,
where known)
• cremation

Fig. 48 Plan of Wasperton

perhaps even burial rites, by the indigenous, British population. They may, in fact, be yet more of the small, family cemeteries which we suggested in Chapter 5 should betoken the presence of that indigenous population.

Even at some of the large, classic, Anglo-Saxon cemeteries of eastern England there may have been a British component. For instance the huge cemetery at Spong Hill (Norfolk)[29] probably originally contained thousands of cremations. Cremation was the preferred mode for disposal of the dead in the continental homelands. But at Spong Hill there were also fifty-seven inhumations, all bar one grouped together.[30] Inhumation was the preferred (Romano-)British mode of disposal. Was there a British element burying at this ostensibly Anglo-Saxon cemetery? Spong Hill contained so many burials that it must have been the focal burial-place for a number of settlements. Were all these settlements Anglo-Saxon? It may be that osteological analysis of the bones from such cemeteries will eventually be able to discriminate between different groupings who used the cemetery.

For Anglo-Saxon settlements also there is now evidence that there may have been a British contribution to their building repertoire[31] as well as the influence on their siting which we have already considered. In the Continental homelands there were three principal building-types. There was a nine- or six-post setting, interpreted as being for raised granaries; there were Grubenhäuser, and there were long, rectangular aisled houses. At one end of these was accommodation for the family; the rest of the building was taken up with stalling for cattle. Excavation of sites in Britain seems to show that the granaries and the long houses did not survive the crossing of the North Sea. Anglo-Saxon settlements in this country consisted of Grubenhäuser and rectangular structures with opposed doors in the middle of their long sides. There are usually referred to as 'hall' buildings. These had no antecedents in the Continental homelands. There are similar if smaller buildings known from Roman and post-Roman farmsteads,[32] and one must wonder if these hall buildings in fact show British influence on the Anglo-Saxons.

We have discussed settlements and cemeteries. The other thing vital to a subsistence agrarian community is landholding. We have already seen in Chapter 4 (p. 159) that there is now evidence from a number of places that field-boundaries of (pre-)Roman date survived into the post-mediaeval period. This must mean that at some time they came into Anglo-Saxon hands. What we do not know is whether large units, such as estates, were also taken over. Estates are another thing which it has been suggested were transmitted from Roman Britain to Anglo-Saxon England.[33] This is probably over-stating the case. It must be remembered that we do not know the boundaries of a single Romano-British estate, nor what an estate actually consisted of (cf. p. 114). But is is possible that the landholdings of the post-Roman population, whether or not they had their origins in the Roman period, could have passed to the Anglo-Saxons.

Cemeteries, settlements, landholdings: for all of these a case can be made that there was British influence on what have traditionally been thought of as Anglo-Saxon institutions. Indeed, they are easier to explain if one envisages such influence than if one tries simply to explain them in terms of

Anglo-Saxon practices. If we accept this, then it is clear that there was the sort of continuity at the level of the basic subsistence economy and social unit of the type that we posited. We must now look to large-scale examination of landscapes, both by extensive survey and by intensive open-area excavation of large sites. In this way we may hope to find the archaeologically-elusive sites of the fifth century. A start in this direction has been made by the Stanwick project in the middle Nene valley. By finding sites of this period we shall be able to refine our knowledge of what it is we are looking for, and thus develop our research and excavation strategies.

If we accept that it was in these areas of activity that there was contact, then it has implications also for the way in which we envisage 'continuity'. In particular it must challenge the traditional view of a direct link between late Roman Britain and early Anglo-Saxon England. These processes will have meant that British sites became Anglo-Saxon. We have seen that some British sites had their origins in the late Roman period. This will mean that some Anglo-Saxon sites may be traced back to late Roman antecedents. Such 'continuity' between Roman Britain and Anglo-Saxon England hardly deserves the name. We would be better employed trying to find and trace the processes of contact between Briton and Saxon at the basic agricultural community level, for this is where there was real continuity.

As yet these indications come from a small number of sites. But their implications are considerable for the way in which we look at the problem of the transition to Anglo-Saxon England. They should also enable us to reinterpret old excavations and to ask new questions of future ones. Our perspective must now be re-focussed away from Roman Britain and onto the societies that succeeded it in the fifth and first half of the sixth centuries. In many ways it makes the Anglo-Saxon experience and achievement the more interesting. Elsewhere in Europe (with the exception of Bavaria, which could be an interesting parallel) Germanic peoples attempted to assimilate themselves to what was left of the Roman empire. For reasons we have seen the Anglo-Saxons were not in a position to do this. Clearly they did not regard the culture of the post-Roman British as a suitable model. Instead they eventually imposed their language, their law, their political system and their material culture on what is now England. Given that the number of Anglo-Saxon migrants to Britain was probably of the order of tens of thousands, as against an indigenous population probably numbering in the millions, the achievement is all the more remarkable. It must mean, in fact, acquiescence or active participation by large numbers of the British population in the Anglo-Saxon order of things. The presence of Anglo-Saxon objects on British sites such as at Wasperton can be seen as acculturation; the acceptance by one group of the material culture and practices of another. But it could well also indicate assimilation, that the population at Wasperton, though genetically British, ceased to regard itself as culturally British and came to think of itself as Anglo-Saxon. It accepted the political, linguistic and perhaps also religious systems of the incoming English. Wasperton happens to lie in an area where the archaeological evidence for Anglo-Saxon settlement is sparse and late. Yet this area was to be part of the heartland of Mercia, one of the greatest of the Anglo-Saxon kingdoms. It must be that many who called themselves Mercian were ethnically British but now regarded themselves, and were regarded, as Anglo-Saxon. It was out of this fusion of post-Roman (not Roman) Briton and Anglo-Saxon that was to arise Anglo-Saxon England.

REFERENCES

1 The Structures of the State (pages 1–15)

1 Jones A.H.M. 1964, 23–4
2 Jones A.H.M. 1964, 24–30
3 Luttwak 1976, 145–54
4 Jones A.H.M. 1964, Ch. XVII; Luttwak 1976, 170–88; MacMullen 1963; Tomlin 1987
5 Luttwak 1976, Ch. 3
6 Duncan-Jones 1978; Tomlin 1987
7 Jones A.H.M. 1964, 649–54
8 Jones A.H.M. 1964, 614–9
9 Jones A.H.M. 1964, 619–23
10 Jones A.H.M. 1964, 620
11 Luttwak 1976, 130–45
12 Johnson S. 1983a
13 Ammianus Marcellinus XXXI, 6, 4
14 Hopkins 1980
15 Jones A.H.M. 1964, Ch. XIII; Hendy 1986
16 Hendy 1986
17 Jones A.H.M. 1964, 803–8; cf. Wickham 1986, 10–11
18 Hendy 1988, 36
19 Kent & Painter eds. 1977, 17–19, *passim*
20 Jones A.H.M. 1964, 438–40; Burnett 1987
21 Reece 1986
22 Jones A.H.M. 1964, 448–62
23 Peacock & Williams 1986, Ch.5
24 Jones A.H.M. 1964, Ch.XII
25 Johnston D. 1985
26 Ward-Perkins 1984, Chs.1, 2
27 Ward-Perkins 1984, 65
28 Jones A.H.M. 1964, 554–7
29 Wightman 1970, 98–123; 1985, 234–9

2 The Continental Background (pages 16–40)

1 Johnson S. 1970; 1983a, 249
2 Casey 1977

3 Wightman 1985, Ch.8; Reece 1981a
4 For location of civil and military commands and installations cf. Jones A.H.M. 1964, Maps I-IV
5 Johnson S. 1983a, Ch.6
6 Johnson S. 1983a, Ch.10
7 Nenquin 1953
8 Lemant 1985
9 Grenier 1931, 362
10 Blagg 1983; Johnson S. 1983a, Ch.5
11 Wood J. 1983
12 Wood J. 1983, 45
13 Johnson S. 1973
14 Wood J. 1983, 45
15 Butler 1961, 44
16 Musée Carnavalet 1984, 326–8, figs. III, XXIX
17 Price 1978, fig. 16; Bayard & Massy 1983, Chs.IX, X
18 Neiss 1984, 184–91
19 *Panegyrici Latini* IX
20 Wightman 1985, 91–7
21 Wightman 1981
22 Chenet 1941
23 Middleton 1979; Peacock & Williams 1986, Ch.5
24 cf. Greene 1979
25 Tortorella 1983, figs. 7, 8
26 Hayes 1972
27 King 1981
28 e.g. le Glay 1975
29 Thompson 1952
30 Carrié 1982
31 Whittaker 1975
32 van Dam 1985, Ch.1
33 Dill 1898; Chadwick 1955
34 Fouet 1983
35 Galliou 1983, Ch.XV
36 Wightman 1985, 43–50
37 Agache 1978, Ch.VIII
38 Wightman 1970, 162–72
39 Wightman 1985, 282–6
40 Wightman 1985, 250–6
41 Ammianus Marcellinus XVIII, 2, 3; Libanius, *Orationes* XVIII, 82–3; Zosimus III, 5, 2
42 Wightman 1985, 269
43 Böhme 1974
44 cf. Lemant 1985, fig.75
45 Mertens & van Impe 1971
46 Hawkes & Dunning 1961
47 Jones A.H.M. 1964, 566

48 Simpson 1976
49 Brown P. 1971, figs.17–20
50 Jones A.H.M. 1968
51 Rivet 1976; Harries 1978
52 Wightman 1985, 286–96
53 Wightman 1970, 110–3
54 Radford 1968
55 Galinié 1981
56 Wightman 1985, fig.44
57 Rheinisches Landesmuseum Trier 1984, 203–10, 232–9, 239–42
58 Radford 1968, 33–4
59 Wightman 1985, 291

3   Britain in the Fourth Century (pages 41–130)

1 Johnson J.S. 1976
2 Breeze and Dobson 1978, 202–9
3 Aurelius Victor: *Epitome de Caesaribus XLI, 3*
4 Casey 1978
5 Libanius: *Orationes* LIX, 139, 141
6 Ammianus Marcellinus XIV, 5, 6–8
7 Ammianus Marcellinus XX, 1
8 Ammianus Marcellinus XXVI, 4, 5 (364); XXVII, 8; XXVIII, 3 (367)
9 Richmond and Gillam 1955, fig.3
10 Webster G. 1969, 223–30
11 Claudian: *de Laudibu Stilichonis* II 247–55; III 138–60
12 Ward 1973; Frere 1987, 225–6
13 *Notitia Dignitatum Occidentalis* VII, XI, XII, XXIII, XXVII, XXVIII, XXIX, XL

Administration

14 *Codex Theodosianus* XI, 7, 2
15 e.g. Dornier 1982
16 Bartholomew 1984, 178–9
17 *Notitia Dignitatum Occidentalis* XI
18 Wild 1967
19 *Notitia Dignitatum Occidentalis* XII

The Army and Frontiers

20 Jones A.H.M. 1964, 411–27
21 Branigan 1977; P.M. Booth pers. comm.
22 Gillam 1961
23 Gillam, Harrison, Newman 1973
24 Dore and Gillam 1979
25 Bidwell 1985
26 Mann 1979, 149–50

27 Frere 1987, 356
28 Breeze & Dobson 1985, 16–17
29 Johnson J.S. 1976, 149, fig.71
30 Johnson J.S. 1976
31 Cunliffe 1968, 244–5
32 Johnson J.S. 1970
33 Philp 1977
34 Cunliffe 1980
35 Cunliffe 1975
36 Johnson J.S. 1976, 56–9
37 Young 1983
38 Johnson A. 1975
39 Johnson J.S. 1976, 133–4
40 Jones G.D.B. & Shotter 1988
41 Johnson J.S. 1976, 134
42 Rankov 1982, 328
43 Breeze & Dobson 1985, fig.10
44 Wheeler 1923
45 Wheeler & Wheeler 1932, 102–3
46 Jones A.H.M. 1964, 631
47 Wilson D.R. 1971, 261
48 Hawkes & Dunning 1961
49 Simpson 1976
50 cf. Böhme 1974
51 Jones R.F.J. 1984
52 Clarke 1979
53 Clarke 1979, 377–403
54 Kirk & Leeds 1954; Cook & Rowley 1985, 30–1
55 Galliou 1983, 244–5
56 Boon 1972, 53–69
57 Strickland 1981, 415–27
58 Strickland 1981, 428–31
59 Sumpter & Coll 1977
60 RCHM(E) 1962, 40–1
61 Whitwell 1976
62 Kenward, Hall, Jones 1986
63 Daniels 1980
64 Dore & Gillam 1979, 65–6
65 Bidwell 1985, 58–72
66 Roach Smith 1850
67 Cunliffe 1975, 422–5
68 Johnson J.S. 1983b, 115–8
69 Johnson J.S. 1976, 56–9
70 Cunliffe 1968, 245–50
71 Vegetius; *Epitoma Rei Militaris* IV, 37
72 James S. 1984
73 Crickmore 1984

74 Corder 1961, 20–33
75 Ammianus Marcellinus XXVIII, 3
76 Casey 1983

The Towns
77 Esmonde Cleary 1985; Burnham 1987
78 cf. Frere 1987, 245–7
79 Reece 1980a
80 Frere 1983, 14–16, 83–276
81 Walthew 1978
82 Down 1978, 41–175
83 McWhirr 1986, 191–259
84 Bidwell 1980, Ch.VI
85 Jones M.J. 1985, 92
86 Wilson D.R. 1984
87 Esmonde Cleary 1987, Ch.8
88 Booth 1980
89 Drury 1976
90 Millett & Graham 1986, 151–60
91 Esmonde Cleary 1987, 142–9
92 Todd 1969
93 Esmonde Cleary 1987, 135
94 Joyce 1881
95 Fulford 1985
96 Atkinson 1942
97 Ashby, Hudd, King 1909
98 Brewer 1988
99 Frere 1971
100 Wacher 1962, 5–8
101 Heighway & Garrod 1980
102 Bidwell 1979
103 Hebditch & Mellor 1973
104 G. Milne, lectures
105 Frere 1971
106 cf. Canterbury Archaeological Trust 1982, Map 1
107 Down 1978, 41–175
108 Goodburn 1979, 327
109 Bidwell 1979, 121–3
110 Kenyon 1948
111 Richmond 1947
112 Nash-Williams 1930
113 St John Hope & Fox 1905
114 G. Webster pers.comm.
115 Barker *et al*. forthcoming. I am grateful to Philip Barker for allowing me
    to see this paper in draft
116 Mackreth 1987
117 Richardson 1944

118 Little 1971
119 Wacher 1964; Brown & McWhirr 1967
120 Fulford 1985, 60–78
121 Bradley 1975
122 White G.M. 1936
123 Frere 1970
124 Crummy 1982
125 Kenyon 1935
126 Blagg 1983
127 cf. Jones A.H.M. 1964, 803–12
128 Jones A.H.M. 1964, 615
129 cf. Hendy 1985, 242–51
130 Smith D.J. 1969
131 cf. Perring 1987
132 Sommer 1984
133 cf. Wacher 1975, fig.82
134 Ashby, Hudd, King 1910
135 cf. Wacher 1975, fig.82
136 Boon 1974a, endpaper
137 McWhirr 1978, 73–7
138 Bidwell 1980, 69–76
139 Biddle 1975, 300–1
140 Bushe-Fox 1914
141 McWhirr 1978, 73–7
142 Esmonde Cleary 1987, Ch.4
143 McWhirr, Viner, Wells 1982
144 Crummy 1982, 264–6
145 Green C.J.S. 1982
146 Clarke 1979
147 Esmonde Cleary 1987, Ch.6
148 Booth 1980, 16
149 Esmonde Cleary 1987, 99
150 Leach 1982
151 Finley 1973; cf. the comments of Hopkins, 1978
152 Milne 1985
153 Dyson ed. 1986
154 Hopkins 1980; Milne 1985, Ch.10
155 Milne 1985, Ch.12
156 Merrifield 1983, 154–67
157 Marsden 1975; 1987
158 Hill, Millett, Blagg 1980
159 Merrifield 1983, Ch.9
160 Esmonde Cleary 1987, 118–20
161 King 1981
162 Hopkins 1980

Pottery

163 Fulford & Bird 1975
164 Galliou, Fulford, Clément 1980
165 Fulford 1987
166 Hodder 1974
167 Fulford 1975a
168 Young 1977
169 Harden & Green 1978
170 Lyne & Jefferies 1979
171 Williams D.F. 1977
172 Corder 1928
173 Fulford 1975b, 295
174 Young 1974
175 Morris P. 1975, Ch.1
176 Jones M. 1981
177 Peacock 1982, Ch.3
178 Peacock 1982, Chs.2, 3
179 Fulford 1973, 172–3
180 Millett 1980
181 Fulford & Hodder 1974
182 Millett 1980
183 Hodder 1974, fig.8
184 Summer 1927
185 Hodder 1974; 1976
186 Hodder 1974, fig.9

Coins and Hoards

187 *Codex Theodosianus* IX, 23, 1
188 Reece 1984b, 173
189 Reece 1972, Table I
190 e.g. Reece 1982; Mann & Reece 1983
191 Walker D. 1988
192 Allason-Jones & MacKay 1985
193 Wheeler & Wheeler 1932, 116, Plate XXXVI
194 Reece 1980b
195 cf. Allason-Jones & MacKay 1985, 67
196 Reece 1972
197 Brickstock 1987
198 Boon 1974b; Brickstock 1987
199 Painter 1977a
200 Painter 1977b
201 Haverfield 1914
202 Burnett & Johns 1972
203 Manning 1972
204 Kennett 1971
205 Painter 1965; Johns & Potter 1985
206 Waugh 1966

207 Painter 1975
208 Johns, Thompson, Wagstaff 1980
209 Johns & Potter 1983
210 Cahn & Kaufmann-Heinimann 1984
211 Shelton 1981
212 Kent & Painter 1977, 50–2
213 Heurgon 1958
214 Toynbee & Painter 1986, 27–8, Plate Xa
215 Curle 1923
216 Bateson 1973
217 Mattingly, Pearce, Kendrick 1933

The Countryside
218 Kenward, Hall, Jones 1986
219 Davies W. 1982, 5–9
220 Jones & Dimbleby eds. 1981; Jones M. 1986
221 Turner J. 1981
222 cf. Buckland 1974
223 Jones M. 1981
224 cf. Cunliffe 1983, 126–33
225 Maltby 1981
226 Maltby 1981, 185–8
227 Grant A. 1975
228 Maltby 1979
229 King A. 1984
230 RCHM(E) 1980
231 RCHM(E) 1978
232 Simco 1984
233 Frere & St Joseph 1983, Plate 124
234 Frere & St Joseph 1983, Plate 134
235 Benson & Miles 1974
236 Johnston D.E. 1978, fig. 2
237 Frere 1982
238 Clarke 1982
239 Goodburn 1972
240 Bulleid & Horne 1926
241 Walters 1981
242 Collingwood & Richmond 1969, 142–3
243 Pollard 1974
244 cf. Smith D.J. 1978, 135–6
245 RCHM(E) 1969
246 Rivet 1969, 209–14
247 Smith D.J. 1975
248 Walthew 1975
249 Smith D.J. 1969
250 Toynbee 1964
251 Davey & Ling 1981

252 Hogg 1980
253 Clack 1982
254 Davies W. 1982
255 Leech 1981
256 Leech 1982
257 Cunliffe 1976
258 cf.Cunliffe 1973, 445
259 Davies W. 1978

Religion

260 Henig 1984
261 Nash 1976
262 Tomlin 1988
263 Lewis 1966; Wilson D.R. 1975; 1980
264 Wheeler & Wheeler 1932
265 Ellison 1980
266 Magilton 1986
267 Harris & Harris 1965; Henig 1984, Ch.5
268 Richmond & Gillam 1951
269 Grimes 1968
270 Toynbee 1986
271 Athanasius: *Epistola ad Jovianum* 2; *Apologia contra Arianos* 1
272 Sulpicius Severus *Chronicon* II, 41
273 Frere 1975
274 King 1983
275 West & Plouviez 1976
276 Brown P.D.C. 1971
277 Meates 1955, Ch.XII
278 Green C.J.S. 1982
279 Crummy 1980
280 Levison 1941; Biddle 1977
281 Painter 1977b
282 Johns 1981
283 Guy 1981

4   The Passing of Roman Britain (pages 131–161)

1 Frere 1972; 1983
2 Down 1978, 45, 81–3, 331–40
3 Crummy 1984, 19, 70
4 Bidwell 1980, 67–76
5 McWhirr 1986
6 Biddle 1975b
7 Blockley 1980
8 Biddle 1983, 111–3
9 Barker *et al*. forthcoming

10 Esmonde Cleary 1987, Ch.VIII
11 Down 1979
12 Neal 1974
13 Webster & Small 1982
14 Branigan 1971, 86–9
15 Magilton 1986, Ch.IX
16 Fulford 1975
17 Young 1977
18 Going 1987
19 Fulford 1979; Tuffreau-Libre 1980
20 Gibbon 1776–81
21 Orosius: *Historia adversus Paganos* VII, 40, 4
22 Zosimus VI, 5, 3
23 Zosimus VI, 10, 2
24 Gallic Chronicle of 452
25 Bartholomew 1982, 261–3
26 Thompson 1983
27 Miller 1978; Muhlberger 1983
28 Kent 1979, 21
29 Burnett 1984, 165–6
30 Archer 1979
31 Burnett 1984
32 Kent 1979, 21–2
33 Eugippius: *Vita Sancti Severini*, in *Monumenta Germaniae Historica* I
34 Mann 1979
35 Daniels 1980; Welsby 1982, Ch.VIII
36 Bidwell, 1985, 76
37 Ferris & Jones 1980; forthcoming. I am grateful to Iain Ferris for allowing me to see this paper in advance of publication
38 Cunliffe 1975; 1976a
39 Cunliffe 1968
40 Reece 1981b
41 Johnson J.S. 1983, 81–8, 115–21
42 Cunliffe 1980, 288
43 Peacock 1973
44 Wacher 1975, Ch.X; Biddle 1976a; Reece 1980a; Brooks 1986
45 Nash-Williams 1930, 257–60
46 Heys & Thomas 1961
47 Parnell 1985
48 Crummy 1984, 18–9
49 Thompson & Whitwell 1973, Plates XXV, XXVI; Jones & Bond 1987, fig.41
50 Biddle 1975a, 116–9
51 Brooks 1986
52 Frere 1983, 93–101
53 Down 1978
54 McWhirr 1986

55 Crummy 1984
56 Bidwell 1980
57 Jones M.J. 1985; Lincoln Archaeological Trust 1984, 31
58 Carver, Donaghey, Sumpter 1978; Ottaway 1984, 32–3
59 MacPhail 1981
60 Limbrey 1975
61 McWhirr, Viner, Wells 1982, 105
62 Green C.J.S. 1982, 67; 1988, 71
63 Clarke 1979, 111–9
64 Frere 1983, 214–26
65 Reece 1980a
66 Blockley 1980, 404–5
67 Bennett 1980, 406–8
68 Bidwell 1979, 109–13
69 Gilmour 1979
70 Barker *et al.* forthcoming
71 Booth 1980
72 Drury 1976
73 Green C.J.S. 1977
74 Leach 1982
75 Rodwell K.A. 1988
76 Millett & Graham 1986
77 Rogerson 1977
78 Lambrick 1980
79 Chambers 1988
80 Leach 1982
81 Rodwell K.A. 1988, 136–7
82 Fulford 1979
83 cf. West 1985, 122
84 R. White pers. comm.
85 Cunliffe & Davenport 1985, 66–75, 157–60, 184–5
86 Heighway 1986
87 Sanders & Esmonde Cleary in prep.
88 Miles & Palmer 1983
89 Clack 1982
90 Leech 1981
91 Williamson 1984; 1986

5   Britons in the Fifth Century (pages 162–187)

1 Thompson 1984
2 *Anglo-Saxon Chronicle*
3 Collingwood & Myers 1936, 320–4
4 Thompson 1984
5 Thompson 1984, 13
6 Prosper of Aquitaine: *Chronicon* §1301

7 cf. Wood I. 1984, 10–11, 13
 8 Dumville 1984
 9 Dumville 1977a
10 Dumville 1977a, 177
11 Hughes 1973
12 Dumville 1977b
13 Dumville 1977a, 180–1
14 Sims-Williams 1983, 26
15 Hodder 1986 and refs.
16 Turner 1981
17 Jones M.E. 1979
18 Todd 1977
19 Wright & Jackson 1968
20 Green C.J.S. 1988, 71–92
21 Garton 1987
22 Alcock 1972; 1982
23 Burrow 1979
24 Burrow 1979, 220–4
25 Rahtz & Fowler 1972, 196–7
26 Wainwright 1962
27 Alcock 1963
28 ApSimon 1965
29 Leech 1980; 1986
30 Ellison 1980
31 Rahtz 1977
32 Frere 1984b, 322
33 Leech 1980, 336–50
34 Meaney 1964
35 Leech 1986
36 Thomas 1981
37 Padel in Thomas 1981, 28–9
38 Thomas 1981 *passim*
39 cf. Hodges 1988
40 Dickinson 1982
41 Lapidge 1984
42 Davies 1978

6   Postscript: Continuity and Change (pages 188–205)

1 Myres & Green 1973
2 Myres 1956
3 Gillam 1979
4 Jobey 1979
5 Brooks 1988
6 Crummy 1981, Ch.1; 1984
7 Merrifield 1983, Ch.10

8　Biddle 1973, 232–7
9　Rowley 1974; Frere 1984a; Cook & Rowley 1985
10　Drury & Wickenden 1982
11　Cunliffe 1976a
12　Mackreth 1978
13　Miles 1984
14　Rodwell & Rodwell 1986
15　Millett 1987
16　West 1985
17　Jones & Jones 1971
18　Losco-Bradley 1977
19　James E. 1988, 53–4
20　Biddle 1976b
21　Boon 1959
22　Biddle 1973, 241
23　Lombard-Jourdan 1972
24　van Dam 1985
25　Ward-Perkins 1984
26　Crawford 1983, 25–7, fig.11
27　Bassett 1982
28　Meaney 1964
29　Hills, Penn, Ricket 1987 and refs.
30　Hills 1984
31　Dixon 1982; James, Marshall, Millett 1984
32　Garton 1987
33　cf. Finberg 1964, Ch.1

BIBLIOGRAPHY

Agache R. 1978: *La Somme Pré-Romaine et Romaine d'après les prospections aériennes á basse altitude*, Amiens

Alcock L. 1963: *Dinas Powys*, Cardiff

Alcock L. 1972: *By South Cadbury that is Camelot . . . Excavations at Cadbury Castle 1966–70*, London

Alcock L. 1982: Cadbury Camelot: A Fifteen-Year Perspective, *Proceedings of the British Academy* LVIII, 355–88

Allason-Jones L. & McKay B. 1985; *Coventina's Well*, Chesters

ApSimon A.M. 1965: The Roman Temple on Brean Down, Somerset, *Proceedings of the University of Bristol Spelaeological Society* X, 195–258

Archer S. 1979: Late Roman gold and silver coin hoards in Britain; a gazetteer, in P.J. Casey ed.: *The End of Roman Britain*, 29–64, BAR British 71, Oxford

Ashby T., Hudd A.E., King F. 1909: Excavations at Caerwent, Monmouthshire, on the Site of the Romano-British City of Venta Silurum, in the years 1907 and 1909, *Archaeologia* LXI ii, 565–82

Ashby T., Hudd A.E. King F. 1910; Excavations at Caerwent, Monmouthshire, on the Site of the Romano-British City of Venta Silurum, in the year 1908, *Archaeologia* LXII, 1–20

Atkinson D. 1942; *Report on Excavations at Wroxeter 1923–1927*, Birmingham

Barker P. *et al*. forthcoming: Wroxeter Baths Basilica: A Preliminary Structural Sequence, *Britannia*

Bartholomew P. 1982; Fifth-Century Facts, *Britannia* XIII, 261–70

Bartholomew P. 1984: Fourth-Century Saxons, *Britannia* XV, 169–85

Bassett S.R. 1982: *Saffron Walden: excavation and research 1972–80*, CBA Research Report 45, London

Bateson J.D. 1973: Roman Material From Ireland: a reconsideration, *Proceedings of the Royal Irish Academy* LXXIII, 21–97

Bayard D. & Massy J-L. 1983: *Amiens Romain*, Amiens

Bennett P. 1980; 68–69a Stour Street, *Archaeologia Cantiana* XCVI, 406–10

Benson D. & Miles D. 1974: *The Upper Thames Valley: an archaeological survey of the river gravels*, Oxford

Biddle M. 1973: Winchester: the development of an early capital, in H. Jankuhn, W. Schlesinger, H. Steuer eds: *Vor- und Frühformen der europäischen Stadt im Mittelalter*, 229–61, Göttingen

Biddle M. 1975a: Excavations at Winchester, 1971: Tenth and Final Interim Report: Part I, *Antiquaries Journal* LV i, 96–126

Biddle M. 1975b: Excavations at Winchester, 1971: Tenth and Final Interim Report: Part II, *Antiquaries Journal* LV ii, 295–337

Biddle M. 1976a: Towns, in D.M. Wilson ed.: *The Archaeology of Anglo-Saxon England*, 99–150, London

Biddle M. 1976b: Hampshire and the Origins of Wessex, in G. Sieveking, I. Longworth, D. Wilson eds: *Problems in Economic and Social Archaeology*, 323–42, London

Biddle M. 1977: Alban and the Anglo-Saxon Church, in R. Runcie ed.: *Cathedral and City: St Albans Ancient and Modern*, 23–42, London

Biddle M. 1983: The Study of Winchester: Archaeology and History in a British Town, *Proceedings of the British Academy* LXIX, 93–135

Bidwell P.T. 1979: *The Legionary Bath-House and Basilica and Forum at Exeter*, Exeter Archaeological Reports I, Exeter

Bidwell P.T. 1980: *Roman Exeter: Fortress and Town*, Exeter

Bidwell P.T. 1985: *The Roman Fort of Vindolanda*, HBMC(E) Archaeological Reports 1, London

Blagg T.F.C. 1983: The reuse of monumental masonry in late Roman defensive walls, in J. Maloney & B. Hobley eds: *Roman Urban Defences in the West*, CBA Research Report 51, 130–5, London

Blockley K. 1980: The Marlowe Car Park Excavations, *Archaeologia Cantiana* XCVI, 402–5

Böhme H.W. 1974: *Germanische Gräbfunde des 4 bis 5 Jahrhunderts zwischen unterer Elbe und Loire*, Munich

Boon G.C. 1959: The latest objects from Silchester, Hampshire, *Medieval Archaeology* III, 79–88

Boon G.C. 1972: *Isca*, Cardiff

Boon G.C. 1974a: *Silchester: The Roman Town of Calleva*, 2nd. edn., Newton Abbott

Boon G.C. 1974b: Counterfeit Coins in Roman Britain, in P.J. Casey & R.M. Reece eds.: *Coins and the Archaeologist*, BAR British 4, 95–171, Oxford

Booth P.M. 1980: *Roman Alcester*, Warwick

Bradley R. 1975: Maumbury Rings, Dorchester: The Excavations of 1908–13, *Archaeologia* CV, 1–98

Branigan K. 1971: *Latimer*, Dorchester

Branigan K. 1977: *Gatcombe Roman Villa*, BAR British 44, Oxford

Breeze D.J. & Dobson B. 1978: *Hadrian's Wall*, 2nd. edn., London.

Breeze D.J. & Dobson B. 1985; Roman Military Deployment in North England, *Britannia* XVI, 1–19

Brewer R. 1988: *Caerwent 1987: Forum-Basilica and Roman Shop*, Cardiff

Brickstock R.J. 1987: *Copies of the Fel Temp Reparatio Coinage in Britain*, BAR British 176, Oxford

Brooks D.A. 1986: A review of the evidence for continuity in British towns in the 5th and 6th centuries, *Oxford Journal of Archaeology* V i, 77–102

Brooks D.A. 1988: The case for continuity in fifth-century Canterbury re-examined, *Oxford Journal of Archaeology* VII i, 99–114

Brown P. 1971: *The World of Late Antiquity*, London

Brown P.D.C. 1971: The Church at Richborough, *Britannia* II, 225–31

Brown P.D.C. & McWhirr A. 1967: Cirencester, 1966, *Antiquaries Journal* XLVII ii, 185–97

Buckland P.C. 1974: Archaeology and environment in York, *Journal of Archaeological Science* I, 303–16

Bulleid A. & Horne E. 1926: The Roman House at Keynsham, Somerset, *Archaeologia* LXXV, 111–38

Burnett A. 1984: Clipped Siliquae and the end of Roman Britain, *Britannia* XV, 163–8

Burnett A. 1987: *Roman Coins*, London

Burnett A. & Johns C.M. 1979: The Whorlton (Yorks) Hoard, in R.A.G. Carson, A. Burnett eds: *Recent Coin Hoards from Roman Britain*, London

Burnham B.C. 1987: The Morphology of Romano-British 'Small Towns', *Archaeological Journal* CXLIV, 156–90

Burrow I. 1979: Roman material from hillforts, in P.J. Casey ed.: *The End of Roman Britain*, BAR British 71, 212–29, Oxford

Bushe-Fox J.P. 1914: *Third Report on the Excavations on the Site of the Roman Town at Wroxeter, Shropshire 1914*, Society of Antiquaries Research Report IV, Oxford

Butler R.M. 1961: Late Roman Town Walls in Gaul, *Archaeological Journal* CXVI, 25–50

Cahn H.A. & Kaufmann-Heinimann A-M. 1984: *Der spätrömische Silberschatz von Kaiseraugst*, Drendingen

Canterbury Archaeological Trust 1982: *Topographical Maps of Canterbury*, 2nd. edn., Canterbury

Carrié J-M. 1982: Le 'colonat du Bas-Empire': un mythe historiographique?, *Opus* I 2, 351–70

Carver M.O.H., Donaghey S., Sumpter A.B. 1978: *Riverside Structures and a Well in Skeldergate and Buildings in Bishophill*, The Archaeology of York 4/1, London

Casey P.J. 1977: Carausius and Allectus — Rulers in Gaul?, *Britannia* VIII, 283–301

Casey P.J. 1978: Constantine the Great in Britain — the evidence of the coinage at the London mint, in J. Bird, H. Chapman, J. Clark eds: *Collectanea Londiniensia*, London and Middlesex Archaeological Society Special Paper 2, 181–93, London

Casey P.J. 1983: Imperial campaigns and 4th century defences in Britain, in J. Maloney, B. Hobley eds: *Roman Urban Defences in the West*, CBA Research Report 51, 121–4, London

Chadwick N.K. 1955: *Poetry and Letters in Early Christian Gaul*, London

Chambers R.A. 1988: The Late- and Sub-Roman Cemetery at Queenford Farm, Dorchester-on-Thames, Oxon, *Oxoniensia* LII, 35–69

Chenet G. 1941: *La Céramique Gallo-Romaine d'Argonne du IVème siècle, et la terre sigillée décorée à la mollette*, Mâcon

Clack P.A.G. 1982: The Northern Frontier: Farmers in the Military Zone, in
  D. Miles ed.: *The Romano-British Countryside*, BAR British 103, 377–402,
  Oxford

Clarke G.N. 1979: *The Roman Cemetery at Lankhills*, in M. Biddle ed.:
  Winchester Studies III: pre-Roman and Roman Winchester: Part ii, Oxford

Clarke G.N. 1982: The Roman Villa at Woodchester, *Britannia XIII*,
  197–228

Collingwood R.G. & Myers J.N.L. 1936: *Roman Britain and the English
  Settlements*, Oxford

Collingwood R.G. & Richmond I.A. 1969: *The Archaeology of Roman
  Britain*, 2nd. edn., London

Cook J. & Rowley T. 1985: *Dorchester through the Ages*, Oxford

Corder P. 1928: *The Roman Pottery at Crambeck*, Roman Malton and
  District Report 1, York

Corder P. 1961: *The Roman Town and Villa at Great Casterton, Rutland:
  Third Report for the Years 1954–1958*, Nottingham

Crawford G. 1983: Excavations at Wasperton, third interim report, *West
  Midlands Archaeology XXVI*, 15–28

Crickmore J. 1984: *Romano-British Urban Defences*, BAR British 126,
  Oxford

Crummy P. 1980: The Temples of Roman Colchester, in W. Rodwell ed.:
  Temples, Churches and Religion in Roman Britain, BAR British 77,
  243–83, Oxford

Crummy P. 1981: *Aspects of Anglo-Saxon and Norman Colchester*, CBA
  Research Report 39, London

Crummy P. 1982: The Roman Theatre at Colchester, *Britannia XIII*, 299–302

Crummy P. 1984: *Excavations at Lion Walk, Balkerne Lane and
  Middleborough, Colchester, Essex*, Colchester Archaeological Report 3,
  Colchester

Cunliffe B.W. 1968: *Fifth Report on the Excavations of the Roman Fort at
  Richborough, Kent*, Society of Antiquaries Research Report XXIII,
  London

Cunliffe B.W. 1973: The Period of Romanization, in *Victoria County History
  of Wiltshire* I ii, 439–52

Cunliffe B.W. 1975: *Excavations at Porchester Castle: I: Roman*, Society of
  Antiquaries Research Report XXXII, London

Cunliffe B.W. 1976a: *Excavations at Portchester Castle: II: Saxon*, Society of
  Antiquaries Research Report XXXIII, London

Cunliffe B.W. 1976b: A Romano-British Village at Chalton, Hants,
  Proceedings of the Hampshire Field Club and Archaeological Society
  XXXIII, 45–67

Cunliffe B.W. 1980: Excavations at the Roman Fort at Lympne, *Britannia*
  XI, 227–88

Cunliffe B.W. 1983: *Danebury: Anatomy of an Iron Age Hillfort*, London

Cunliffe B.W. & Davenport P. 1988: *The Temple of Sulis Minerva at Bath:
  Volume 1: The Site*, Oxford

Curle A.O. 1923: *The Treasure of Traprain*, Glasgow

Daniels C.M. 1980: Excavations at Wallsend and the fourth-century barracks on Hadrian's Wall, in W.S. Hanson, L.J.F. Keppie eds: *Roman Frontier Studies 1979*, BAR International 71, 173–93, Oxford

Davey N. & Ling R. 1981: *Wall-painting in Roman Britain*, Britannia Monograph Series 3, London

Davies W. 1978: *An Early Welsh Microcosm*, London

Davies W. 1982: *Wales in the Early Middle Ages*, Leicester

Dickinson T.M. 1982: Fowler's Type G Penannular Brooches Reconsidered, *Medieval Archaeology* XXVI, 41–68

Dill S. 1898: *Roman Society in the Last Century of the Western Empire*, London

Dixon P. 1982: How Saxon is a Saxon House?, in P. Drury ed.: *Structural Reconstruction*, BAR British 110, 275–88, Oxford

Dore J.N. & Gillam J.P. 1981: *The Roman Fort at South Shields*, Newcastle

Dornier A. 1982: The Province of Valentia, *Britannia* XIII, 253–60

Down A. 1978: *Chichester Excavations 3*, Chichester

Down A. 1979: *The Roman Villas at Chilgrove and Upmarden*, Chichester Excavations 4, Chichester

Drury P.J. 1976: Braintree: Excavations and Research, 1971–76, *Essex Archaeology and History* VIII, 1–143

Drury P.J. & Wickenden N.P. 1982: An early Saxon Settlement within the Romano-British Small Town at Heybridge, Essex, *Medieval Archaeology* XXVI, 1–40

Dumville D.N. 1977a: Sub-Roman Britain: History and Legend, *History* LXII, 173–92

Dumville D.N. 1977b: Kingship, Genealogies and Regnal Lists, in P. Sawyer, I. Wood eds.: *Early Medieval Kingship*, 72–104, Leeds

Dumville D.N. 1984; Gildas and Maelgwn: problems of dating, in M. Lapidge, D.N. Dumville eds: *Gildas: New Approaches*, 51–9, Woodbridge

Duncan-Jones R. 1978: Pay and Numbers in Diocletian's Army, *Chiron* VIII, 173–93

Dyson A. ed. 1986: *The Roman Quay at St Magnus House London*, London and Middlesex Archaeological Society Special Papers 8, London

Ellison A. 1980: Natives, Romans and Christians on West Hill, Uley: An Interim Report on the Excavation of a Ritual Complex of the First Millennium AD, in W. Rodwell ed.: *Temples, Churches and Religion in Roman Britain*, BAR British 77, 305–28, Oxford

Esmonde Cleary A.S. 1985: The quick and the dead: suburbs, cemeteries and the town, in F. Grew, B. Hobley eds: *Roman Urban Topography in Britain and the Western Empire*, CBA Research Report 59, 74–7, London

Esmonde Cleary A.S. 1987: *Extra-Mural Areas of Romano-British Towns*, BAR British 169, Oxford

Ferris I.M. & Jones R.F.J. 1980: Excavations at Binchester 1976–9, in W.S. Hanson, L.J.F. Keppie eds: *Roman Frontier Studies 1979*, BAR International 71, 233–54, Oxford

Ferris I.M. & Jones R.F.J. forthcoming: Binchester — a northern fort and vicus, in R.F.J. Jones ed.: *Britain in the Roman period*, Sheffield

Finberg H.P.R. 1964: *Lucerna: Studies of some problems in the early history of England*, London

Finley M. 1973: *The Roman Economy*, London

Fouet G. 1969: *La Villa Gallo-Romaine de Montmaurin (Haute Garonne)*, Supplément XX à Gallia, Paris

Frere S.S. 1970: The Roman Theatre at Canterbury, *Britannia* I, 88–113

Frere S.S. 1971: The Forum and Baths of Caistor-by-Norwich, *Britannia* II, 1–26

Frere S.S. 1972: *Verulamium Excavations: Volume I*, Society of Antiquaries Research Report XXVIII, London

Frere S.S. 1975: The Silchester Church: The Excavation by Sir Ian Richmond in 1961, *Archaeologia* CV, 277–302

Frere S.S. 1982: The Bignor Villa, *Britannia* XIII, 135–95

Frere S.S. 1983: *Verulamium Excavations: Volume II*, Society of Antiquaries Research Report XLI, London

Frere S.S. 1984a; Excavations at Dorchester-on-Thames 1963, *Archaeological Journal* CXLI, 91–174

Frere S.S. 1984b: Roman Britain in 1983: Part I: Sites Explored, *Britannia* XV, 266–332

Frere S.S. 1987: *Britannia: a history of Roman Britain*, 3rd. edn., London

Frere S.S. & St Joseph J.K. 1983: *Roman Britain from the Air*, Cambridge

Fulford M. 1973: The Dating and Distribution of New Forest Pottery, *Britannia* IV, 160–78

Fulford M. 1975a: *New Forest Roman Pottery*, BAR British 17, Oxford

Fulford M. 1975b: The Pottery, in B.W. Cunliffe: *Excavations at Porchester Castle: I: Roman*, 270–367

Fulford M. 1979; Pottery production and trade at the end of Roman Britain: the case against continuity, in P.J. Casey ed.: *The End of Roman Britain*, BAR British 71, 120–32, Oxford

Fulford M. 1985: Excavations on the Sites of the Amphitheatre and Forum-Basilica at Silchester, Hampshire: an Interim Report, *Antiquaries Journal*, LXV I, 39–81

Fulford M. 1987: La céramique et les échanges commerciaux sur La Manche à l'époque romaine, in L. Rivet ed.: *Société Francaise d'Etude de la Céramique Antique en Gaule: Actes du Congres de Caen*, 95–106

Fulford M. & Bird J. 1975: Imported pottery from Germany in late Roman Britain, *Britannia* VI, 171–81

Fulford M. & Hodder I. 1974: A Regression Analysis of some Late Romano-British Pottery: A Case Study, *Oxoniensia* XXXIX, 26–33

Galinié H. 1981: Fouilles archéologiques à Tours 1981; rapport préliminaire, *Bulletin de la Société Archéologique de Touraine* XXXIX, 1041–84

Galliou P. 1983: *L'Armorique Romaine*, Braspars

Galliou P., Fulford M., Clément M. 1980: La diffusion de la céramique 'à l'éponge' dans le nord-ouest de l'empire romain, *Gallia* XXVIII ii, 265–78

Garton D. 1987: Dunston's Clump and the Brickwork Plan Field Systems at Babworth, Nottinghamshire: Excavations 1981, *Transactions of the Thoroton Society* XCI, 16–73

Gibbon E. 1776–81: *The Decline and Fall of the Roman Empire*, London

Gillam J.P. 1961: Excavations at Halton Chesters, 1961, *University of Durham Gazette* n.s. IX, 2

Gillam J.P. 1979: Romano-Saxon Pottery: an alternative explanation, in P.J. Casey ed.: *The End of Roman Britain*, BAR British 71, 103–18, Oxford

Gillam J.P., Harrison R.M., Newman T.G. 1973: Interim Report on Excavations at the Roman Fort of Rudchester, *Archaeologia Aeliana*[5] I, 81–5

Gilmour B. 1979: The Anglo-Saxon Church at St Paul-in-the-Bail, Lincoln, *Mediaeval Archaeology* XXIII, 214–8

Going C.J. 1987: *The Mansio and other sites in the south-eastern sector of Caesaromagus: the Roman pottery*, CBA Research Report 62, London

Goodburn R. 1972: *The Roman Villa Chedworth*, London

Goodburn R. 1979: Roman Britain in 1978: I: Sites Explored, *Britannia* X, 268–338

Grant A. 1975: The Animal Bones, in B.W. Cunliffe: *Excavations at Portchester Castle: I: Roman*, 378–408

Green C.J.S. 1977: Excavations in the Roman kiln field at Brampton, *East Anglian Archaeology* 5, 31–95, Gressenhall

Green C.J.S. 1982: The Cemetery of a Romano-British Community at Poundbury, Dorchester, Dorset, in S.M. Pearce ed.: *The Early Church in Western Britain and Ireland*, BAR British 102, 61–76, Oxford

Green C.J.S. 1988: *Excavations at Poundbury: Volume I: The Settlements*, Dorset Natural History and Archaeological Society Monograph VII, Dorchester

Greene K. 1979: *Report on the Excavations at Usk 1965–1976: The Pre-Flavian Fine Wares*, Cardiff

Grenier A. 1931: *Manuel d'archéologie Gallo-Romaine*, Paris

Grimes W.F. 1968: The Temple of Mithras and its Surroundings, in *The excavation of Roman and Mediaeval London*, 92–117, London

Guy C.J. 1981: Roman Lead Circular Tanks in Britain, *Britannia* XII, 271–6

Harden D.B. & Green C. 1978: A late Roman grave-group from The Minories, Aldgate, in J. Bird, H. Chapman, J. Clark eds: *Collectanea Londiniensia*, London and Middlesex Archaeological Society Special Paper 2, 163–75, London

Harries J. 1978: Church and State in the *Notitia Galliarum, Journal of Roman Studies* LXVIII, 26–43

Harris E. & Harris J.R. 1965: *The Oriental Cults in Roman Britain*, Leiden

Haverfield F.W. 1914: Roman Silver in Northumberland, *Journal of Roman Studies* IV, 1–12

Hawkes S.C. & Dunning G.C. 1961: Soldiers and Settlers in Britain, fourth to fifth century: with a catalogue of animal-ornamented buckles and related belt-fittings, *Medieval Archaeology* V, 1–70

Hayes J. 1972: *Late Roman Pottery*, London

Hebditch M. & Mellor J. 1973: The Forum and Basilica of Roman Leicester, *Britannia* IV, 1–83

Heighway C.M. 1987: *Anglo-Saxon Gloucestershire*, Gloucester

Heighway C.M. & Garrod P. 1980: Excavations at Nos. 1 and 30 Westgate Street, Gloucester, *Britannia* XI, 73–114

Hendy M. 1986: *Studies in the Byzantine Monetary Economy: c.300–1450*, Cambridge

Hendy M. 1988: From Public to Private: The Western Barbarian Coinages as a Mirror of the Disintegration of Late Roman State Structures, *Viator* XIX, 29–78

Henig M. 1984: *Religion in Roman Britain*, London

Heurgon J. 1958: *Le Trésor de Ténès*, Paris

Heys F.G. & Thomas M.J. 1961: Excavations on the defences of the Romano-British town at Kenchester, Final Report, *Transactions of the Woolhope Naturalists Field Club* XXXVII, 149–78

Hill C., Millett M., Blagg T.F.C. 1980: *The Roman Riverside Wall and Monumental Arch in London*, London and Middlesex Archaeological Society Special Paper 3, London

Hills C.M. 1984: *Spong Hill: Part III: Catalogue of Inhumations*, East Anglian Archaeology 21, Gressenhall

Hills C.M., Penn K., Rickett R. 1987: *The Anglo-Saxon Cemetery at Spong Hill, North Elmham: Part IV: Catalogue of Cremations*, East Anglian Archaeology 34, Gressenhall

Hodder I. 1974: Some marketing models for Romano-British coarse pottery, *Britannia* V, 340–59

Hodder I. 1976: The distribution of Savernake ware, *Wiltshire Archaeological Magazine* LXIX, 67–84

Hodder I. 1986: *Reading the Past*, Cambridge

Hodges R. 1988: *Primitive and Peasant Markets*, Oxford

Hogg A.H.A. 1962: Garn Boduan and Tre'r Ceiri: Two Caernarvonshire Hill-forts, *Archaeological Journal* CXVII, 1–39

Hopkins K. 1978: Economic Growth and Towns in Classical Antiquity, in P. Abrams, E.A. Wrigley eds: *Towns in Societies*, 35–77, Cambridge

Hopkins K. 1980: Taxes and trade in the Roman Empire, *Journal of Roman Studies* LXX, 101–25

Hughes K. 1973: The Welsh Latin Chronicles: *Annales Cambriae* and related texts, *Proceedings of the British Academy* LIX, 233–58

James E. 1988: *The Franks*, Oxford

James S. 1984: Britain and the late Roman army, in T.F.C. Blagg & A.C. King eds: *Military and Civilian in Roman Britain*, BAR British 136, 161–86, Oxford

James S., Marshall A., Millett M. 1984: An Early Medieval Building Tradition, *Archaeological Journal* CXLI, 182–215

Jobey I.M. 1979: Housesteads Ware — a Frisian tradition on Hadrian's Wall, *Archaeologia Aeliana*[5] VII

Johns C. 1981: The Risley Park silver lanx: a lost antiquity from Roman Britain, *Antiquaries Journal* LI i, 53–72

Johns C. & Potter T. 1983: *The Thetford Treasure: Roman Jewellery and Silver*, London

Johns C. & Potter T. 1985: The Canterbury late Roman Treasure, *Antiquaries Journal* LXV ii, 313–52

Johns C., Thompson F., Wagstaff P. 1980: The Wincle, Cheshire, hoard of Roman gold jewellery, *Antiquaries Journal* L i, 48–58

Johnson A. 1975: A Roman Signal Tower at Shadwell, E.1., an interim note, *Transactions of the London and Middlesex Archaeological Society* XXVI, 278–80

Johnson J.S. 1970: The Date of the Construction of the Saxon Shore Fort at Richborough, *Britannia* I, 240–8

Johnson J.S. 1973: A Group of Late Roman City Walls in Gallia Belgica, *Britannia* IV, 210–23

Johnson J.S. 1976: *The Roman Forts of the Saxon Shore*, London

Johnson J.S. 1980: A Late Roman Helmet from Burgh Castle, *Britannia* XI, 303–12

Johnson J.S. 1983a: *Late Roman Fortifications*, London

Johnson J.S. 1983b: *Burgh Castle: Excavations by Charles Green, 1958–61*, East Anglian Archaeology 20, Gressenhall

Johnston D. 1985: Munificence and *Municipia*: Bequests to Towns in Classical Roman Law, *Journal of Roman Studies* LXXV, 105–25

Johnston D.E. 1978: Villas of Hampshire and the Isle of Wight, in M. Todd ed.: *Studies in the Romano-British Villa*, 71–92, Leicester

Jones A.H.M. 1964: *The Later Roman Empire, 284–602*, Oxford

Jones G.D.B. & Shotter D.G.A. 1988: *Roman Lancaster*, Gloucester

Jones M. 1981: The development of crop husbandry, in M. Jones & G. Dimbleby eds: *The Environment of Man: the Iron Age to the Anglo-Saxon Period*, BAR British 87, 95–127, Oxford

Jones M. 1986: *England Before Domesday*, London

Jones M. & Dimbleby G. eds 1981: *The Environment of Man: the Iron Age to the Anglo-Saxon Period*, BAR British 87, Oxford

Jones M.E. 1979: Climate, nutrition and disease: an hypothesis of Romano-British population, in P.J. Casey ed.: *The End of Roman Britain*, BAR British 71, 231–51, Oxford

Jones M.J. 1985: New streets for old: the topography of Roman Lincoln, in F. Grew, B. Hobley eds: *Roman Urban Topography in Britain and the Western Empire*, CBA Research Report 59, 86–93, London

Jones M.J. & Bond C.J. 1987: Urban defences, in J. Schofield, R. Leech eds: *Urban Archaeology in Britain*, CBA Research Report 61, 81–116, London

Jones R.F.J. 1984: Death and distinction, in T.F.C. Blagg, A.C. King eds: *Military and Civilian in Roman Britain*, BAR British 136, 219–25, Oxford

Jones W. & Jones M.U. 1974: The Early Saxon Landscape at Mucking,

Essex, in T. Rowley ed.: *Anglo-Saxon Settlement and Landscape*, BAR
British 6, 20–35, Oxford
Joyce J.G. 1881: Third account of excavations at Silchester, *Archaeologia*
XLVI ii, 349–65

Kennett D.H. 1971: Late Roman bronze vessel hoards in Britain, *Jahrbuch
des Römisch-Germanischen Zentralmuseums Mainz* XVI, 123–48
Kent J.P.C. 1979: The end of Roman Britain: the literary and numismatic
evidence reviewed, in P.J. Casey ed.: *The End of Roman Britain*, BAR
British 71, 15–27, Oxford
Kent J.P.C. & Painter K. eds. 1977: *The Wealth of the Roman World*, London
Kenward H.K., Hall A.R., Jones A.K.G. 1986: *Environmental Evidence
from a Roman Well and Anglian Pits in the Legionary Fortress*, The
Archaeology of York 14/5, London
Kenyon K.M. 1935: The Roman Theatre at Verulamium, St Albans,
Archaeologia LXXXIV, 213–61
Kenyon K.M. 1948: *Excavations at the Jewry Wall Site, Leicester*, Society of
Antiquaries Research Report XV, Oxford
King A.C. 1981: The decline of samian ware manufacture in the North-West
Provinces: problems of chronology and interpretation, in A.C. King &
M. Henig eds: *The Roman West in the Third Century*, BAR International
109, 55–78, Oxford
King A.C. 1983: The Roman Church at Silchester Reconsidered, *Oxford
Journal of Archaeology* II ii, 225–38
King A.C. 1984; Animal Bones and the Dietary Identity of Military and
Civilian Groups in Roman Britain, in T.F.C. Blagg, A.C. King eds:
Military and Civilian in Roman Britain, BAR British 136, 187–207, Oxford
Kirk J.P. & Leeds E.T. 1954: Three early Saxon graves from Dorchester,
Oxon, *Oxoniensia* XVII–XVIII, 63–76

Lambrick G. 1980: Excavations in Park Street, Towcester, *Northamptonshire
Archaeology* XV, 35–118
Lapidge M. 1984: Gildas's education and the Latin culture of sub-Roman
Britain, in M. Lapidge, D.N. Dumville eds: *Gildas: New Approaches*,
27–50, Woodbridge
le Glay M. 1975: La Gaule Romanisée, in G. Duby ed.: *Histoire de la France
Rurale* I, 275–85, Paris
Leach P. 1982: *Ilchester: Volume I: Excavations 1974–5*, Bristol
Leech R. 1980: Religion and Burials in South Somerset and North Dorset, in
W. Rodwell ed.: *Temples, Churches and Religion in Roman Britain*, BAR
British 77, 329–66, Oxford
Leech R. 1981: The Excavation of a Romano-British Farmstead and
Cemetery on Bradley Hill, Somerton, Somerset, *Britannia* XII, 177–252
Leech R. 1982: *Excavations at Catsgore 1970–1973: A Romano-British
Village*, Bristol
Leech R. 1986: The Excavation of a Romano-Celtic temple and a Later
Cemetery on Lamyatt Beacon, Somerset, *Britannia* XVII, 259–328

Lemant J-P. 1985: *Le Cimitière et la Fortification du Bas-Empire de Vireux-Molhain, Dep. Ardennes*, Mainz

Levison W. 1941: St Alban and St Albans, *Antiquity* XV, 337–59

Lewis M.J.T. 1966; *Temples in Roman Britain*, Cambridge

Limbrey S. 1975: *Soil Science and Archaeology*, London

Lincoln Archaeological Trust 1984: *Lincoln: 21 Centuries of Living History*, Lincoln

Little J.H. 1971: The Carmarthen Amphitheatre, *The Carmarthen Antiquary* VII, 58–63

Lombard-Jourdan A. 1972: Oppidum et Banlieue. Sur l'origine et la dimension du territoire urbain, *Annales* XXVII, 373–95

Losco-Bradley S. 1977: Catholme, *Current Archaeology* LIX, 358–64

Luttwak E. 1976: *The Grand Strategy of the Roman Empire*, Baltimore

Lyne M.A.B. & Jefferies R.S. 1979: *The Alice Holt/Farnham Roman Pottery Industry*, CBA Research Report 30, London

Mackreth D.F. 1978: Orton Hall Farm, Peterborough: A Roman and Saxon Settlement, in M. Todd ed.: *Studies in the Romano-British Villa*, 209–38, Leicester

Mackreth D.F. 1987: Roman public buildings, in J. Schofield, R. Leech eds: *Urban Archaeology in Britain*, CBA Research Report 61, 133–46, London

MacMullen R. 1963: *Soldier and Civilian in the Later Roman Empire*, Harvard

MacPhail R. 1981: Soil and botanical studies of the 'Dark Earth', in M. Jones, G. Dimbleby eds: *The Environment of Man: the Iron Age to the Anglo-Saxon Period*, BAR British 87, 309–31, Oxford

McWhirr A. 1978: Cirencester 1973–6: Tenth Interim Report, *Antiquaries Journal* LVIII i, 61–80

McWhirr A. 1986: *Houses in Roman Cirencester*, Cirencester Excavations III, Gloucester

McWhirr A., Viner L., Wells C. 1982: *Romano-British Cemeteries at Cirencester*, Cirencester Excavations II, Cirencester

Magilton J. 1986: *Paganism in Late Roman Britain*, unpublished M. Phil thesis, University of Birmingham

Maltby M. 1979: *The Animal Bones from Exeter*, Exeter Archaeological Reports 2, Sheffield

Maltby M. 1981: Iron Age, Romano-British and Anglo-Saxon Animal Husbandry: A Review of the Evidence, in M. Jones, G. Dimbleby eds: *The Environment of Man: The Iron Age to the Anglo-Saxon Period*, BAR British 87, 151–203, Oxford

Mann J.C. 1979: Hadrian's Wall: the last phase, in P.J. Casey ed.: *The End of Roman Britain*, BAR British 71, 144–51, Oxford

Mann J.E. & Reece R.M. 1983: *Roman Coins from Lincoln 1970–1979*, The Archaeology of Lincoln VI 2, London

Manning W. 1972: Iron Work Hoards in Iron Age and Roman Britain, *Britannia* III, 224–50

Marsden P.R.V. 1975: The Excavation of a Roman Palace Site in London,

Transactions of the London and Middlesex Archaeological Society XXVI, 1–102

Mattingly H., Pearce J., Kendrick T.D. 1933: The Coleraine Hoard, *Antiquity* XI, 39–45

Meaney A. 1964: *Gazetteer of Early Anglo-Saxon Burial Sites*, London

Meates G.W. 1955: *Lullingstone Roman Villa*, London

Merrifield R. 1983: *London: City of the Romans*, London

Mertens J. & van Impe L. 1971: Het Laat-Romeins Grafveld von Oudenburg, *Archaeologia Belgica* CXXXV, Brussels

Middleton P.S. 1979: Army Supply in Roman Gaul: An Hypothesis for Roman Britain, in B.C. Burnham & H.B. Johnson eds: *Invasion and Response: the Case of Roman Britain*, BAR British 73, 81–98, Oxford

Miles D. 1984: *Archaeology at Barton Court Farm Abingdon, Oxon*, CBA Research Report 50, London

Miles D. & Palmer S. 1983: *Figures in a Landscape: archaeological excavations at Claydon Pike, an interim report*, Oxford

Miller M. 1978: The Last British Entry in the 'Gallic Chronicles', *Britannia* IX, 315–8

Millett M. 1980: Aspects of Roman Pottery in West Sussex, *Sussex Archaeological Collections* CXVIII, 57–68

Millett M. 1987: The Question of Continuity: Rivenhall Reviewed, *Archaeological Journal* CXLIV, 434–8

Millett M. & Graham D. 1986: *Excavations on the Romano-British Small Town at Neatham*, Hampshire Field Club Monograph 3, Gloucester

Milne G. 1985: *The Port of Roman London*, London

Morris P.: *Agricultural Buildings in Roman Britain*, BAR British 70, Oxford

Muhlberger S. 1983: The Gallic Chronicle of 452 and its Authority for British Events, *Britannia* XIV, 23–33

Musée Carnavalet 1984: *Lutèce: Paris de César à Clovis*, Paris

Myres J.N.L. 1956: Romano-Saxon Pottery, in D.B. Harden ed.: *Dark-Age Britain*, 16–39, London

Myres J.N.L. & Green B. 1973: *The Anglo-Saxon Cemeteries of Caistor-by-Norwich and Markshall*, Society of Antiquaries Research Report XXX, London

Nash D. 1976: Reconstructing Poseidonios' Celtic Ethnography; some considerations, *Britannia* VII, 111–26

Nash-Williams V.E. 1930: Further Excavations at Caerwent, Monmouthshire, 1923–5, *Archaeologia* LXXX, 229–88

Neal D.S. 1974: *The Excavation of the Roman Villa in Gadebridge Park Hemel Hempstead 1963–8*, Society of Antiquaries Research Report XXXI, London

Neiss R. 1984: La structure urbaine de Reims antique et son évolution du Ier au IIIe siècle ap. JC. in *Les Villes de la Gaule Belgique au Haut Empire*, Revue Archéologique de Picardie III–IV

Nenquin J. 1953: *La Nécropole de Furfooz*, Namur

Ottaway P. 1984: Colonia Eburacensis: A Review of Recent Work, in
P.V. Addyman, V.E. Black eds: *Archaeological Papers from York
Presented to M.W. Barley*, 28–33, York

Painter K.S. 1965: A Roman silver treasure from Canterbury, *Journal of the
British Archaeological Association*[3] XXVIII, 1–15
Painter K.S. 1975: A Roman Christian silver treasure from Biddulph,
Staffordshire, *Antiquaries Journal* LV i, 62–9
Painter K.S. 1977a: *The Mildenhall Treasure*, London
Painter K.S. 1977b: *The Water Newton Early Christian Silver*, London
Parnell G. 1985: The Roman and Medieval Defences and Later Development
of the Inmost Ward, Tower of London: Excavations 1955–77, *Transactions
of the London and Middlesex Archaeological Society* XXVI, 1–79
Peacock D.P.S. 1973; Forged brick-stamps from Pevensey, *Antiquity* XLVII
ii, 138–40
Peacock D.P.S. 1982: *Pottery in the Roman World: an ethnoarchaeological
approach*, London
Peacock D.P.S. & Williams D.F. 1986: *Amphorae in the Roman Economy*,
London
Perring D. 1987: Domestic buildings in Romano-British towns, in
J. Schofield, R. Leech eds: *Urban Archaeology in Britain*, CBA Research
Report 61, 147–55, London
Philp B. 1977: Dover, in D.E. Johnston ed.: *The Saxon Shore*, CBA
Research Report 18, 20–1, London
Pollard S.M.H. 1972: A Late Iron Age settlement and a Romano-British villa
at Holcombe, near Uplyme, Devon, *Proceedings of the Devon
Archaeological Society* XXXII, 59–161
Price J. 1978: Trade in glass, in J. du Plat Taylor, H.F. Cleere eds: *Roman
shipping and trade: Britain and the Rhine provinces*, CBA Research Report
24, 70–8, London

Radford C.A.R. 1968: The Archaeological Background on the Continent, in
M.W. Barley, R.P.C. Hanson eds.: *Christianity in Britain 300–700*, 19–36,
Leicester
Rahtz P.A. 1977: Late Roman cemeteries and beyond, in R.M. Reece ed.:
Burial in the Roman World, CBA Research Report 2, 53–64, London
Rahtz P. & Fowler P. 1972: Somerset AD 400–700, in P. Fowler ed.:
Archaeology and the Landscape, 187–221, London
Rankov N.B. 1982: Roman Britain in 1981: I: Sites Explored, *Britannia* XIII,
328–95
Reece R.M. 1972: A short Survey of the Roman coins found on Fourteen
Sites in Britain, *Britannia* III, 169–76
Reece R.M. 1980a: Town and country; the end of Roman Britain, *World
Archaeology* XII i, 77–92
Reece R.M. 1980b: Religion, Coins and Temples, in W. Rodwell ed.:
Temples, Churches and Religion in Roman Britain, BAR British 77,
115–28, Oxford

Reece R.M. 1981a: Coinage and Currency in the Third Century, in A.C.King & M. Henig eds: *The Roman West in the Third Century*, BAR International 109, 79–88, Oxford

Reece R.M. 1981b: The Roman Coins from Richborough – A Summary, *Bulletin of the Institute of Archaeology, University of London* XVIII, 49–71

Reece R.M. 1982: The coins from the Cow Roast, Herts. — a commentary, *Hertfordshire Archaeology* VIII, 60–6

Reece R.M. 1984a: Mints, Markets and the Military, in T.F.C. Blagg, A.C. King eds: *Military and Civilian in Roman Britain*, BAR British 136, 143–60, Oxford

Reece R.M. 1984b: Coins, in H. Hurst & S. Roskams: *Excavations at Carthage: The British Mission, Volume I.1*, 171–81

Rheinisches Landesmuseum Trier 1984: *Trier; Kaisserresidenz und Bischofssitz*, Mainz

Richardson K.M. 1944: Report on Excavations at Verulamium: Insula XVII, 1938, *Archaeologia* XC, 81–126

Richmond I.A. 1947: The Roman City of Lincoln, *Archaeological Journal* CIII, 26–56

Richmond I.A. & Gillam J.P. 1951: The Temple of Mithras at Carrawburgh, *Archaeologia Aeliana*[4] XXIX, 1–92

Richmond I.A. & Gillam J.P. 1955: Some excavations at Corbridge, 1952–1954, *Archaeologia Aeliana*[4] XXXIII, 218–52

Rivet A.L.F. 1969: Social and Economic Aspects, in A.L.F. Rivet ed.: *The Roman Villa in Britain*, 173–216, London

Rivet A.L.F. 1976: The Notitia Galliarum: some questions, in R. Goodburn, P. Bartholomew eds: *Aspects of the Notitia Dignitatum*, BAR International 15, 119–41, Oxford

Roach Smith C. 1850: *The Antiquities of Reculver, Richborough and Lympne*, London

Rodwell K.A. 1988: *The prehistoric and Roman settlement at Kelvedon, Essex*, CBA Research Report 63, London

Rodwell W.J. & Rodwell K.A. 1986: *Rivenhall: investigations of a villa, church and village, 1950–1977*, CBA Research Report 55, London

Rogerson A. 1977: Excavations at Scole, 1973, *East Anglian Archaeology* 5, 97–224, Gressenhall

Rowley R.T. 1974, Early Saxon Settlement in Dorchester, in R.T. Rowley ed.: *Anglo-Saxon Settlement and Landscape*, BAR British 6, 42–50, Oxford

RCHM(E) (Royal Commission on Historical Monuments for England) 1962: *Eburacum: Roman York*, London

RCHM(E) 1969: *Peterborough New Town*, London

RCHM(E) 1978: *The Gloucestershire Cotswolds*, London

RCHM(E) 1980: *Northamptonshire: An Archaeological Atlas*, London

St John Hope W.H. & Fox G.E. 1905: Excavations on the Site of the Roman City at Silchester, Hants, in 1903 and 1904, *Archaeologia* LIX ii, 333–70

Sanders I.F. & Esmonde Cleary A.S. in preparation: *Excavations at Thenford 1971–3*

Shelton K.J. 1981: *The Esquiline Treasure*, London

Simco A. 1984: *Survey of Bedfordshire: The Roman Period*, Bedford

Simpson C.J. 1976: Belt-Buckles and Strap-Ends of the later Roman Empire; a preliminary survey of several new groups, *Britannia* VII, 192–223

Sims-Williams P. 1983: The Settlement of England in Bede and the *Chronicle*, *Anglo-Saxon England* XII, 1–41

Smith D.J. 1969: The Mosaic Pavements in A.L.F. Rivet ed.: *The Roman Villa in Britain*, 71–126, London

Smith D.J. 1975: Roman mosaics in Britain before the fourth century, in H. Stern, M. leGlay eds: *La Mosaique Gréco-Romaine*, 269–90, Paris

Smith D.J. 1978: Regional aspects of the winged corridor villa in Britain, in M. Todd ed.: *Studies in the Romano-British Villa*, 117–47, Leicester

Sommer C.S. 1984: *The Military Vici in Roman Britain*, BAR British 129, Oxford

Strickland T.J. 1981: Third century Chester, in A.C. King, M. Henig eds: *The Roman West in the Third Century*, BAR International 109, 415–44, Oxford

Sumner H. 1927: *Excavations in New Forest Roman Pottery Sites*, London

Sumpter A.B. & Coll S. 1977: *Interval Tower SW5 and the South-west Defences*, The Archaeology of York 3/2, London

Thomas C. 1981: *A Provisional List of Imported Pottery in Post-Roman Western Britain and Ireland*, Redruth

Thompson E.A. 1952: Peasant revolts in late Roman Gaul and Spain, *Past and Present* II, 11–23

Thompson E.A. 1983; Fifth-century Facts?, *Britannia* XIV, 272–4

Thompson E.A. 1984: *Saint Germanus of Auxerre and the End of Roman Britain*, Woodbridge

Thompson F.H. & Whitwell J.B. 1973: The Gates of Roman Lincoln, *Archaeologia* CIV, 129–207

Todd M. 1969: The Roman Settlement at Margidunum. *Transactions of the Thoroton Society* LXXIII, 7–110

Todd M. 1977: *Famosa Pestis* and Britain in the Fifth Century, *Britannia* VIII, 319–25

Tomlin R.S.O. 1987: The Army of the Late Empire, in J.S. Wacher ed.: *The Roman World*, 107–34, London

Tomlin R.S.O. 1988: The Curse Tablets, in B.W. Cunliffe ed.: *The Temple of Sulis Minerva at Bath: Volume 2: The Finds from the Sacred Spring*, 59–277, Oxford

Tortorella S. 1983: Produzione e circolazione della ceramica africana di Cartagine (V–VII sec.), *Opus* II i, 15–30

Toynbee J.M.C. 1964; A New Roman Mosaic Pavement found in Dorset, *Journal of Roman Studies* LIV, 7–14

Toynbee J.M.C. 1986: *The Roman Art Treasures from the Temple of Mithras*, London and Middlesex Archaeological Society Special Papers 7, London

Toynbee J.M.C. & Painter K.S. 1986: Silver Picture Plates of Late Antiquity, *Archaeologia* CVIII, 15–65

Tuffreau-Libre M. 1980: *La Céramique Commune Gallo-Romaine dans le Nord de la France*, Lille
Turner J. 1981: The Vegetation, in M. Jones, G. Dimbleby eds: *The Environment of Man: the Iron Age to the Anglo-Saxon Period*, BAR British 87, 67–73, Oxford

van Dam 1985: *Leadership and Community in Late Antique Gaul*, Berkeley

Wacher J.S. 1962: Cirencester 1961: Second Interim Report, *Antiquaries Journal* XLII ii, 1–14
Wacher J.S. 1964: Cirencester, 1963. Fourth Interim Report, *Antiquaries Journal* XLIV i, 9–18
Wacher J.S. 1975: *The Towns of Roman Britain*, London
Wainwright G.J. 1962: *Coygan Camp*, Cardiff
Walker D. 1988: The Roman Coins, in B.W. Cunliffe ed.: *The Temple of Sulis Minerva at Bath: Volume 2: The Finds from the Sacred Spring*, 281–337, Oxford
Walters B. 1981: Littlecote, *Current Archaeology* LXXX, 264–8
Walthew C.V. 1975: The Town House and the Villa House in Roman Britain, *Britannia* VI, 189–205
Ward J.H. 1973: The British Sections of the *Notitia Dignitatum*: an Alternative Interpretation, *Britannia* IV, 253–63
Ward-Perkins B.R. 1984: *From Classical Antiquity to the Middle Ages, urban public building in Northern and Central Italy*, Oxford
Waugh H. 1966: The hoard of Roman silver from Great Horwood, Buckinghamshire, *Antiquaries Journal* XLVI i, 60–71
Webster G. 1969: The Future of Villa Studies, in A.L.F. Rivet ed.: *The Roman Villa in Britain*, 217–49, London
Webster G. & Smith L. 1982: The Excavation of a Romano-British Rural Establishment at Barnsley Park, Gloucestershire, 1961–1979, Part II, c.A.D.360–400, *Transactions of the Bristol and Gloucestershire Archaeological Society* C, 65–189
Welsby D.A. 1982: *The Roman military defence of the British provinces in its later phases*, BAR British 101, Oxford
West S.E. 1985: *West Stow: The Anglo-Saxon Village*, East Anglian Archaeology 24, Ipswich
West S.E. & Plouviez J. 1976: The Roman Site at Icklingham, *East Anglian Archaeology* 3, 63–125, Ipswich
Wheeler R.E.M. 1923: Segontium and the Roman Occupation of Wales, *Y Cymmrodor* XXXIII
Wheeler R.E.M. & Wheeler T.V. 1932: *Report of the Excavation of the Prehistoric, Roman and Post-Roman site in Lydney Park, Gloucestershire*, Society of Antiquaries Research Report IX, London
White G.M. 1936: The Chichester Amphitheatre: Preliminary Excavations, *Antiquaries Journal* XVI ii, 149–59
Whittaker C. 1975: *Agri deserti*, in M. Finley ed.: *Studies in Roman Property*, Cambridge

Whitwell J.B. 1976: *The Church Street Sewer and an Adjacent Building*, The Archaeology of York 3/1, London

Wickham C.J. 1986: The Other Transition: from the Ancient World to Feudalism, *Past and Present* CIII, 3–36

Wightman E.M. 1970: *Roman Trier and the Treveri*, London

Wightman E.M. 1981: The fate of Gallo-Roman villages in the third century, in A.C. King, M. Henig eds: *The Roman West in the Third Century*, BAR International 109, 237–43, Oxford

Wightman E.M. 1985: *Gallia Belgica*, London

Wild J.P. 1967: The gynaeceum at Venta and its context, *Latomus* XXVI, 648–76

Williams D.F. 1977: The Romano-British black-burnished industry: an essay on characterisation by heavy mineral analysis, in D.P.S. Peacock ed.: *Pottery and Early Commerce: Characterisation and Trade in Roman and Later Ceramics*, 163–220, London

Williamson T.M. 1984: The Roman Countryside: Settlement and Agriculture in N.W. Essex, *Britannia* XV, 225–30

Williamson T.M. 1986: Parish boundaries and early fields: continuity and discontinuity, *Journal of Historical Geography* XII iii, 2421–8

Wilson D.R. 1971: Roman Britain in 1970: I: Sites Explored, *Britannia* II, 243–88

Wilson D.R. 1975: Romano-Celtic temple architecture, *Journal of the British Archaeological Association*[3] XXXVIII, 3–27

Wilson D.R. 1980: Romano-Celtic temple architecture: how much do we actually know?, in W. Rodwell ed.: *Temples, Churches and Religion in Roman Britain*, BAR British 77, 5–30, Oxford

Wilson D.R. 1984: The Plan of Viroconium Cornoviorum, *Antiquity* LVIII, 117–20

Wood I. 1984: The end of Roman Britain: Continental evidence and parallels, in M. Lapidge, D.N. Dumville eds: *Gildas: New Approaches*, 1–26, Woodbridge

Wood J. 1983: *Le castrum de Tours. Etude architecturale de Rempart du Bas-Empire*, Tours

Wright R.P. & Jackson K.A. 1968: A Late Inscription from Wroxeter, *Antiquaries Journal* XLVIII ii, 296–300

Young C.J. 1974: Excavations at the Churchill Hospital, 1973; Interim Report, *Oxoniensia* XXXIX, 1–11

Young C.J. 1977: *Oxfordshire Roman Pottery*, BAR British 43, Oxford

Young C.J. 1983: The Lower Enclosure at Carisbrooke Castle, Isle of Wight, in B.R. Hartley, J.S. Wacher eds.: *Rome and Her Northern Provinces*, 290–301, Leicester

INDEX

Administration, 8–13, 18–20, 47–50, 64, 71–4, 138–9, 197–9
Aegelsthrep, 163, 171
Aetius, 163, 167
African Red Slip ware, 12, 28, 90, 179, 185
Agri Decumates, 16
Agri Deserti, 28–30
Alamanni, 1, 6, 17, 18, 34, 43, 50, 136
Alaric, 137–8
Alcester, 48, 50, 68, 80, 132, 153; fig. 15
Alchester, 91; fig. 15
Alice Holt/Farnham pottery, 86, 91; fig. 22
Allectus, 17, 43
Ambrosius Aurelianus, 163
Amiens, 20, 22, 27, 35, 45; figs 4, 6
Ammianus Marcellinus, 7, 44, 45, 46, 47, 48, 63
Amphitheatre, 22, 72
Amphorae, 12, 28, 82, 179, 185
Anglo-Saxons, 34, 43, 46, 55, 137, 141, 143, 146, 155, 160, 161, 162, 163, 167, 174, 175, 178, 179, 187, 188–205
Anglo-Saxon Chronicle, 171
Annales Cambriae, 169
Annona, 8,10
Arcadius, 138, Pl. 2 & 3.
Arcani, 44, 51
Argonne pottery, 28, 83; fig. 21
Arles, 20, 82, 136, 142, 160. Council of, 35, 47, 121; fig. 4
Armorica, see Brittany
Army, 4–8, 11, 14, 50–63, 117, 140, 142–44; Supply, 12, 28, 48, 85, 90, 102, 115
Arthur, 163, 168, 169
Athanasius, 121
Attacotti, 44, 51
Augustine of Canterbury, 164, 199
Augustine of Hippo, 128
Aurelian, 4, 17
Aurum Coronarium, 9

Aurum Oblaticium, 9
Ausonius, 13, 14, 27, 30, 35, 46, 110
Autun, 27; fig. 4
Auxerre, 24, 36; fig. 4 see also Germanus of Auxerre

Bacaudae, 29–30
Bacchus, 120
Badon, 163, 168, 169
Balline, 99; fig. 24
Ballinrees, 99; fig. 24
Ballistaria, 59
Baptistery, 124
Barbarians, 6, 7, 17, 22, 27, 41, 44–5, 129, 136–37, 174 see also Alamanni, Anglo-Saxons, Burgundiones, Foederati, Franks, Germans, Goths, Laeti, Vandals, Visigoths
Barbarian Conspiracy, 44–5
Barbarous Radiates, 95
Barnack, 108; fig. 25
Barnsley Park, 94, 134; fig. 25
Barton Court Farm, 196; fig. 25
Basilica, 64, 71, 152, 199
Bath, 90, 94, 106, 154, 155–7, 164, 171; figs 15, 37; Pl. 11
Baths, 72, 75, 132, 152, 178
Bavai, 22; fig. 4
Beauvais, 24; fig. 4
Bedcanford, 163
Bede, 163, 170
Belgica II, 10, 33, 47
Belts, 33, 34, 54–6, 155, 191
Beranburh, 163
Bewcastle, 51; fig. 10
Biddulph, 99; fig. 24
Bignor, 108; fig. 25
Binchester, 143; fig. 10
Birdoswald, 50; fig. 10
Bishops, 22, 24, 34, 36, 47, 121, 124, 128, 162
Bitterne, 53

Black-Burnished pottery, 86; fig. 22
Bonn, 36, 38, 127; fig. 4
Bordeaux, 27
Boulogne, 17
Boundaries, 198
Brading, 110; fig. 25
Bradley Hill, 111, 158–9; figs 25, 28
Bradwell, 53; fig. 11
Braintree, 68, 153; fig. 15
Brampton, 132, 153; fig. 15
Brancaster, 53, 61; fig. 11
Brean Down, 179, 184
Brittany, 29, 32, 56, 137
Bruttium, 138
Burgh Castle, 53, 61, 95, 143; fig. 11
Burgi, 7, 27
Burgundiones, 137
Burials, 151, 152–3 *see also* Cemeteries

Cadbury Congresbury, 179, 186
Caer Gybi, 54
Caerleon, 57
Caernarfon, 54, 59
Caerwent, 48, 63, 71, 72, 75–6, 145; fig. 15
Caistor-by-Norwich, 48, 71, 72, 189; figs 15, 44
Cambrai, 35
Camlann, 169
Cannington, 184, 186, 187, 201; fig. 43
Canterbury, 63, 72, 97, 117, 132, 147, 148, 151, 153, 171, 193; figs 15, 45. Hoard, 99, 128, 139; fig. 24
Capitus, 10
Caracalla, 50
Carausius, 17, 43, 57
Cardiff, 53
Carisbrooke, 53, 171
Carmarthen, 72; fig. 15
Carrawburgh, 94, 120; fig. 10
Carthage treasure, 99
Cathedrals, 35
Catholme, 197
Catsgore, 111; fig. 25
Catterick, 132
Cattle, 48, 103–4, 111, 115
Ceawlin, 163, 164
Cella Memoriae, 36, 127
Cemeteries, 32, 55–6, 80–1, 124, 125–6, 134, 146, 148, 151, 153, 154, 155, 159, 178, 184, 198
Cemetery churches, 26, 38, 127, 199
Céramique à l'éponge, 83
Cerdic, 163, 170, 171

Chalets, 59
Châlons-sur-Marne, 35
Chalton, 111; figs 25, 29
Charterhouse-on-Mendip, 90
Chedworth, 108; fig. 25
Chester, 57. Battle of, 164
Chi-Rho, 124–25, 127, 128
Chichester, 68, 72, 90, 91, 132, 134, 147; fig. 15
Chilgrove, 134
Chiragan, 30, 41
Chisenbury Warren, 111; Fig. 25.
Christ, 110, 125
Christianity, 34, 116, 117, 120–8, 135, 175, 184
Churches, 13, 36, 124–25, 199
Church councils, 35, 121 *see also* Ariminium, 121. Arles, 35, 47, 121. Nicaea, 121, 125. Serdica, 121
Cirencester, 47, 68, 71, 72, 75, 77, 80, 90, 91, 106, 110, 132, 134, 147, 148, 164, 171; fig. 15
Civil Service, 8, 12, 55
Civitas, 13, 22, 34, 63, 71, 72, 137
Civitas-capital, 22, 27, 35, 41, 63, 64, 75, 82, 129, 189
Claudian, 46
Claudius II, 95
Clipping of coins, 139
Clochmabenstane, 51
Coinage, 2, 9, 10, 11, 24, 41, 45, 72, 73, 74, 91–6, 135, 138, 142, 143, 155, 157 *see also* Clipping, Counterfeiting, Follis, Hoards, Milliarense, Minimissimi, Siliqua
Coinmail, 164
Colchester, 47, 80, 85, 125–7, 132, 145, 147, 193; fig. 15
Coleshill, 119
Collatio Glebalis, 9
Collatio Lustralis, 9
Collectarii, 11 *see also* Nummularii.
Cologne, 16, 36, 38, 82; fig. 4
Coloni, 10, 15, 28–9, 114
Comes Britanniarum, 46, 50, 54, 55, 56, 61, 64, 142
Comes Litoris Saxonici, 45, 50, 61 *see also* Nectaridus
Comes Sacrarum Largitionum, 10, 11, 20, 48
Comitatenses, 5, 7, 18, 41, 44, 45, 46, 50, 54–6, 64, 142
Condidan, 164
Constans, 4, 18, 44, 155; Pl. 3

Constantine I, 2, 5, 8, 11, 13, 18, 20, 27, 34, 43, 44, 47, 117, 136; Pl. 3.
Constantine II, 4, 18; Pl. 3
Constantine III, 136–9, 142, 160, 161, 162, 167; Pl. 3
Constantinople, 8
Constantius I (Chlorus), 2, 17, 18, 43, 47, 59; Pl. 1 & 3
Constantius II, 4, 18, 44, 121; Pl. 3
Constantius (Patrician), 137, 142, 160
Constantius of Lyon, 165–6, 168, 170
Consularis, 13, 47
Corbridge, 98; fig. 15
Corrector, 13, 22
Counterfeiting, 95–6, 135, 140
Countryside, 28, 33, 41, 82, 93, 94, 100–16
Coventina's Well, 94
Coygan Camp, 179
Crambeck/Malton pottery, 86, 91, 143; fig. 22
Crecganford, 163, 171
Crispus, 18
Crocus, 43
Crops, 102–3
Cunei, 5
Curiales, 10, 13, 14, 15, 71, 129, 141, 144, 145 see also 8, 79–80, 81, 173–4
Cursus Publicus, 9, 73
Cybele, 120
Cynric, 163, 170, 171

Dark Earth, 83, 146, 147–8
Dating, 45, 85, 134, 142, 151, 152, 153, 154, 155–7
Decapitation, 134
Decentius, 44
Deforestation, 102
Deorham, 163, 164, 171
Dinas Powys, 179
Diocletian, 1, 2, 11, 13, 15, 18, 73; Pl. 3
Dionysos, 120
Donatives, 10
Dorchester (Dorset), 72, 75, 80, 90, 91, 110, 157; fig. 15 see also Poundbury
Dorchester-on-Thames, 55, 91, 154, 193–6; figs 15, 46
Dover, 53; fig. 11
Dux Belgicae Secundae, 20; fig. 3
Dux Britanniarum, 44, 50, 51, 59, 61; fig 3 see also Fullofaudes
Dux Moguntiacensis, 20; fig. 3
Dux Sequanici, 20; fig. 3

Dux Tractus Armoricani et Nervicani, 20; fig. 3

Elne, 44
Esquiline treasure, 99
Exeter, 41, 68, 71, 72, 77, 104, 132, 147, 148, 151–2, 153, 197; fig. 15

Farmsteads, 41, 100, 106, 110–14, 158–9, 175
Faunus, 99
Fausta, 18
Faustus of Riez, 174
Fields, 159, 203
Fleet, 43, 61
Foederati, 6, 33, 34, 55–6, 191, 197
Follis, 93
Forts, 5, 7, 9, 20, 41, 51, 54, 56–61, 73, 95, 199
Forum, 64, 71–2, 75, 83, 152, 198, 199
Frampton, 125, 127; fig. 25
Franks, 1, 6, 18, 34, 44, 50, 159–60, 191, 198, 200
Frisian, 196
Fritigern, 8
Frocester Court, 94, 158; fig. 25
Fullofaudes, 44
Furfooz, 22; fig. 4

Gadebridge, 134; fig. 25
Gallic Chronicle of AD 452, 138, 165
Garn Boduan, 111
Gatcombe, 48
Genealogies, 169–70
Germans, 33–4, 191
Germanus of Auxerre 162, 163, 165–6, 167, 168
Gildas, 46, 166–9, 170, 173, 174, 175, 186, 197
Gloucester, 71, 90, 147, 164, 171; fig. 15
Gododdin, 168
Goths, 1, 7
Grain, 12, 33, 48, 85,102–3
Gratian, 7, 14, 18, 34, 46, 116; Pl. 3
Great Casterton, 63; fig. 15
Great Chesterford, 198
Great Horwood, 99; fig. 24
Gregory of Tours, 174
Grubenhäuser, 143, 193, 196, 203
Gynaecium, 48

Hacksilber, 99
Hadrian's Wall, 17, 41, 43, 45, 50, 53, 54, 59–60, 95, 130, 142–3, 167; fig. 10

Halton Chesters, 50; fig. 10
Hengest, 163
Henley Wood, 184, 185
Heybridge, 196
High Rochester, 51, 59; fig. 10
Hillforts, 22, 179, 184
Hinton St Mary, 110, 125, 127; fig. 25; Pl. 6
Hoards, 11, 17, 96–9, 139–40, 143
Holcombe, 108; fig. 25
Honestiores, 15, 30
Honorius, 6, 46, 137, 138, 144, 148; Pl. 2 & 3
Horncastle, 63; fig. 15
Horsa, 163
House of Constantine, 4. Coins of, 24, 92, 93, 95
House of Theodosius, 4. Coins of, 98, 131, 132, 142, 146, 153, 155, 157
House of Valentinian 4. Coins of, 93, 96, 131, 135, 152, 153
Housesteads, 61, 142, 191; fig. 10
Humiliores, 15, 30

Icklingham, 124, 125; fig. 32
Ida of Northumbria, 170, 171
Ilchester, 81, 90, 106, 132, 153, 154; fig. 15
Ingots, 11
Irchester, 80; fig. 15. Hoard, 99
Isis, 120

Julian, 4, 6, 10, 18, 22, 33, 34, 44, 116; Pl. 3

Kaiseraugst treasure, 99
Kelvedon, 153, 154; fig. 15
Kenchester, 132, 145; fig. 15
Kent (Kingdom of), 171
Keynsham, 108; figs 25, 27
King-lists, 169–70
Knaresborough hoard, 99

Laeti, 6, 29, 30, 33
Lamyatt Beacon, 179, 184, 185; fig. 42
Lancaster, 53–4
Lankhills, 55, 134, 148; fig. 34
Latimer, 134
Le Mans, 24; fig. 4; Pl. 4
Lead tanks, 124, 128
Legion, 5, 56–7
Legio II Augusta, 57
Legio VI Victrix, 56, 57–8
Legio XX Valeria Victrix, 57

Legumes, 102–3
Leicester, 63, 71, 71; fig. 15
Limitanei, 4, 18, 20, 41, 50, 54, 55, 56–61, 142, 144
Lincoln, 47, 48, 68, 72, 145–6, 147, 148, 151–2, 153, 197; figs 14, 15
Littlecote, 108, 110, 120; fig. 25; Pl. 7
Llandaff charters, 114, 186–7
Loca, 51
Locus Maponi, 51
London, 20, 41, 43, 44, 45, 47, 48, 53, 63, 71, 82–3, 120, 145, 147, 193, 197; fig. 15
Loveden, 184
Low Ham, 110; fig. 25
Lufton, 108; fig. 25
Lullingstone, 124–5; fig. 25
Lupicinus, 44
Lupus of Troyes, 162
Lydney, 54, 94, 96; fig. 30
Lympne, 53, 61, 95, 143; fig. 11
Lyon, 20, 82; fig. 4

Maeatae, 50
Maelgwn of Gwynedd, 167
Magister, 5, 20, 44
Magnentius, 18, 24, 44, 92, 93, 95, 98, 125; Pl. 3
Magnus Maximus, 18, 46, 142, 167, 169; Pl. 3
Mainz, 16, 136; figs 3, 4
Malton, 59, 86, 91; fig. 10
Mancetter pottery, 85; fig. 22
Margidunum, 68; fig. 15
Marketing, 75, 88–91, 145, 148, 154
Marmoutier, 38
Martin of Tours, 15, 27, 32, 35, 36, 38, 121, 165
Martinus, 44
Martiobarbuli, 54
Martyrium, 36, 127
Maximian, 2, 17, 18, 20, 47; Pl. 3
Mayen pottery, 83
Mercia (Kingdom of), 171, 204, 205
Medraut, 169
Melania the Younger, 114
Metal-working, 71, 75, 77, 134, 152, 179
Metz, 35, 38; fig. 4
Mildenhall (Suffolk) treasure, 98, 99, 128, 139
Mildenhall (Wilts.), 63
Milliarense, 11
Minimissimi, 94, 96
Mints, 11, 20, 43, 44, 93, 138
Mithras, 120

Montmaurin, 30, 31, 41, 108; figs 4, 7
Mosaics, 41, 75, 77, 108–9, 134, 148
Much Hadham pottery, 86, 91; fig. 22
Mucking, 197
Munus, 12
Mystery religions, 120–1, 128

Neatham, 68, 153; fig. 15
Nectaridus, 44–5, 53
Negotiatores, 12, 91
Nene Valley pottery, 85, 86, 135, 154;
    fig. 22
Nennius, 168–9
Nervii, 36
Netherby, 51
New Forest pottery, 86, 88, 90–1, 135,
    154; figs 22, 23
North Leigh, 108; fig. 25
North Mendip, 139
Notitia Dignitatum, 20, 46, 48, 50, 51, 57
Notitia Galliarum, 35
Nummularii, 11, 74, 96

Olympiodorus of Thebes, 137
Orosius, 137, 165, 167
Orpheus, 110, 120
Orton Hall Farm, 150, 196; fig. 47
Ostrogoths, 159
Oudenburg, 33; fig. 4
Oxfordshire pottery, 86, 88, 90–1, 135,
    154; figs 22, 23

Pacatianus, 47
Paganism, 38–40, 117–20, 125, 175, 184
Paris, 27, 44; fig. 4
Parochia, 35
Patrick, 163, 166
Paul, 44
Paulinus of Nola, 13, 30, 35
Pay, 8, 10, 12, 48
Pelagianism, 121, 128, 162, 166, 167
Périgueux, 22; fig. 4
Persia, 1, 4, 5, 6
Pevensey, 53, 61, 90, 143–4, 163; fig. 11
Picts, 44, 46, 50, 168
Plague, 174–5
Plate, 10, 11, 12, 74, 98–9
Plough, 102
Pope, Celestine, 162. Leo, 163, 185
Population, 80, 81, 100, 104, 115–6, 136,
    145, 148, 158, 174–5
Port, 171
Portchester, 53, 54, 61, 86, 95, 104, 143;
    196; figs 11, 13, Pl. 5

Postumus, 17
Pottery, 12, 28, 75, 78, 85–91, 135, 140,
    141–2, 154–7, 159; figs 21, 22, 23 see
    also African Red slip Ware,
    Amphorae, Argonne, Black-
    Burnished, Céramique à l'éponge,
    Crambeck/Malton, Mancetter, Mayen,
    Much Hadham, Nene Valley, New
    Forest, Oxfordshire, Romano-Saxon
Poundbury, 125–7, 134, 148, 178–9, 184,
    186, 187; figs 33, 40
Praefectus Reliquationis, 54
Praeses, 13, 14, 47
Praetorian Prefect, 10, 11, 12, 14, 15, 18,
    19
Primus Pilus, 12, 13, 20, 48
Probus, 4
Prosper of Aquitaine, 166
Pulborough, 90

Rationalis, 20, 48, 96
Reculver, 53, 61; fig. 11
Reims, 27, 35, 47; fig. 4
Religion, 34–40, 116–28
Remigius, 160, 173
Rents, 9, 73
Rescript, 47, 137
Re-used stonework, 22, 42, 72
Rhodri ap Hywel Dda, 169
Richborough, 45, 53–7, 61, 124, 143;
    fig. 11
Riothamus, 174
Risingham, 51; fig. 10
Risley Park, 128
Rivenhall, 196
Rochester, 106; fig. 15
Romano-Saxon pottery, 189–91
Rome, 8, 12, 93, 96, 124, 138
Rudchester, 50; fig. 10
Rudston, 110; fig. 25
Rutilius Namatianus, 30

Saexneat, 169
Saffron Walden, 201
Saloninus, 16
Samian, 82–3, 85, 86
Sancton, 184
Sarapis, 120
Saxon Shore, 41, 43, 45, 50, 53, 62, 90,
    95, 142, 143–44; fig. 11
Scole, 153
Scotti, 44, 46, 51
Sea Mills, 90
Searoburh, 163

Selgovae, 50
Senators, 9, 14
Senlis, 24; fig. 4
Severinus, 142
Severus Alexander, 1, 16
Severus of Trier, 163, 165
Shadwell, 53; fig. 11
Sidonius Apollinaris, 13, 30, 174
Signal stations, 51–2, 53
Silchester, 63, 71, 72, 75–6, 78, 91, 124, 196, 198; figs 15, 18, 19, 31; Pl. 9
Siliqua, 11, 139, 148
Soissons, 24; fig. 4
Sol Invictus, 120, 125
Solidus, 11, 73
Somme, 32
South Cadbury, 179, 187, 201; fig. 41
South Shields, 50, 59; fig. 10
Southsea, 139
Spong Hill, 184, 203
Squatter occupation, 134
Stanwick, 204
State factories, 10, 15, 20, 24, 48
Stilicho, 6, 46
Stipendium, 10, 11
Strasbourg, 18; fig. 3
Strategy, 1, 4–8, 20, 51, 64
Stretton-on-Fosse, 201
Strip-buildings, 64, 68, 75, 77, 78, 81, 82
Sulis Minerva, 119, 155
Sulpicius Severus, 27, 30, 32, 38, 110, 121, 165
Superindiction, 9
Sussex (Kingdom of), 163, 170,171

Temple, 8, 32, 92, 93, 94, 99, 119–20, 135 see also Bath, Coleshill, Coventina's Well, Lydney, Thetford, Uley
Ténès, 99
Tetrarchy, 2, 43, 47, 50
Tetricus, 17
Thames Valley, 105, 158
Theatres, 72
Thenford, 158
Theodosius (Comes), 45–6, 47, 48, 63
Theodosius I, 4, 40, 46; Pl. 2 & 3
Thesaurus, 48
Thetford treasure, 99, 139; Pl. 8
Thruxton, 110; fig. 25
Tintagel, 18–86
Titulus, 35, 36, 124
Tongeren, 63; fig. 4
Tours, 22, 24, 36; fig. 4
Towcester, 153; fig. 15

Town defences, 22, 24, 36, 63–4, 72, 82, 83, 145–6
Town houses, 64, 68, 78–81, 148–51
Town, functions of, 9, 20, 28, 63–85, 90, 106, 115–16, 140, 141, 144–5. large, 64, 68, 74, 78, 80, 82, 83, 93, 94, 129, 144–53, 193. small, 27, 41, 55, 64, 68, 74, 78, 80, 82, 90, 93, 94, 129, 153–4, 193
Toxandria, 18
Trade, 12, 27, 28, 82, 83–4, 85, 88–91, 103 see also marketing
Traprain Law, 99; fig. 24
Tre'r Ceiri, 111
Trier, 14–15, 18, 20, 32, 35, 36, 38, 40–1, 45, 46, 47, 54, 82, 138, 160, 163; figs 4, 8
Tripontium, 68; fig. 15

Uley, 119, 179–80
Ulwell, 184

Valens, Pl. 3
Valentia, 47, 48
Valentinian I, 4, 5, 11, 14, 18, 20, 22, 45, 46, 48; Pl. 3
Valentinian III, 161
Valentinus, 45
Valerian, 2, 16
Vandals, 6, 136, 159, 200
Verdun, 35
Verulamium, 66–8, 72, 77, 91, 127, 131–2, 146–7, 148–51, 152, 153, 154, 162, 166, 178, 196, 199; figs 15, 35
Vexillations, 5, 56–7
Vicarius, 13
Vicarius Britanniarum, 44, 47, 82
Victorinus, 17
Vitricius of Rouen, 36, 38, 121
Villa, 30, 32, 41, 48, 55, 94, 100, 106–10, 114–15, 124, 129, 134, 158, 188, 196
Vindolanda, 59, 143; fig. 10
Vireux-Molhain, 22; fig. 4
Visigoths, 159–60, 191, 200
Vortigern, 163

Waffengräber, 22, 32, 33–4, 55–6, 155, 191
Wallsend, 59; fig. 12
Walton, 53; fig. 11
Wasperton, 201, 204; fig. 48
Water Newton, 68, 75, 106, 132; figs 15, 17. Treasure, 98, 127–28
Wessex (Kingdom of) 163, 171
West Stow, 196–7

Whorlton, 99; fig. 24
Wihtgar, 171
Winchester, 48, 55, 63, 77, 80, 91, 103,
    132, 146, 148, 193, 197, 198; fig. 15 *see
    also* Lankhills
Wincle, 99; fig. 24
Woden, 169
Woodchester, 41, 108, 110; figs 25, 26
Wroxeter, 54, 68, 71, 72, 77, 132, 148,
    152–3, 154, 158–9, 178, 187, 196; figs
    15, 38, 39, Pl. 10

Xanten, 36, 38, 63, 127; figs 4, 9

York, 2, 41, 43, 47, 48, 57, 59, 75, 100,
    136, 247, 197; fig. 10

Zosimus, 137–38, 165